The Faber Monographs on Pottery and Porcelain
Former Editors: W. B. Honey *and* Arthur Lane
Present Editors: Sir Harry Garner *and* R. J. Charleston

★

DERBY PORCELAIN

A. HARLEQUIN GROUP
Date 1756–60   Height 6¾ in.
*Reproduced by permission of the Syndics of the Fitzwilliam Museum,
Cambridge   See pages 19, 25*

DERBY PORCELAIN
1750–1848

by
FRANKLIN A. BARRETT
and
ARTHUR L. THORPE

FABER AND FABER
3 Queen Square
London

First published in 1971
by Faber and Faber Limited
3 Queen Square London W.C.1
Printed in Great Britain by
R. MacLehose and Company Limited
The University Press Glasgow
All rights reserved

ISBN 0 571 09577 1

FOREWORD

The Derby factory had a longer continuous existence on one site than any other English porcelain manufacture. The exact circumstances surrounding its foundation are still shrouded in mystery, but it emerges from these shadows by the middle of the eighteenth century, and thenceforth its history is, at least in the main, clear. Unlike Worcester, its only near rival in point of longevity, Derby from the beginning laid as much (if not more) emphasis on figure-making as it did on the manufacture of useful wares, and with this side of its production in mind, took to itself the proud title of 'the Second Dresden'. It was the direct heir of Chelsea when that pre-eminent factory was bought by William Duesbury of Derby in 1769, and in this 'Chelsea-Derby' period (1770–84) it made some of the most beautiful tablewares ever produced in England. Then and thereafter it employed many of the best porcelain painters in the country, and, with Worcester, maintained a standard of porcelain decoration unsurpassed, and seldom rivalled, in contemporary Europe.

A factory which has contributed so much at different periods to the English porcelain tradition deserves a book to itself. John Haslem's *The Old Derby China Factory* (1876) was a precious source of information gleaned by one who had himself worked in the factory and whose personal recollections and memories of factory tradition went back a very long way. Documentary material to complement Haslem's was added by W. Bemrose's *Bow, Chelsea and Derby Porcelain* (1898), but neither of these writers could be the beneficiary of the sifting process carried out by a later generation of scholars and connoisseurs in so far as the Derby wares and figures themselves are concerned.

Mr. Franklin A. Barrett, author of several books on English porcelain, and Mr. A. L. Thorpe, Curator of the Derby Museum and Art Gallery, have both devoted many years of study to the subject of

FOREWORD

Derby porcelain, and their survey of the source-material combines with their discrimination in the matter of the porcelain itself to produce the first balanced picture of the Derby factory in its activity from before the middle of the eighteenth century until the beginning of the Victorian period, when new values and a new approach to 'Art manufactures' made a break with earlier traditions.

R. J. CHARLESTON

ACKNOWLEDGMENTS

The authors wish to record their grateful thanks to the private owners and museums who have allowed pieces in their collections to be reproduced as illustrations in this book. We are also indebted to these owners and the officials of these museums for the trouble they have taken to supply information and answer our numerous queries. In particular, we would like to thank Mr. E. Bletcher, until his recent retirement Borough Librarian, for the facilities provided for the study of the Duesbury Papers housed in the Derby Public Library.

CONTENTS

ILLUSTRATIONS

COLOUR PLATES

MONOCHROME PLATES
at the end of the book

1
ANDREW PLANCHÉ
1750–1756

The first recorded mention of the possible manufacture of china in the town of Derby is contained in a postscript to a letter written from Derby by the second Earl Cowper, whilst on a tour of England, to his sister. The letter is headed:

'Derby, Sunday, 22nd September, 1728'

and the postscript reads:

> 'If 2 portmantoes should come to you
> I desire you to take them in—
> 'I have bespoke a Set of China from the
> Man who makes it here in England.'[1]

The letter, of course, antedates the earliest known manufacture of porcelain in this country, about 1744/45, and the letter itself is couched in terms that are tantalisingly obscure, so that we have to conjecture whether the phrase 'here in England' denotes the place from which the letter was written, namely, Derby, or somewhere else 'in England'. And if only 'the man' had been named! Nor should it be too readily assumed that the use of the term 'China' at that time meant porcelain or china proper. John Dwight in his patent application of 1671 described his product as 'transparent earthenware commonly known by the names of porcelaine or china', whereas the ware he made was salt-glazed stoneware which, if sufficiently thin, was sometimes translucent. Others had, during the late seventeenth and early eighteenth centuries, applied themselves to solving the 'mystery' of porcelain, mainly by an admixture of crushed Chinese porcelain, quicklime and other ingredients.[2] Tin-glazed earthenware ('delftware')

---

[1] Documents in the County Record Office, Hertfordshire County Council. (Reproduced in part in the *Manchester Guardian Weekly* of 25th August, 1955, under the title 'An English Journey of 1728'.)

[2] *British Museum Catalogue of English Porcelain, 1905*, pp. XVI–XVII.

was also sometimes referred to as 'porcelain'. All efforts to follow up the reference in the Earl Cowper's letter have proved abortive, and nothing in the extensive collection of English porcelain belonging to the Cowper family, which was largely amassed during the eighteenth century, can be linked with that referred to by the second Earl.

So we simply have the letter as written by Earl Cowper. It would be perverse, in the absence of other evidence, to do anything but accept as a fact that the 'set of China' ordered by the writer was made in Derby and not elsewhere. That it was 'China' as we know it must be open to doubt, but even so the existence of a pottery in Derby— whether it was making earthenware, stoneware or porcelain—as early as 1728 has not previously been recorded and the disclosure represents an addition to the scanty record of early eighteenth century potting in that town.

The development of porcelain manufacture in Derby during the eighteenth century is associated with the proprietorship of William Duesbury, and subsequently with that of his son of the same name. The commencement of the former is, by general consent, fixed by an unsigned partnership agreement dated 1st January 1756, naming as the partners John Heath of Derby, 'Gentleman'; Andrew Planché of Derby, 'China Maker'; and William Duesbury of Longton, 'Enamel-lor'.[1] But there exists ample evidence that china manufacture was carried on in Derby prior to this. In point of time, the first documentary reference is a report in the *Derby Mercury* for 26th January 1753, concerning the drowning of a workman from the China Works on Christmas Eve, 1752. The report reads as follows:

'Derby Mercury, Friday, January 26th, 1753. We hear that yesterday morning the Body of a man who appeared to have lain a considerable time in the Water, was taken out of the River near Borrowash.[2] 'Tis said he was one of the Workmen belonging to the China Works near Mary Bridge, and he had been missing since Christmas Eve, at which time the Waters being much out 'tis thought he fell in accidentally near the said Bridge and was drowned.'

From the report it is reasonable to deduce that the China Works was, at the time of the occurrence, well-known locally and therefore well-established.

The next documentary reference is contained in the Parish Registers of St. Alkmund's Church in Derby (a church formerly situated on the road leading down to St. Mary's Bridge and therefore

---

[1] Appendix VII.
[2] On the River Derwent, about three miles below Derby.

close to the China Works)[1] which record the baptism of Andrew Planché's first son, Paul Edmund, on 21st September 1751 and his second son, James, on 12th October 1754; and also the burial of the latter on 11th December 1754. Not only do we have proof here of Andrew Planché's presence in Derby before 1756, but his being described in the Partnership Agreement of 1756 as 'of Derby', 'China Maker', is evidence enough that he was already actively engaged in china manufacture in the town. Further entries in St. Alkmund's Church Registers are:

'1756 March 4 Bap. James, the bastard son of Andrew Planché and
        Margaret Burroughs'
'1756 July 3 Bap. William, the son of Andrew Planché and Sarah
        his wife.'[2]

Additionally, the Registers of St. Werbergh's Church in Derby record the marriage on 3rd June 1754 of William Whitehall, 'labourer at the China House'.[3]

More direct evidence of the actual manufacture of china in Derby prior to 1756 are references in William Duesbury's London Account Book to Derby china painted by him whilst working in London as an independent decorator.[4] The Accounts cover a period from late 1750 (22nd November is the first date entered) to August 1753, and among the many hundreds of items entered there appear the following eight which are positively identified as of Derby manufacture:

Page 47	'Mr. Morgan	
Joun 6 (1753)	1 Darbeyshire seson	1–0
August	3 pr. of Darbishire sesons	6–0
21	2 pr. of Dansers Darby figars	6–0'
Page 71	'Mr. Proctor	
Augoust 18	1 pr. of Dansars Darbey	
(? 1753)	figures	3–0
20	1 pr. of Larg Darbey figars	4–6
	7 pr. of Small Single figars	10–6
	1 pr. of Small Single figars	1–6'
Page 78	'Mr. Foy	
May 5 (1753)	1 pr. of Darbey figars large	
	(to enamell)	— '

[1] St. Alkmund's Church was demolished in 1967 to make way for a new road.
[2] L. Jewitt, *The Ceramic Art of Great Britain*, 1878, vol. II, p. 65.
[3] F. Williamson, *Museums Journal*, vol. XXII, p. 141.
[4] *William Duesbury's London Account Book, 1751–1753*, English Porcelain Circle Monograph, 1931.

Besides these there are others which, though not described as 'Derby', may well be from that factory: for example, large numbers of 'Staggs' and a pair of 'Boors'.

Three well-known white cream jugs, small in size, one of which bears on the base the incised date 1750 with a script 'D' (Plate 1), another the 'D' without the date, and the third the word 'Derby' incised,[1] comprise the only known datable specimens of this early period. Of these jugs, with a highly translucent pinkish body, decorated at the foot with moulded leaves and strawberry fruits and in a style not unlike some triangle Chelsea, Mrs. Donald MacAlister, in a paper read to the English Porcelain Circle on 5th March 1929, observed that, in contrast to other early Derby porcelain, they had no lead in their composition.[2] However, more recent spectrographic analysis is stated to have shown a relatively high lead content.[3]

Last in the chain of evidence in favour of china manufacture in Derby before 1755 is a letter written in 1775 in which George Holmes, modeller, and Constantine Smith, enameller, seeking employment at Wedgwood's, claimed to have worked at Derby for twenty-eight years, which, if taken at its face value, would take us back to 1747.[4]

The productions assumed to have been made in Derby prior to Duesbury's advent in 1755/6 will be discussed in due course, but two other questions first need examination; namely, who actually made the Derby figures that were decorated by Duesbury in London and where, in Derby, was the site of the manufactury? The productions in question are in general classified as 'Planché figures', on account of the evidence for Andrew Planché's presence in Derby as 'China Maker' at the time, and at present there exists no good reason to quarrel with this attribution, though it has to be admitted that final proof is still lacking. Claims have been made for Thomas Briand,[5] partially on the evidence of an entry in the Baptismal Registers of All Saints, Derby, for 20th May 1745,[6] but the name is *Byard* not Briand, and this alleged evidence in favour of Briand having been repeated many

---

[1] The first is in the Victoria and Albert Museum (E. F. Broderip gift); and the second is in the British Museum. The whereabouts of the third jug is not known but it is believed to be in a private collection.

[2] MacAlister, 'The Early Work of Planché and Duesbury', *E. P. C. Trans.*, 1929, no. II, p. 59.

[3] Bernard Watney, 'Pre-1756 Derby Domestic Wares', *Burlington Magazine*, vol. CIX, no. 766, 1967 p. 19.

[4] W. H. Tapp, 'Thomas Hughes, First Enameller of English China, of Clerkenwell', *E. C. C. Trans.*, 1939, vol. 2, no. 6, p. 60, and Wedgwood archives at Keele University.

[5] W. H. Tapp, 'The Earliest Days of the Derby China Factory', *Apollo*, August 1933, p. 97.

[6] W. H. Tapp, 'The History of Derby Porcelain Figures', *Apollo*, Dec. 1934, p. 1.

times since the publication of the late Major Tapp's article, it is as well that it should now be discarded. The name of Thomas Briand is, however, linked with Derby in another, somewhat circumstantial way, through a biscuit plaque, made at Champion's Bristol factory, and bearing the initials 'G.G.', on the back of which, according to Hugh Owen,[1] was pasted a label inscribed 'Specimen of Bristol china modelled by Thomas Briand of Derby, 1777'. This Thomas Briand may have been the same Briand who, thirty-four years earlier, exhibited before the Royal Society some specimens of what appear to have been frit-paste porcelain,[2] but the lapse of time interposes an element of uncertainty, and there is no proof that the label is contemporary with the Bristol plaque.[3] Apart from this label there exists no other evidence that Briand was concerned with china manufacture in Derby and in the absence of more reliable information his claims can be dismissed in favour of Planché, 'the foreigner' who, according to a tradition in the factory, modelled 'small articles of china about 1745'.[4]

The little we know about Andrew Planché was set out by Mrs. MacAlister in her paper read to the former English Porcelain Circle.[5] Born 14th March 1727–8, of French refugee parents, he came to Derby at some date unspecified. Llewellyn Jewitt stated that he had proof that Planché was in Derby eight years ('how much longer I know not') but, exasperatingly, he failed to provide the evidence for this. Coincidentally, however, if Jewitt's eight years are reckoned as immediately prior to 1756 (the date of the unsigned Agreement with Heath and Duesbury) this would take us back to 1748, the year after Holmes and Smith claimed to have commenced work at Derby. There is no record of Planché's continuing to work at Derby under Heath and Duesbury, though he may have done so, and we next learn that he was living at Bath and was buried at St. James' Church, Bath, 10th January 1805, being then named as Andrew Planché Floor.[6]

The actual site of the manufacture of the Derby figures decorated in London by William Duesbury has been the subject of much conjecture,

[1] Owen, *Two Centuries of Ceramic Art in Bristol*, London, 1873, p. 87.

[2] Royal Society's *Journal Book*, 10th Feb. 1742–3.

[3] A recent paper read by Mr. Arnold Mountford to the English Ceramic Circle indicates that a Mr. Thomas Briand, likely to be the one who appeared before the Royal Society, was potting at Lane Delph, Staffordshire, in February, 1746, and died in February, 1747: 'Thomas Briand—A Stranger', *E. C. C. Trans.*, vol. 7, part 2, pp. 87–99.

[4] According to a note made by Samuel Keys, a workman at the factory at the end of the 18th century, the original of which is now in the Derby Public Library (Duesbury Manuscripts).

[5] MacAlister, loc. cit., p. 50.

[6] Jewitt, op. cit., vol. 1, p. 66.

the favourite claim being that of Cockpit Hill, Derby, where in 1751 there commenced a partnership between William Butts, John Heath, Thomas Rivett and Ralph Steane which was known as the 'Derby Pot-Works'. This date does not of course embrace the 1750 cream jugs, but it is possible that the manufacture antedated the formation of the partnership. The claim on behalf of Cockpit Hill is readily understandable, but the only wares positively identified as having been made at Cockpit Hill are of creamware, dating from the 1760s; other likely productions of Cockpit Hill are tortoiseshell and other coloured-glaze wares as well as white and brown saltglaze. It is true that the nature of the productions of the first ten or twelve years at Cockpit Hill is still speculative and a case has been advanced for the manufacture of domestic china there;[1] future excavation of the site, should opportunity offer, may throw further light on the question. At the moment, however, there exist considerations that are opposed to Cockpit Hill being the source of the Planché wares. It will be recollected that the newspaper report of the drowning of a workman 'belonging to the China Works' went on to describe these works as 'near Mary Bridge'. It is inconceivable that the reference could have been to Cockpit Hill, which lies a considerable distance down river from St. Mary's Bridge. By no stretch of the imagination would a local reporter describe Cockpit Hill as being 'near Mary Bridge'. Then there is the tradition, handed down by workpeople at Duesbury's factory: 'The site first occupied by William Duesbury when he commenced . . . in 1750 . . . was near to the foot of St. Mary's Bridge. In the course of a few years . . . a piece of ground about 100 yards Eastwards from the Bridge was purchased.'[2] Although we know the reference to Duesbury's commencing 'in 1750' to be incorrect, it has been shown[3] that Duesbury did indeed purchase land further to the east of St. Mary's Bridge and tradition is likely to be reliable in regard to the site itself.

Further, we know, from an advertisement in the *Derby Mercury* for 30th July 1756 (only seven months after the date of the unsigned partnership Agreement) that property described as 'near St. Mary's Bridge' was, at the date of the advertisement, occupied as a China Manufactory by 'Mr. Heath and Company'; the advertisement reads:

'To be sold, a freehold estate consisting of seven houses and a barn, situate all together near St. Mary's Bridge, Derby, which are now

[1] For a full account of Cockpit Hill productions see Donald Towner, 'The Cockpit Hill Pottery Derby', *E. C. C. Trans.*, 1967, vol. 6, part 3, p. 254.

[2] John Haslem, *The Old Derby China Factory*, 1876, p. 31.

[3] F. A. Barrett, 'The Derby China Factory Sites on Nottingham Road', *E.C.C. Trans.*, 1959, vol. 4, part 5, pp. 26–44.

occupied by Mr. Heath and Company in the China Manufactory and let at £10 per annum exclusive of all taxes.'

There can be little doubt that the 'China Manufactory' of the advertisement is that referred to in the report of the drowned workman, and it is clear that 'Mr. Heath and Company' were tenants, not owners, of the property. Now the property was not sold as a result of the advertisement of 30th July 1756, and was again offered for sale on 25th October in the same year, this time by public auction. The owner of the property in question was named in the advertisement as 'Charles Shepherdson at Kings Newton, five miles from Derby', and a contemporary extract from a conveyance dated 1st August 1780[1] recited a number of earlier Deeds, among them one dated 19th November 1756 conveying from Charles Shepherdson of Kings Newton and others to John Heath a property described as 'beyond St. Mary's Bridge', that is to say, on the eastward side of the bridge, which exactly describes the position of the Nottingham Road factory site. The proximity in dates of the indenture (19th November) and that of the auction sale (25th October) poses a coincidence too great to be ignored and there seems little doubt that the properties were one and the same, 'Mr. Heath and Company' purchasing the property as sitting tenants.

It has not so far proved possible to ascertain the date on which Mr. Heath and Company first became tenants of the Shepherdson property, but since it is implied by the July advertisement that the manufactory was well-established at that date, it is not at all unlikely that it was in fact carried on there before 1st January 1756. Both John Heath and Planché were resident in Derby prior to the date of the Partnership Agreement, the former as a banker, whilst Duesbury was a newcomer to the town, having arrived from Longton at about the date of the Agreement,[2] and this would seem to point to an earlier association between Heath and Planché, an inference which is strengthened by the continued manufacture in later years at Heath and Duesbury's factory of some Planché models, and also to a continuity of manufacture on this site. The evidence is overwhelmingly in favour of Planché, financed by John Heath, manufacturing his china figures here on Nottingham Road under the name of 'Heath and Company'.

The identification of the productions of 'Heath and Company', or as they are better known, of Andrew Planché,[3] relies mainly upon four facts. First, the existence of several figures of early date which reappear as later Derby productions, examples being a *putto* (Plate 12),

[1] British Museum, Department of British and Mediaeval Antiquities, papers relating to the Derby China Factory (Bemrose papers).
[2] Jewitt, op. cit., pp. 66–67.
[3] See Appendix IX, List of Figures Attributed to Andrew Planché.

representative of *Autumn*, utilised for a candlestick of about 1760; *Pluto and Cerberus* (Plate 47), a *Dancing Youth*, and figures of *St. Thomas* and *St. Philip*. Second, the evidence of William Duesbury's London Account Book. Third, the results of chemical or other analysis, a high lead content (for example) being indicative of a Derby origin. Fourth, the survival of a few pressings from moulds which were disposed of at the closure of the Nottingham Road factory in 1848. These include some heads of figures, one of which matches that of the female of a *chinoiserie* group in the British Museum (Plate 16).[1]

Additionally, there are the three white cream jugs, which were long a puzzle and regarded as atypical. Dr. Ainslie, however, more recently drew attention to the presence, on each of three figures of *Kitty Clive*[2] (Plate 3) of a sprig of prunus blossom similar to that on the cream jugs; these figures, previously considered to be of Bow origin, now take their place as Derby figures of the pre-Duesbury period, the evidence of the prunus sprigs being supported by analysis showing 7·2% lead oxide in the body of the ware.[3]

The moulded flowers of the 1750 cream jugs, as well as those on the bases of the Derby *Kitty Clive*, have the peculiarity that the petals, of which there are four to each flower, are primitively modelled in a fan-shape with a raised and crinkled edge. Somewhat similar prunus sprigs, having a raised edge but more than four petals, and of more refined modelling, appear on an early bowl, square in shape with lobed corners, in the Derby Museum (Plate 2). This has early moth painting not unlike that on a rare teapot[4] also at Derby, though with a more brilliant glaze and crisper potting. Moth painting became a feature of Derby porcelain during the first years of Duesbury's proprietorship, and may have preceded Duesbury's advent, for an entry in his London Account Book reads:

'2 flower pots with moths on 8d.'

though the factory of origin is not named. Even closer to the 1750 cream jugs is a lobed cup at the Victoria and Albert Museum with sprigged florets painted in iron-red,[5] which appears to be of a date contemporary with these early productions.

[1] Another is illustrated in Yvonne Hackenbroch, *Chelsea and Other English Porcelain, Pottery and Enamel in the Irwin Untermyer Collection*, 1957, Plate 269.
[2] One is in the Schreiber Collection (Catalogue I, no. 1a), the other two are in private collections.
[3] The evidence is fully set out by Hugh Tait in 'Some Consequences of the Bow Exhibition', *Apollo*, vol. LXXI, 1960, pp. 42–43, and by Dr. Watney, loc. cit., p. 19.
[4] A similar lobed teapot in the Cecil Higgins Museum at Bedford has the incised date '1756'.
[5] Victoria and Albert Museum, no. C 19–1959.

Applied prunus decoration is well-known on early English porcelain, and particularly that of Bow, being derived from Chinese Fukien porcelain. The Bow flowers have raised edges to the petals very like those on the Derby Museum bowl.[1] It is possible that some early Derby table-wares may yet be masquerading as Bow, as were the non-phosphatic *Kitty Clive* figures, and a bone-ash test applied to some of these wares might conceivably result in the discovery of further additions to the few recognisable Planché table-wares. Dr. Watney, in a recent article[2] drew attention to two white wall brackets in the collections of Mr. D. Harris and Mr. A. F. Green respectively,[3] which, he points out, are both crisply modelled and slip-cast, besides possessing other characteristics of the 'dry-edge' figures which bring them into the Planché category. A coloured shell-shaped sauceboat with cray-fish handle from the collection at Althorp[4] is of a type variously attributed to Chelsea and Longton Hall but is close to 'dry-edge' Derby as regards paste and glaze. Also allied to these sauceboats are some shell centrepieces of which Dr. Watney illustrates[5] a coloured specimen in his collection and comments upon the similarity of its colour to that of the coral and shell incrustation of a 'dry-edge' Derby *chinoiserie* figure in the Untermyer Collection.[6] This in itself might merely indicate a common decorator such as William Duesbury, but analysis of the former shows a non-phosphatic body with a high lead content consistent with a Derby (Planché) origin.[7] However, even with the addition of the specimens for which Dr. Watney presents a strong case, there yet remains a virtual absence of those wares which we commonly associate with domestic use as table-wares and which can be ascribed to Derby prior to 1756.

The situation regarding figures is vastly different, upwards of fifty different models, animal and human, being attributed to Planché. Many are white, some are coloured and of the latter the decoration of a number may be regarded as the work of Duesbury's London decorating establishment. The figures which are nowadays attributed to Planché are in many instances far removed from the kind of article described by Samuel Keys[8] as 'small articles . . . such as Birds-Cats-

---

[1] Chelsea also used this Chinese motif, as did most Continental factories.
[2] Watney, *Burlington Magazine*, vol. CIX, no. 766, pp. 19–20.
[3] Another is at the Victoria and Albert Museum (Plate 22).
[4] R. J. Charleston, 'Porcelain in the Collection of Earl Spencer at Althorp', *Connoisseur*, Jan. 1967, Plate 14.
[5] Watney, *Burlington Magazine*, loc. cit.
[6] Yvonne Hackenbroch, op. cit., Plate 269.
[7] Watney, *Burlington Magazine*, loc. cit.
[8] Samuel Keys, in a note on the origins of the Derby China Factory, stated that small china models of animals were made by 'an individual in humble circumstances in Lodge Lane, Derby' (Derby Public Library MSS).

Dogs-Lambs-Sheep and other Animals'. Certainly figures of animals are represented among the Planché productions though some are not particularly small—the well-known Florentine *Boars*, for example (Plates 18 and 19). The figures regarded as Planché's, whether human or animal, are notable for a dynamic quality approaching in some instance the liveliness and verve of some of the best Continental models. They are characterised by a feeling of spontaneity alien to the more static appearance of most of their successors and this, together with certain physical qualities, has made them easier to recognise.

The modelling of these figures is generally sharp and clean, particularly in regard to the folds of garments and the body texture of the animals; sometimes the figures have a tendency to lean over. The glaze may be remarkably clean and bright, or it may be speckled or discoloured, or at times lacking in brilliance, with a candle-grease appearance. They are, without exception, slip-cast and therefore relatively thin, the hollow interior following the contours of the external modelling.

The process of slip-casting was carried on by Derby both during the Planché period and during the proprietorship of the two Duesbury's, father and son. Briefly, it involved the assembling of plaster moulds for the various parts of a figure—head, limbs etc.—and the pouring of liquid 'slip', i.e. the clay in liquid form, through a hole, usually in the base. The mould absorbed a proportion of the water in the slip, leaving a 'lining' of clay within the mould. After an interval the residue of the slip was poured away, the mould taken apart and the casting removed.[1] Before firing the base was normally closed with a piece of clay save for a small hole serving to release the steam generated during the firing.

The first, or biscuit, firing having then been successfully accomplished, the figures were ready for glazing after a little cleaning up. It is evident that the biscuit figure was dipped upside down into the glaze and was then stood on its base when the glaze would run down irregularly, resulting in the well-known 'dry-edge' characteristic of many, though not all, of the Planché figures. Where it appears, the glaze stops short of the foot in an irregular line revealing the biscuit body at the lower extremity. The whiteness of the glaze is also characteristic of Planché figures: it is somewhat opaque and apparently contained a proportion of tin oxide to ensure the clean, white appearance of the figure. The bases of the figures attributed to Andrew Planché are generally of 'bun' or mounded type, though some show slight rococo moulding, the latter perhaps being nearer to the time of Duesbury's advent.

[1] A full description of the technique of slip-casting is given in *Pottery and Ceramics* by Ernst Rosenthal, Penguin Books, no. A201, 1949, p. 95.

The remaining physical characteristic of the figures attributed to Planché is the so-called 'screw-hole', which is nothing more than the hole pierced through the base of the figure to allow the escape of steam during firing. The particular shape of this hole, which seems peculiar to Derby, and which is similar to a hole that might be drilled in a piece of wood to receive the shank of a countersunk screw, was evidently due to the use of a tool, tapering in shape, with which the hole was pierced in the raw clay. This is clearly shown in the case of a rare figure of a *Chinese Boy*, one of a set representing *The Elements*, beneath the base of which is incised the word 'Water'. On this piece the screw-hole has been driven through the inscription, partly obliterating it (Plate 13). Not all of the figures classified as Planché, however, have the screw-hole. In some examples the hole has straight sides, whilst others, some of the *chinoiseries* among them, have larger apertures occasionally leading to a smaller hole that may itself be of screw-hole type. A figure of Planché type in the Derby Museum has no hole in the base, which is unusual.

That the characteristic Planché screw-hole persisted into the succeeding 'pale' period (so called from the pale enamel colours used) is indicated by a pair of seated figures in the Derby Museum representing *Spring* and *Autumn*, which possess both the screw-hole and the 'patch marks' characteristic of the later period, and have star-like florets and applied flowers of two kinds—on the boy, flat and open, and on the girl, the petals half open and with slight gilding (Plate 48).

One feature of the modelling of these early figures which is fairly constant is that the mouths of the human figures are generally over-large, a characteristic that becomes emphasised when they are coloured, a typical example of this being the so-called *Dancing Shepherdess* at the Victoria and Albert Museum.[1]

Many Planché figures are white, but quite a number of coloured examples have survived and in some instances both white and coloured versions of the same figure exist, some of the former having perhaps been originally decorated in unfired pigments that have, in the course of time, become worn away. Whether any of the coloured decoration on Planché figures was executed at Derby, it is impossible to say. We know, however, from the entries in William Duesbury's London Account Book, that some were painted in his London workshop. The rather primitive painting of flowers and herbage on the bases of such examples as a pair of charging *Bulls* (Plate 20), as well as that on the coloured *Boars* and *Stags* (Plate 21), is usually attributed to Duesbury, and singularly unskilled it appears to be. From the Account Book we know that he painted 'Dancers Derby

[1] Arthur Lane, *English Porcelain Figures of the 18th Century*, 1961, Plate 61A.

11

figars' and the costumes of some of these bear simple, yet neat, floral sprig and star-like decoration. Similar sprigged ornamentation is seen on the dresses of *chinoiserie* figures and one may note that on 14th May 1751 Duesbury charged 1s. 6d. for painting '1 pair of large Chines men', though here the factory of origin is not recorded. At the same time it is noteworthy that the colouring of the Chinese groups in fresh yellow, puce and other colours is applied in a manner that is broad and effective.

Painting similar to the flower-sprig and star decoration on Planché figures is also to be found on certain Chelsea figures, generally those with the red anchor mark, made during the period when Duesbury was in London and perhaps decorated by him, and also on Longton Hall during its Middle Period between 1754 and 1757, whilst Duesbury was engaged there as an 'Enamellor'.[1]

Round holes, as distinct from the similarly placed square holes in Bow figures, were sometimes pierced in the back of Derby figures to hold metal branches to carry porcelain flowers.[2]

[1] For an example of the former see F. S. MacKenna, *Chelsea Porcelain—the Red Anchor Wares*, fig. 119, and of the latter B. Watney, *Longton Hall Porcelain*, figs. 34, 45a, 55a etc.
[2] The *chinoiserie* figure of *Water* described on pages 11 and 96 is an example.

2
WILLIAM DUESBURY I
1756–1769

There exists no evidence as to whether Andrew Planché continued, either as principal or employee, with the Derby manufactory after 1st January 1756, the date of the well-known unsigned Agreement; the latest record of his presence in Derby is on 3rd July 1756, when his son, William, was baptised at St. Alkmund's, near the China Works. John Heath, a local banker and partner in the nearby potworks at Cockpit Hill, undoubtedly provided the finance and gave his name to the business of 'Heath and Company'. During the year 1756, the works were extended by the acquisition of adjoining properties, and further property was acquired eight years later on 29th August 1764 by his leasing for twenty-one years a site known as Calver Close, immediately to the east of the manufactory. The Calver Close property, however, was not adapted for the manufacture of china until after the end of the century, when it was under the proprietorship of Michael Kean. But we are advancing too far and must return to April 1756, on the 19th of which month a number of properties adjacent to the Shepherdson property[1] were acquired by John Heath and

> 'were . . . converted into *and then continued to be* Workshops used and employed by the Sd. W. Duesbury and Company as such in the making of China.'[2]

The manufacture was carried on in these premises for some fifty years, further extensions taking place in 1781 and 1785,[3] and the whole of the site later became known as 'The Old China Manufactory' to distinguish it from 'The New Works' erected on Calver Close by Kean in 1798.

When considering the early productions of the new partnership we

[1] See p. 7.
[2] Duesbury MSS at the British Museum (Bemrose Collection). Conveyance dated 1st August 1780.
[3] Derby Co-operative Society Deeds, Conveyance 20th November 1840.

are obliged, through lack of positive evidence in the shape of dated or documentary pieces to group them in a general way according to their characteristics, and to conjecture as best we may their probable date.

First, there exists a rather small class of figures, which Lane considered to date from before 1756, the modelling of which retained much of the spontaneity and vigour of those which we associate with Andrew Planché, combined with a rather dirty, speckled glaze, and suitably termed 'transitional'. These 'transitional' productions probably overlapped the commencement of the Heath-Duesbury partnership, gradually giving place to a more defined factory product. Typical of this group is a taperstick in the form of a long-necked, plumed bird standing on a rococo base and coloured in a palette in which are prominent a fresh yellow, pale green and puce. Two examples of this taperstick are recorded, one in the Untermyer Collection[1] which is painted with a small group of flowers on the base, the other from the Foden Collection which possesses the added interest of a small vignette of figures in place of the flowers (Plate 23). The glaze of these tapersticks is speckled owing to foreign bodies from either the glazing or enamelling kiln, probably the latter, and perhaps indicates decoration outside the factory. In shape the birds of the tapersticks are not unlike some white Bow examples of even more fantastic shape, perhaps the 'hosterredg' (ostrich) of Duesbury's London Account Book.

A *Dancing Youth*, standing on a pierced rococo base, with typical Derby colouring of the period and beribboned in a manner much favoured by the factory both for figures and vases, has the unusual incised mark of a triangle within a circle, enclosing what looks like a letter 'Y'; the base shows 'patch marks' more usual on slightly later wares.[2] A figure described as the *Goddess Cybele*, with a lion, symbolic of 'Earth', standing on a high, mounded base, is also of 'transitional' type with pale gilding at the hem of the skirt (Plate 24).[3] Gilding is not common at so early a date in the history of the Derby factory, but slight gilding, pale in colour, appears also at the hem of the skirt on a 'dry-edge' figure of the *Lady with a Basket* at South Kensington.[4] A watchstand, the space for the timepiece being incorporated in extravagant rococo modelling, which has as its principal theme a Chinaman in flowered costume and a boy, whose blouse with frilled collar has the star-shaped florets already noted on Planché figures, is executed with great vigour both as regards the figures and the high

[1] Yvonne Hackenbroch, op. cit., Plate 280.
[2] Victoria and Albert Museum, Hutton Bequest (Cat. no. C540—1921). Illustrated in Lane, op. cit., Plate 62B.
[3] *Ibid.* (Cat. no. C45—1959), ex MacAlister Collection.
[4] *Ibid.* (Cat. no. C1410—1924), ex Broderip Collection.

B. DOVECOTE
Date about 1760   Height 21½ in.   'Patch marks'
Rous Lench Collection   See pages 25, 151, 173

pierced rococo base,[1] and possesses the dynamic quality of Planché figures, but the colouring and the rococo feeling suggest a later date. A pair of *Dancing Figures* with linked arms at the Fitzwilliam Museum have the large mouths of Planché figures but probably date from between 1756 and 1760.[2] Derived from Meissen the model is also found in Chelsea (red anchor period) and Bow. There is even a Chinese version at the Fitzwilliam. A pair of figures of a *Youth and Girl with Dogs*, the former having a strange, long-tailed bird perched upon his arm, at the British Museum, are mounted on pierced rococo bases very similar to that of the *Dancing Youth* at the Victoria and Albert Museum.[3] A figure of a *Chinese Boy Climbing a Tree* appears also to belong to this period (Plate 25), as does a *Youth with Dog* at the Fitzwilliam (Plate 26).

The application of flowers modelled in the round dates from this time, the flowers at first being rather large with wide-open petals coloured in puce, yellow and other shades and often with a 'hot cross bun' centre. Similar flowers together with ribbons (as on the beribboned youth already described) are a feature of some early globular vases with spreading feet, moulded in a mildly rococo manner and painted with vignettes of flowers or figure subjects (Plate 29). These vases are of a shape common also to Chelsea of the late red anchor or early gold anchor period about 1758, an example of the latter in the Schreiber Collection[4] at South Kensington having the neck pierced but lacking the ribbons and applied flowers of the Derby vases. Some of the Derby examples exhibit 'patch marks'—usually rather pale—caused by pads of clay, three in number, upon which the vases stood whilst in the glazing kiln. Vases, of rococo or other form, perhaps the *parfum* pots of the early catalogues, had covers of modelled flowers, and bear vignettes of figures, flowers and, occasionally, fables (Plate 28). Applied flowers of an early type are also a feature of a *Shepherdess* (Plate 27) whose skirts are painted with flowers and display a crispness of modelling comparable with the best Planché figures. Important in this transitional class is a candelabra of two branches in the Derby Museum, the candlestick being in the form of a flowering tree supporting a nesting bird while beneath the branches stand male and female figures wearing gaily flowered costumes (Plate 30). The flowers on tunics, coats and skirts of the earlier figures of Duesbury's proprietorship were at first simple sprigged or star-shaped florets of the kind found on the polychrome 'dry-edge' figures; soon, however, a

[1] Gilhespy, *Crown Derby China*, Plate 140.
[2] There exists some doubt as to the Derby origin of this group, but in the absence of analysis its appearance seems to support a Derby attribution.
[3] Lane, op. cit., Plate 62A.
[4] Schreiber Catalogue, I, no. 220.

more sophisticated manner appears with flowers drawn close to nature, though in colours rather arbitrarily dictated by the palette available, a strong iron-red being especially prominent, with the fine, threadlike stalks of the cotton-stem painter (Colour Plate C).

As the palette widened, so the painters were enabled to depict their floral decoration more naturally and in greater variety. Here we find ourselves entering on the first really distinctive Derby style of flower painting. In a manner derived from Meissen, this floral decoration of the costumes of figures is even more familiar on a considerable range of early Duesbury domestic wares. Sauceboats modelled as overlapping leaves with stalk handles, similar in shape to some Longton Hall examples, are relatively common. Others are fluted and have a low foot. Coffee cups and saucers, fluted or plain teapots (scarce because of their propensity for cracking) (Plate 35), plates with plain, moulded or perforated rims (Plates 31 and 32), a delightful double-handled cup and *trembleuse* saucer with perforated gallery (Plate 33), and other useful china, were all decorated with flowers by the 'cotton-stem' painter —at first in the palette already described with its characteristic iron-red and an ochreous yellow of somewhat hard appearance, the enamels lying often incompletely absorbed by the glaze. A second, and very attractive class of early flower painting is of much softer appearance, the artist utilising a wider palette including a clear yellow, pale blue, violet, indigo and rose-pink, and here the colours have largely been absorbed by the soft glaze that often gives an appearance of great richness and beauty. A bottle, or 'guglet' as the contemporary sale catalogues named such articles, with collared neck and bulbous body at the Victoria and Albert Museum has fine flower groups of this kind, including a particularly well-drawn iris with 'flared-out' petals. Other examples of this attractive decoration are to be found in the Derby Museum and elsewhere (Plate 34).

The scarcity of early Derby teapots has already been noted, but a small number of lobed teapots has survived, including the documentary example now in the Cecil Higgins Museum at Bedford with the incised date 1756. Unusually for Derby, this teapot is painted with Chinese figures and furniture very similar to some well-known Worcester decoration, and no doubt taken from a common Oriental source. An undated teapot of identical shape in the Derby Museum has a bird subject painted in rather heavy colours including a purplish blue (Plate 36), a colour which is also seen on a jug in the same collection, on the reverse of which is a bird subject of a kind that seems often to be associated with flowers of the 'cotton-stalk' painter. The same palette was used for both subjects, perhaps implying that the same painter was responsible for both the bird and the flower decoration, and a similar bird subject is seen on a bell-shaped mug a few years later in date (Plate 37). Some hand candlesticks, as well as dishes with scalloped rims, are delicately moulded with scrolls and flowers in garlands, reminiscent of the Chelsea 'damasked wares'. Not infrequently such wares exhibit lighter patches or 'moons' similar to those on Chelsea red anchor porcelain. Spouts and handles of teapots, some of a large size being 'punch kettles' rather than teapots, and those of the even scarcer coffee pots, were decorated with moulded foliate additions (Plate 39) and are sometimes fluted (Plate 38). Knops may be conical or floral, whilst a 'punch kettle' with puce decoration after the Japanese, probably by way of Meissen, has its knop in the shape of a lemon[1]. Other examples of porcelain fruit are rare in Derby, but a fine toilet pot of this period in the form of a peach is in the Derby Museum (Plate 40) and another is at the Victoria and Albert Museum. Dessert baskets were either perforated or had moulded basketwork and were painted in the interior with long-legged birds, flowers, fruit and other subjects. They have double-looped rope twist handles, which distinguish them from the Worcester baskets, and reeded feet, with applied florets at the intersections of the perforated sides (Plate 82). Fruit painting is large and bold, and is usually associated with large moths typical of early Derby, which appear on many wares (Plate 44). Jugs with rather prominent lips were evidently much in demand during this early period of the factory's history and are the vehicle for some vigorous and interesting decoration. One such, in Dr. and Mrs. Bold's collection, has a bounding hound in pursuit of a hare (Plate 46); others have delicately pencilled ears of corn, birds and flowers. A bright yellow is prominent in the palette of some of these wares similar to that of the contemporary figures. Butter tubs, oblong-octagonal in shape, were also made and painted with flowers or birds of the kind described; some have rather spidery-looking Chinese figures with an iron-red or slightly gilt border. Dishes modelled and coloured to simulate a fully open sunflower (Plate 41) are more likely to be derived from the similar Longton Hall examples than from Chelsea. Other possible links with Longton are the small asymmetrical vases already described and later, about 1760, some larger vases of somewhat similar shape, reeded and with frills picked out in a rather discoloured green enamel and poor gilding, their reserves painted with flowers or birds (Plate 75). Some oval dishes, their sides moulded as fruiting vines, are also somewhat reminiscent of Longton (Plate 45). Such resemblance is not surprising since Duesbury himself was at Longton Hall and the two places are not far apart.

The early figure production of the Heath and Duesbury partnership,

[1] In the Royal Crown Derby Porcelain Company's Museum.

if we exclude the 'transitional' figures already described (which may belong to the period either immediately before or that following the commencement of the Duesbury partnership), was labelled by the late W. B. Honey 'the pale-coloured family', which aptly describes the appearance. The glaze of these figures is sometimes unpleasantly blued, and overlies a light-weight chalky body; 'screw-holes' in the base are occasionally met with, a legacy from pre-Duesbury days, as on a figure of *Mars* or some seated *Seasons* on broad rococo bases, of which *Spring* and *Autumn* can be seen in the Museum at Derby (Plate 48).[1] The costumes of these figures, moreover, are painted with star-like florets in deep red-brown calling to mind the very similar decoration on some 'dry-edge' figures of the earlier period. Similar slight floral painting occurs on a 'pale' period *Pluto and Cerberus*, representing a later version of the Planché group of the same subject; this 'pale' period example is noteworthy for the deep turquoise lining to the cloak, being an early use of this colour at Derby, and for the large 'tears' of glaze that have accumulated here and there, particularly in the jaws of the dog *Cerberus* (Plate 47). A *Drummer* at Derby, playing a fife, stands on a shell-moulded base (Plate 49), whereas for the most part the smaller figures of this period are on bun, or mildly rococo bases. The majority of 'pale' period figures average six or seven inches in height, though a *Shepherdess* at Derby stands ten inches high on a five-footed rococo base with branches on either side (Plate 53), as does her companion at the Victoria and Albert Museum,[2] and a set of *Seasons* on square bases from a Meissen model is of a similar height (Plate 50).[3]

The palette used by the Derby painters to decorate these figures was similar to that found, and already described, on the early domestic wares. In particular, however, there is the persistent use of a deep yellow, which at times becomes strident, though use was also made of a softer yellow with very satisfactory results. Slight gilding, usually round the brims of hats and hems of skirts, is generally present, and among the floral patterns of dresses and costumes the hand of the 'cotton-stalk' painter is easily discernible (Plate 51). An important group of *Lovers and Clown* in the Untermyer Collection[4] was adapted from a Meissen group modelled by Johann Joachim Kaendler, and reappears about ten years later from new moulds as a 'patch' period group (Plate 57).

[1] Compare the similar Longton Hall models illustrated in Watney, *Longton Hall Porcelain*, Plates 34B and C.

[2] Lane, op. cit., Plate 63.

[3] Chelsea-Derby examples of the same model have rococo bases (see Schreiber Cat., vol. I, no. 341).

[4] Yvonne Hackenbroch, op. cit., Plate 272.

The frequent use of an over-blued glaze detracts from the appearance of many of these 'pale' period figures, its cold, starchy colour failing to harmonise with the bright yellows and other colours employed. Why the Derby artists refrained from colouring the cheeks of the 'pale family' is difficult to understand; some do possess a little colouring, but many were left untouched.

During the 'pale' period there first appeared a number of models that were continued during subsequent periods, in some instances almost to the end of the factory's existence. Among these were the ever-popular *Shakespeare*, after Scheemakers' monument in Westminster Abbey (1741), and *Milton*, also probably after Scheemakers.[1] Some charming and colourful *Harlequins* and *Columbines* from the Italian Comedy belong to this period, too (Colour Plate A), as do some of the small, and much sought after, blue tits, goldfinches and other birds (Plate 54). Such, in brief, were the figures heralded by Derby in 1756 as 'after the finest Dresden models', 'the nearest to Dresden', and 'the Second Dresden'.

As yet there existed no system of marking to denote the Derby origin of the factory's products. Some incised marks occur in the shape of crosses, probably workmen's marks; more obscure are those incised on a group of a *Sportsman and Companion* at the British Museum, consisting of a triangle with the letters 'T x T', and on another early figure in the British Museum where the triangle is accompanied by the letters 'T.T.L.'.[2] In the absence of other evidence these, too, are likely to be workmen's marks. In the Derby Museum the male figure of a pair known as *Gardener and Companion* (though more probably they are *Seasons*) (Plate 52) has incised in the base 'New D', which has been interpreted as referring to the new factory buildings set up at Derby in 1756 following the commencement of the Heath and Duesbury partnership,[3] or may be an abbreviation of 'New Dresden'.[4]

Documentary evidence concerning the Derby factory prior to 1770 is rather sparse. The large quantity of Derby China Factory papers, mainly business correspondence, preserved at the Derby Public Library and at the British and Victoria and Albert Museums, is mainly post 1770, among the few exceptions being some Apprenticeship Deeds, the earliest, dated 10th March 1765, being that of George Bradbury, apprenticed for seven years to 'China Repairing', and another on 23rd September of that year of Joseph Bullock to 'Painting on China or Porcelain', also for seven years. There is an agreement of

[1] Lane, op. cit., p. 33.
[2] British Museum no. C/D No. 63.
[3] A. L. Thorpe 'Some early Derby porcelain', *Connoisseur*, CXLVI, 1960, pp. 260–4.
[4] Note reference to Derby as 'the Second Dresden' in sale notices: see p. 21.

31st May 1769, between Duesbury and Robert Moad Wilmot, a Derbyshire landowner, for 'Oaktrees at Chaddesden Wood', which would be for the purpose of providing fuel for the enamel kilns, probably as charcoal. Charcoal was used at Derby at least as late as 1790, for on 20th May Leonard Lead, wood collier of Belper, near Derby, agreed with Duesbury 'to burn manufacture and convert into charcoal . . . cord wood'.[1]

A number of contemporary sale notices of the period have been unearthed and published, mainly by J. E. Nightingale,[2] though the catalogues themselves have not survived; catalogues of later sales, however, are fortunately extant and have been reproduced, in whole or in part, in the same publication.[3]

The earliest sale notice available is one of June 1756, and was first quoted by the late Edward Hyam.[4] The sale took place at 54 Richmond Wells, in Surrey, and, occurring so soon following the commencement of the Heath-Duesbury proprietorship, this notice, though brief, is necessarily of particular interest. The relevant part reads:

'. . . the greatest variety of the Derby Porcelain, in Figures, Jars, Candlesticks, Sauceboats, Lettices, Leaves, Roses, and several curious Pieces for Desserts, finely enamelled in Dresden Flowers, reckoned by Judges who have been Purchasers to excel, if not exceed, anything of the Kind in England.'

A notice in the *Public Advertiser* announced a further Sale of Derby Porcelain on 14th December in the same year, as follows:

'To be Sold by Auction
By Mr. Bellamy
By Order of the Proprietors of the DERBY PORCELAIN Manufactory at a commodious House in Princes Street, Cavendish Square. This and three following days. A curious collection of fine figures, jars, sauceboats, Services for deserts, and a great Variety of other useful and ornamental Porcelain after the finest Dresden models all exquisitely painted in Enamel, with Flowers, Insects, India Plants, etc.'

The descriptions of the articles sold at these two sales are similar to one another, as might be expected, the latter providing a little more information concerning the decoration of the wares, and emphasising

---

[1] Derby Public Library, Duesbury Manuscripts.
[2] Nightingale, *Contributions towards the History of Early English Porcelain from Contemporary Sources*, 1881.
[3] Extracts from these are contained in Appendix VI.
[4] Hyam, *The Early Period of Derby Porcelain*, 1926.

that they were coloured in 'enamel', that is, the colours were fired into the porcelain, as distinct from the 'cold' colours sometimes applied without firing and so liable, if not certain, to wear off. Among the first productions of the new partnership already discussed may be recognised some of the items described: figures 'after the Dresden models' (Plate 50), sauceboats of leaf and other shapes, rococo vases (perhaps the 'jars' of the sale notices) (Plate 29), candlesticks with figures, birds or animals (Plate 58), and leaf dishes (Plate 45). 'Lettices' and 'Roses' were, presumably, tureens or other containers so modelled, 'Roses' being very likely toilet or pomade pots after the Chelsea models. Tea-table wares are notably absent from the sale notices, though the teapot in the Cecil Higgins Museum bears the date 1756,[1] and some fluted tea and coffee cups also seem to belong to this early period. 'Services for desert' would include such wares as plates with basketwork or perforated rims, sunflower dishes and dessert baskets (Plates 31, 32 and 41).

In the Spring of 1757 a sale took place on 17th May; *The Public Advertiser* describing the event stated:

'. . . the largest Variety of the Derby or Second Dresden, with Chelsea, Worcester, Bow, Longton Hall, Birmingham, etc. At the large Auction Room facing Craig's Court near the Admiralty, Whitehall, there were Numbers of Quality and Gentry, who expressed great satisfaction at seeing the extensive Number of foreign, and the great Variety of the English China Manufactories; and admired at the great Perfection the Derby Figures in particular are arrived to, that many good Judges could not distinguish them from the real Dresden.'

This notice is particularly interesting in claiming Derby as the 'Second Dresden', and the figures already discussed as belonging to the so-called 'pale' period were, indeed, largely derived from 'Dresden' originals. The reference to 'Birmingham' china is obscure, but may refer to porcelain made elsewhere though decorated in that city by artists engaged chiefly in the painting of 'Enamels' from Bilston or Birmingham itself.[2]

On 28th January and again on 11th February 1758, the *Public Advertiser* announced as follows:

'The Proprietors of the DERBY China Company beg leave to acquaint the nobility and Gentry that they have fix'd their

[1] See p. 16.
[2] R. J. Charleston and B. Watney, 'Birmingham, The Great Toyshop of Europe', *E.C.C. Trans.*, 1966, vol. 6, part 2.

Porcelain to be sold by their Factor, *Mr. Williams*, at his large Foreign China Warehouse up one Pair of Stairs, formerly known by the name of Oliver Cromwell's Drawing Room, facing Craig's Court near the Admiralty, consisting of a great Variety of Figures, the nearest the Dresden, and curious Pieces for Deserts and all mark'd at the Factory's lowest Prices . . . the great Demand (for them) has encouraged the Proprietors to enlarge their Manufactory, and have engaged double the number of Hands they used to employ, which will enable them to send to the said Warehouse every week great Variety of new Goods, and much cheaper than anything of equal Quality made in England.'

On 6th March 1758, Mr. Williams followed up this announcement by advertising:

'that he has this day unpacked the greatest Variety of new Figures from Derby . . . and several curious Wares in Leaves, Baskets, etc., for Deserts, finely painted in Dresden flowers, and all warranted true enamel.'

'Wares in Leaves, Baskets, etc.' would probably comprise the well-known plates and baskets with perforated rims, moulded in the centre with over-lapping vine leaves (Plate 31), some very like Longton Hall models, baskets with or without pierced sides, sunflower dishes (Plate 41) and small pots in the shape of peaches (Plate 40) and other fruits.

Mr. Williams' China Warehouse facing Craig's Court was short-lived, for on 6th April 1758 it was announced:

' 'Tis assured that the large China Warehouse facing Craig's Court, Charing Cross, must soon be pulled down to widen the Way . . . Mr. Williams having received Warning to quit the Premises in a Short Time. There is to be sold at the above Warehouse the greatest variety in England of the Derby Porcelain or Second Dresden, foreign China etc. . . .'

Mr. Williams evidently transferred his business to Pall Mall since a notice quoted by Nightingale, and dated January 1763, describes him as 'China Dealer, Pall Mall'.[1]

About 1760, it appears, the 'pale' period figures gave way to a class of figures in which the so-called 'patch marks', resulting from the practice of standing figures and other articles upon pads of clay during the firing of the glaze, became particularly prominent. These 'patch marks', usually three or four in number, show as dark patches beneath the bases of figures and also of domestic wares, though in the

---

[1] Nightingale, op. cit., p. xxii.

case of the latter are generally confined to the larger wares. Their occurrence is not restricted to the period from 1760 to 1770 which we are now considering, but they appear to a lesser degree on productions belonging to the 'pale' period, and continue into the succeeding, Chelsea-Derby, period. It seems that the use of clay pads in this way during the glaze firing was not peculiar to Derby, since some Gold Anchor Chelsea productions show similar 'patch marks'; but so consistent is their appearance on the Derby productions at this time, that they are virtually accepted as evidence of a Derby origin (See Plate 56.)

Apart from the occurrence of 'patch marks' between 1760 and 1770, the figures made during this period differ from those of the 'pale' period in several ways: many were considerably larger,[1] indeed some were extremely large, as much as nineteen inches high, and were made in several sizes. The larger size of these figures became possible due to a change of body from that of the chalky paste of the preceding years to one of more substance and weight; the glaze often gathered thickly within the hollows of the rococo modelling and elsewhere, giving rise to crazing in such positions. The larger size also gave opportunity for a more elaborate decoration of costumes, but was accompanied by a greatly reduced vitality, the subjects being generally stiffly posed. Faces instead of appearing pale or colourless became ruddy-cheeked. Following the example of gold-anchor Chelsea, the addition of 'bocage', leafy or flowering backgrounds, to figures and groups became customary, and Derby bocage can often be recognised by the flowers having half-open, pointed petals tipped with colour, most often blue. Bases were generally heavy and scrolled, the scrolling being picked out in gold, puce-pink and a dirty looking turquoise. The latter colour evidently caused trouble in firing and is rarely, if ever, clear, but appears muddy and olive green in patches. Gilding was lavish, especially on the dresses and costumes of the figures, all following the Chelsea example, to which factory at one time all these figures were erroneously attributed. An important pair of *Musicians* (Plate 72) in Derby Museum are seated within pagodas reminiscent of Chinese Chippendale mirrors, one of which has 'cold' (unfired) decoration.

The great variety of figures and other wares produced at this time is indicated in a reference by Jewitt[2] to the sending to London in 1763 of no less than forty-two large boxes of Derby China. Jewitt lists some

[1] As in the case of the 'patch mark' group *Lovers and Clown* at the Royal Crown Derby Porcelain Company Museum (Plate 57), the earlier 'pale' period version being little more than half the size.
[2] Jewitt, op. cit., pp. 68–9.

of the articles thus despatched and it is worthwhile reproducing some
of them here:

'*Box No. 41*
8 Large Flower Jars
3 Large Ink Stands
1 Small ditto
4 Large Brittanias
6 Second size Huzzars
4 Large Pidgeons
12 Small Rabbits
12 Chickens
16 Small Baskets

Box No. 19
4 Large Quarters
2 Jupiters
2 Junos
5 Ledas
1 Europa
2 Bird Catchers
12 Sixth-sized Solid Baskets
18 Second-sized Boys

Box No. 31
4 Large Quarters

4 Shakespeares
6 Miltons
24 Bucks on Pedestals

Box No. 11
24 Enamelled, round fourth-sized open-worked Baskets
12 Blue ditto
12 Open-worked Spectacle Baskets
9 Second-sized Sage-leaf boats'

Also,

'blue fluted boats, mosaic boats, sage-leaf boats, potting pots, caudle
cups, blue strawberry pots, fig-leaf sauce boats, octagon fruit
plates, vine-leaf plates, coffee cups, flower vases, standing sheep,
feeding sheep, cats, sunflower bowls, pedestals, honeycomb jars,
coffee pots, blue guglets, and basins to ditto, butter tubs, Chelsea
jars, teapots, honeycomb pots, figures of Mars and Minerva, sets
of Elements, Spanish Shepherds, Neptune, The Muses, bucks,
tumblers, roses, Jupiter, Diana, boys, garland Shepherd, Spaniards,
Chelsea-pattern candlesticks, Dresden ditto, jars and beakers,
polyanthus pots, etc.'

Some of the figures named are familiar enough to us; the *Shakespeares*
and *Miltons*, and also those of classical myth and legend, often
representing sets of the *Elements*, *Muses* and other abstractions such
as a fine figure of *Jupiter* holding a thunderbolt and accompanied by
an eagle—a large example of which is in the Derby Museum, as is
another of *Leda and the Swan* (Plate 59), a seemingly vulnerable
model with a slender curved swan's neck. *Mars*, *Venus* (Plate 60),
Minerva, *Neptune*, *Diana* and others are examples of a long series of
classical figures which continued to be produced over many years. A
figure of a young man holding a dagger and with a cannon at his feet,
representative of *War*, is an uncommon model (Plate 61). Others are

less easily recognised; for example, what are we to make of 'Bird Catchers', 'Spanish Shepherds', 'tumblers' and 'Huzzars'? As to 'Bird Catchers', there are the groups of lovers generally called *Liberty and Matrimony*, with their symbolic birdcage. We have shepherds, certainly, but why 'Spanish'? 'Tumblers' might be Harlequins from the Italian Comedy, of which Derby made a number of models in various sizes (Plate 64 and Colour Plate A).

Pigeons, rabbits and chickens are scarce to-day, yet there is no mention of the goldfinches, linnets, owls and other small figures of birds, many of which have 'patch marks', as in the case of a pair of *Owls* at Bedford and two small *Parrots* at Rous Lench. A lively *Leopard* at Derby is also of this period, as is a large and imaginative *Dovecote* at Rous Lench (Colour Plate B), a later version of which is included in a sale list of 10th May 1781 (see p. 173).

Returning to human models, in addition to the *Shakespeares* and *Miltons*, there are ceramic 'portraits' of *James Quinn as Falstaff* (Plate 62), after a mezzotint by James McArdell, and of *David Garrick as Tancred* (Plate 63) from Thompson's *Tancred and Sigismunda*, in which play Garrick first appeared in 1744–5.[1] A series of *Blackamoors* (Plates 65 and 66) was probably copied from contemporary book illustrations, as were many other figures. In satirical vein is the *Tithe Pig* group in which the farmer and his wife are offering to the parson the child in place of the pig as tithe (Plate 67); barbed wit aimed at the clerics of the day was popular amongst countryfolk in particular but is more commonly portrayed in the earthenware figures of the Staffordshire potters, and in prints on creamware and other domestic pots. Here, however, the theme is reproduced on the more sophisticated porcelain and it is interesting that Derby also issued the three figures of the *Tithe Pig* group separately. Far removed from the earthy nature of the farmer and his family are the tall *Ranelagh* figures, splendidly attired in fancy dress, the female of the pair wearing a miniature said to represent an admission ticket to the Ranelagh Gardens. Aubrey Toppin identifies the figure with a mezzotint of Mary, Duchess of Ancaster, by McArdell after Hudson published in 1757.[2]

With contemporary entertainment we may also associate a bold pair of 'patch mark' figures at Derby known as the *Duet Singers*, the origin of which has not been found. Dressed in flowered costume they stand on robust rocky bases holding in upraised hands the music of their song, but unfortunately words and music are represented only by wavy lines (Plate 68).

[1] Schreiber Collection Catalogue, I, no. 301.
[2] *E.C.C. Trans.*, 1951, vol. 3, part 1, p. 70.

The production of 'romantic' *Shepherdesses* and other country figures continued, many with highly decorative, even sophisticated costumes, plentifully bedecked with flowers modelled in the round (Plate 70). Of this class is a figure of a standing *Shepherd* in fancy dress which was sold in America in 1926 from the Leverhulme Collection and which is a documentary example of the period by virtue of an incised inscription on the base: 'George Holmes did this figer 1765'. The present whereabouts of the figure does not appear to be known. A group of two standing figures, a young man and a young woman, in the collection of the Royal Crown Derby Porcelain Company, possesses much charm. The woman holding a fold of her apron filled with fruit may represent *Autumn* from a set of *Seasons* (Plate 71). Allied to these 'folk' figures are those of *Street Sellers*, of which Derby Museum has an attractive pair of *Map-sellers* (Plate 69) derived from Meissen, probably by way of Chelsea, where similar representations were made. Also, a figure of a woman, richly dressed in flowered skirt and coat trimmed with ermine, a scarf round her head, apparently selling objects from the basket she holds, is commonly regarded as the actress Mrs. Cibber in the character of a *Vivandière* (Plate 63), but Lane has shown that the association is not supported by evidence.[1]

Of the domestic wares listed by Jewitt as being amongst those sent to London in 1763, baskets of various sizes, both 'solid' and pierced, also the so-called chestnut baskets with pierced covers (Plate 74), are well-known, decorated with birds, flowers and moths, or in blue and white. 'Blue fluted boats' may well be the low-footed, fluted sauce-boats painted in underglaze blue with oriental scenes and elaborate borders. Other similar sauceboats are from the early period and are painted with the typical early Derby bird subjects and 'cotton-stalk' flowers, the shape continuing into the Chelsea-Derby period. 'Fig-leaf sauceboats' were probably the rather robust sauceboats with low foot ring, moulded panels, and a high, strongly grooved handle from the base of which depend leaves and fruit. These are to be found in both polychrome and blue-and-white. 'Octagon fruit plates' have moulded cell diapers touched out in colour on the rims; or moulded basketwork, with florets at the intersections, may be found on them as well as on round plates, often painted boldly with fruit; the vine-leaf plates were moulded with overlapping vine leaves touched out in sickly yellow and yellowish-green and embellished with flower-sprays by the 'cotton-stalk' painter. The earliest coffee-pots were lobed, as were the teapots already described, and had a foliate or scroll moulding on the spout. They were painted with the usual subjects or, less often, with

[1] Lane, op. cit., p. 103.

C. MUG
Date about 1756   Height $4\frac{3}{8}$ in.
Victoria and Albert Museum   (Herbert Allen Collection)   See page 16

Chinese figures, as were some rather uncommon tall and fluted examples (Plate 38) upon which were painted elongated *Lange Liszen* figures (Long Elizas) in a fresh palette by an artist who painted almost identical subjects on a Cockpit Hill (Derby) creamware teapot at Temple Newsam. 'Guglets' were water bottles of globular shape with long necks having a swelling near the top, the name being descriptive of the sound made by water being poured from such a vessel. It is evident, therefore, that the table-wares sent to London in 1763 were largely the same models as those made from the commencement of Duesbury's proprietorship, but whereas the earliest examples were of a rather coarse body, with a tinned glaze, the corresponding wares of the 'patch' period are more translucent and 'patch marks' are usual—except that in the case of those possessing a foot-ring the marks left by the clay pads are likely to be less conspicuous, or even missing altogether. Very elegant are some well-proportioned condiment sets with silver covers, one set being at the Victoria and Albert Museum and a single sugar caster in the Derby Museum (Plate 73). Trouble was, however, experienced in eliminating air bubbles from the paste, and at times the body erupted in blisters, sometimes of a large size, and firecracks are common.

Shell centrepieces, consisting of tiers of scallop shells mounted on massive rockwork bases encrusted with smaller shells of all descriptions, belong to the 'patch' period and are often of a large size and heavy in weight. Sometimes they were made in two sections, one to be mounted upon the other (Plate 84). The best proportioned are those surmounted by a well-modelled kingfisher, and these may be decorated in polychrome or underglaze blue. One polychrome example has a seated male figure as a finial. These Derby shell centrepieces are to be distinguished from the somewhat similar Bow and Worcester ones, particularly the blue-and-white ones, by their very substantial and heavy bases, usually with well-defined 'patch marks', and the colour of the cobalt, which may be of a rich violet-blue tone, or a very dark colour that is frequently of a dry appearance, not being fully covered by the glaze. The fashion for porcelain modelled as rockwork, seaweed and shells was first introduced in this country in the early days of the Chelsea factory and was originally derived from silverware of the more ornate type. The shells themselves are said to have been modelled from natural marine shells and, at best, they certainly reproduce in a most realistic way the shapes of a large number of different types. They serve also as bases for such classical figures as *Neptune* and *Venus* (Plate 60).

Prominent among the 'patch marked' wares are the sets of vases popularly known as 'frill' vases; these are lavishly ornamented with

27

applied flowers, have female masks on either side, and a 'frill' around the lower part of the vase which, in the case of the centre vase of a garniture, is globular with a perforated cover and (usually) a bird finial (Plate 76), whilst the flanking vases are beaker-shaped, the bodies of all being pierced in a decorative manner. One such vase is inscribed on the foot 'Jonathon Boot 1764',[1] confirming the date of such 'patch mark' productions. Other rather rare 'patch mark' vases have a deep underglaze blue ground with gilding in the Chelsea manner, heavy rococo handles embellished, as are the covers, with flowers modelled in the round. One such vase, in the Derby Museum, is painted on a large scale with the subject of *Birdcatchers* (Plate 77).[2] Unusual for Derby is a fine pair of rococo wall vases of cornucopia shape, the scrollwork picked out in turquoise and gold and painted with dishevelled birds (Plate 78). The excellence of the turquoise enamel on these vases suggests that they were made about the time of the acquisition by Duesbury of the Chelsea establishment.

Reference has been made to Derby table-wares painted in underglaze blue. It was long believed that blue-and-white porcelain was only made at Derby on a small scale. Contemporaneously both Bow and Worcester, not to mention Lowestoft, were engaged to a very great extent in supplying a ready market with the English counterpart of Chinese blue-painted china, of which immense quantities were imported into this country. There existed a great demand for utility wares so decorated and it would have been surprising if Duesbury had not endeavoured to obtain a share of the business. At one time considered to be very scarce, an increasing quantity of Derby blue-and-white has been identified, and although the output must have been small by comparison with that of Worcester, Bow, Lowestoft and Caughley, Derby blue-and-white is nowadays accepted as forming a not inconsiderable part of the factory's output. It has been suggested that Derby experienced difficulties due to the blue running in the soft glaze, and for that reason Duesbury did not persevere with it. However, surviving specimens hardly bear this out, many being technically of excellent quality. A more likely reason to account for the smaller quantity of surviving Derby blue-and-white is that the ware itself was insufficiently robust to withstand daily domestic use (the scarcity of early teapots has been noted). It may well be that, for this reason, the quantity made was relatively small, or it may be that

[1] In Mrs. Esmé Godkin's Collection, and see Sotheby Catalogue of 18th April 1967, Lot 133, where Jonathon Boot is described as having been a modeller at Cobridge in Staffordshire, and is said to have learnt his trade at Derby. His apprenticeship papers, however, are not among the surviving papers of the factory.

[2] Vases of this type have the appearance of the work of an outside decorator.

a larger proportion than usual has succumbed to the hazards of two hundred years of domestic use.[1]

Derby blue-painting naturally followed the popular forms derived from Chinese export porcelain. There are three main types. One, which appears to be the earliest, is a rather spidery portrayal of the familiar Chinese watery landscapes of islands and pagodas, commonly found in the interior of perforated baskets of which the moulded florets and reeded foot, and sometimes the ribs of the basketwork, are picked out in blue (Plate 82); this 'spidery' decoration often has a 'dry' appearance, being insufficiently covered by the thin glaze. The second type is a soft-toned blue of considerable beauty, beneath a full, bright glaze (Plate 81); and the third a heavily applied, very dark violet-blue, at times rising through the glaze, at other times appearing very deep and rich beneath a brilliant glaze (Plate 83). Whether the varying results of painting in underglaze blue were deliberate or accidental it is hard to say. It is probable that all three types were contemporary and therefore most likely the result of batches of cobalt of varying purity and/or unstable kiln conditions.

Much less common than blue-painting on Derby are the few examples of blue-printing. In 1764, Richard Holdship came from Worcester to Derby and undertook to teach enamelling 'in blew', and it can be fairly deduced that such blue-printing as appears on Derby porcelain resulted from his advent. Whether Holdship himself engraved copper plates at Derby is uncertain; probably he did not. Jewitt quotes[2] a bill from one John Lodge for engraving plates with Chinese figures and borders in 1771. The known designs are: a version of the *Chinaman Riding an Ox*, with a very tall pagoda and swans on the reverse of the piece; a rare portrait of Queen Charlotte; a heavily printed flower basket group; a poorly composed Chinese scene; and a version of the 'red bull' or 'spinning maiden' pattern of Worcester and Liverpool. These Derby blue-prints are characterised by an uncertain line and a general smudginess, an exception being the flower basket subject on some dessert plates with feather-moulded edge. But of all blue-printed Derby none can compare for quality with that of a seemingly unique 'patch mark' jug in Derby Museum, printed in a soft blue with a stag at lodge within a paled fence—representing, in fact, the arms of the town of Derby and known locally as the *Buck in the Park* (Plate 81). Richard Holdship, in addition to his agreement to teach blue-printing to the Derby hands, also undertook to sell to Heath and Duesbury his 'secret process' for

[1] It is noteworthy that among the wares sent to London in 1763 were a number described as 'blue' (p. 24).

[2] Jewitt, op. cit., vol. II, p. 89.

making china using soapstone and to supply them with 'sufficient quantities of soapy rock at fair prices'.[1] Derby appears to have used soapstone for a short period, since examples from about 1765 are recorded as showing magnesia on analysis.[2] In 1770 Derby adopted a bone-ash formula.

Blue-and-white china continued to be produced at Derby well into the Chelsea-Derby period, later examples possessing the fine body of that period; but blue-and-white did not survive, it seems, the death of the elder Duesbury in 1786.[3] There are a number of references in the sale catalogues[4] to wares decorated solely in underglaze blue, e.g. 'twelve double-shape coffee cups, blue Nankin pattern', 'one pair of potting pots and 6 large scallop'd shells blue and white', 'large coffee pot, blue Nankin pattern', 'six scallop shells, asparagus servers and 6 artichoke cups, blue and white'. Yet not only are these but a tiny proportion of the whole, but, with the exception of the coffee-pot and the 'French shape cup and saucers', the types of wares mentioned are small both in size and importance.

In contrast to most other English factories, Derby made little use of Oriental decoration in its earlier years. Indeed, not until towards the end of the century did the Oriental theme appear in quantity. There are some sparsely executed pagoda scenes, as on a dish at Derby with a 'dirty turquoise' border (Plate 79), and the occurrence on early teapots and coffee-pots of Long Elizas has been noted; some of these are very much in the Worcester manner. Some 'patch mark' mugs and other wares have rather stiffly painted Chinese figures with a formalised palm tree and a more extensive treatment of the same theme is found on a desk writing-set in the Derby Museum portraying sketchy landscapes and anglicised Chinese figures (Plate 80). Similar treatment is afforded some rare, and perhaps earlier, mustard pots, pounce pots and bulbous salts.[5] Further decoration in the Oriental style appears, as we shall see, during the ensuing Chelsea-Derby period.

By way of contrast to the china made at Worcester, only a relatively small proportion of the Derby wares made under Duesbury's proprietorship seems to have been painted by independent decorators. William Duesbury appears to have lent financial assistance to the

[1] Jewitt, op. cit., vol. II, p. 89. It will also be remembered that Holdship held the rights to mine soapstone at Gew Graze in Cornwall. (Barrett, *Worcester Porcelain and Lund's Bristol*, p. 4.)

[2] In *E.C.C. Trans.*, 1964, vol. 5, part 4, p. 248, Mr. Dudley Delevigne refers to two Derby analyses disclosing magnesia 'in good quantity'.

[3] For a fuller account of Derby blue-and-white see Bernard Watney, *English Blue and White Porcelain of the Eighteenth Century*, ch. 6., 1963.

[4] Nightingale, op. cit. and Appendix VI.

[5] Gilhespy, op. cit., Plates 11, 12 and 14.

London decorator James Giles, and the dishevelled birds appearing on some rather puzzling plates may be from his workshop; the paste and glaze of these plates are of early appearance, with 'moons' visible by transmitted light and the plates themselves are frequently distorted. Possibly Giles obtained some of the old undecorated stock from Derby, or they may have been old Chelsea stock taken over by Derby in 1769, for the mould was common to both factories. One such plate has the signature 'Thos.F. . . .' (the surname is unfortunately illegible) hidden in the wing of a moth, but so far the painter has not been identified (Plates 42 and 43).

3

CHELSEA–DERBY PERIOD
1770–1784
(i) INTRODUCTION

If, as the proverb says, imitation is the sincerest form of flattery, then Duesbury must have had a high regard for the porcelain made at Chelsea and it is not surprising that when, in 1769, the opportunity arose of acquiring the Chelsea works, Duesbury and Heath seized their chance. Sprimont, the proprietor of Chelsea, had indeed offered his manufactory for sale as early as 1763, but presumably at that time the Derby proprietors had not felt justified in making the purchase. As it happened, the sale did not take place and even in 1769, when Sprimont advertised for a second time, the Chelsea works did not pass directly to Duesbury. They were first sold to a James Cox, an exporter of musical boxes, musical clocks and other automata, who it has been suggested (correspondence between Wedgwood and Bentley supports this) intended associating with Matthew Boulton in the marketing of porcelain wares mounted in ormolu. However, on the death after a very short time of Francis Thomas, who had been works manager for Sprimont, Cox, having no practical knowledge of the porcelain trade, decided to sell out, and in February 1770 Duesbury and Heath became the proprietors of the china factory which had been their main competitor and on many occasions, let it be said, their guide and inspiration.

Although the output from the Chelsea factory in its declining years cannot have been large, there nevertheless existed amongst its artists and craftsmen a considerable wealth of artistic talent, technical knowledge and experience, and Duesbury lost no time in making this expertise available to his Derby works. One result was that bone-ash was introduced for the first time into the china body, this ingredient having been used at Chelsea since about 1758; a bill dated March–July 1770, from one William Johnson, reads: 'To 10 Bags of Bonash from London.' The result of these developments was a marked improvement in the quality of the paste, the thinness of the potting, the evenness of the glaze and the colour of the enamels. The Derby turquoise lost its smudgy, dirty look and approached more nearly the pleasant shade seen on gold-anchor Chelsea wares. On the other hand, the rich Chelsea claret colour deteriorated, perhaps because the craftsman responsible for it migrated to Worcester, where a beautifully controlled claret ground was most effectively employed. It is noteworthy that in 1768 Worcester had announced the recruitment of 'the best painters from Chelsea'. Be that as it may, Duesbury must have been successful in keeping some of Chelsea's skilled workmen, sharing them out between the London and Derby factories, since the quality of the wares rose considerably in the 1770s.

Collectors and ceramic historians have for long been intrigued by the possibility of distinguishing the wares made at Derby from those made at Chelsea during the period 1770 to 1784, whilst both manufactories were in production. It has been suggested that a clue might be found in the two quite distinct factory marks used during this time. It is a fact that on acquiring the London works Duesbury found himself the proprietor of a factory which had for over twenty years possessed a factory mark: the anchor in relief or in colour or gold. His own factory, which had been in existence almost as long, had not marked its wares. Naturally Duesbury would not wish this situation to continue and he was therefore faced with the necessity of creating a mark which would publicly distinguish the Derby wares from any other. Tradition has it[1] that a visit by George III in 1773—presumably to the London showrooms since there is no record of a royal visit to Derby in that year—gave Duesbury the right to mark his wares with the royal crown. This symbol alone of course could indicate no more than that Duesbury had received royal patronage. The privilege did, however, enable Duesbury to incorporate the royal symbol in the factory mark. This mark took the form of a crown surmounting a script 'D' usually painted in blue but occasionally in puce. Contemporarily there was another mark done in gold in which an anchor was conjoined in a monogram with a script 'D'. It is not certain whether the 'D' stands for 'Derby' or 'Duesbury'; the fact that it is part of both marks would seem to support the latter. In any case the description 'Duesbury-Chelsea' would be a much better way of describing the wares made at Chelsea during Duesbury's proprietorship. 'Chelsea-Derby' would seem to be a term unknown in Duesbury's day and is a name first used by nineteenth century

[1] Haslem, op. cit., p. 23.

writers.[1] It would be logical to assume that those wares marked with the anchor and 'D' had a Chelsea origin—or were at least decorated at Chelsea, since it is usually at the decorating stage that the mark is applied—while those bearing a crown and 'D' had been made or decorated at Derby. Despite the absence of definite proof, and after recognising the possibility that some wares may well have been manufactured at one factory and decorated at the other, it is hard to believe that two such distinct marks, known to be contemporary, should have been applied without some plan or purpose. Yet another mystery surrounds the use of these marks. Why are they absent from the very considerable output of figures which are today classed as 'Chelsea-Derby'? There exist a number of figures and groups, as well as vases, which bear the anchor in gold without the script 'D' and which on technical and stylistic grounds can reasonably be attributed to Derby rather than Chelsea before the amalgamation; these are usually Duesbury's copies of Sprimont's models.[2] For a period of not less than ten years, during which time the production of figures at Derby, in biscuit as well as glazed, became established on a firm commercial as well as artistic basis, as evidenced by the practice then introduced of cataloguing and numbering each model, none of the figures carried a factory mark. Many did, however, bear the model number, incised, of the Derby Factory Price List: some, where the same figure was produced in different sizes (usually three, but at times five or six) carry the incised word 'small' or 'large'.

The weekly statements of work done at Chelsea show that the number of hands there, hardly more than a dozen, was tiny compared to the number at Derby.[3] Nevertheless it is evident, since he renewed the lease several times, that Duesbury looked upon the Chelsea works as making an important contribution to his business. Indeed, in April 1771, on the occasion of his first public sale after becoming proprietor of both works, Duesbury gave Chelsea priority of place in the sale catalogue, describing them in the order 'Chelsea and Derby'.

The evidence of the weekly statements quoted by Jewitt might seem to lead to the conclusion that the output of Chelsea after its acquisition by Derby consisted almost wholly of seals and other

[1] It would perhaps be pertinent to mention that the term 'Crown-Derby' is also a late nineteenth century term; it was not used by any of the eighteenth century topographical writers describing the industries of the town nor even by Haslem or Jewitt writing in the 1870s.

[2] R. J. Charleston (ed.), *English Porcelain*, 1965, Plate 7B, shows a crimson ground vase in gold anchor Chelsea style, painted with Vertumnus and Pomona copied from an engraving published in 1771, i.e. after Duesbury's acquisition of the Chelsea factory.

[3] Jewitt, op. cit., vol. I, pp. 180–182, vol. II, pp. 70–71. See also Appendix V, pp. 150–3.

'toys'. However it will be noted that all the examples cited occur within the years 1770 to 1773 and it is hard to believe that some at least of the services and perhaps the figures and decorative pieces such as vases were not made at the Chelsea works between, say, 1775 and 1783.

From the Duesbury papers in the Derby Public Library[1] it would seem that at the Chelsea works the potting and glazing were the responsibility of Richard Boyer and Richard Barton, with the assistance of the workmen Inglefield, Roberts and Piggot. In the weekly bills sent from London to Duesbury in Derby we find Inglefield 'Cleaning of the Bisket Work to be Glas^d', Roberts making 'Soports for the inhamil (enamel) Kiln', and Piggot 'Grinding of the Case Clay and Working the Bruisers', besides Barton 'Glazing of the Work' and Boyer 'Making of 1 perfume Jarr on 4 feet', also making seals and other small 'toys'.

Most, if not all, of these wares were decorated at Chelsea by Zachariah Boreman, Wollams, Jenks and Snowden, all named in the Weekly Bills between 1770 and 1773. Richard Askew, whose *Putti in Clouds* had already made their appearance on gold anchor Chelsea wares, also painted for Duesbury at this time, though apparently as an independent artist, since he rendered his own bills for work done. On the cessation of manufacture at Lawrence Street, Chelsea, Boreman, on 26th August 1783, entered into an agreement with Duesbury to serve him as a painter on china.

A modeller named Gauron appears for the first time in June 1773, and was the highest paid workmen in Chelsea at that time, receiving 8s. 9d. per day, compared with Boreman's 5s. 3d. per day. Three years earlier one Thomas Morgan, who appears in some capacity to have been looking after Duesbury's interests at Chelsea, wrote to Duesbury saying he had been informed by a 'Mr. De Viveur', of Tournai, of a modeller named 'Mr. Garon' at Tournai who was willing to come to England.[2] 'Mr. De Viveur' was doubtless the china painter Henri Joseph Duvivier, of Tournai, whose nephew, Fidèle, had in October 1769 undertaken to paint on china for William Duesbury for a period of four years. Fidèle's work on Derby porcelain remains yet to be positively identified, though his signed painting on porcelain of other factories, notably that of Worcester, Caughley/Coalport and New Hall is recorded.[3]

Sales of Chelsea and Derby china were held in London from 1771

---

[1] See Appendix V.

[2] Duesbury MSS at Derby Public Library, Appendix V, pp. 150–3.

[3] A notable contribution is by Margaret Foden in *Antique Dealer and Collector's Guide*, July 1968, p. 56.

onwards, including those on 5th May 1778, when there was offered for sale 'The Remainder of the Valuable Stock of the Chelsea Porcelain Manufactory', and in December 1783, offering 'All the remaining Finished and Unfinished Stock of the Chelsea Porcelain Manufactory in Laurence Street, near the Church, Chelsea', with 'All the Buildings and Fixtures thereto belonging'. On 16th December, the news of the sale having reached Derby, William Duesbury wrote to his son, William, in London, 'I am very glad to here (sic) the Sale went so well at Chelsea'. Even after this apparently final farewell there appeared the announcement of yet another sale by auction, on 17th May 1784, of 'The Derby and Chelsea Porcelain'.

On 18th February 1784, however, Richard Boyer wrote to Duesbury informing him that 'we are pretty forward in the pulling down of the bildings (sic) at Chelsea', and on the 2nd March the removal of equipment to Derby was under way.

Meantime at Derby the future of the manufactory was being assured by the apprenticing of a number of younger men, and by the engagement of experienced workmen also under agreement for a period of years, as was the custom at that time. Among them were Jacob Spooner, kiln man (who later went to Pinxton with Billingsley); William Gadsby, mould maker; Thomas Mason, repairer; and William Smith, the latter being apprenticed to his father, Constantine Smith, to learn 'that same art or mistery (sic) of preparing colours, painting and enamelling on Porcelain'.[1] Most of these pass briefly across the scene, and are known only through the chance survival of their indentures or agreements, and are not again heard of, but one young man engaged by Duesbury at this time was destined to become famous both in his own lifetime and down to the present day for his skill in flower painting on porcelain—William Billingsley, who was apprenticed for five years on 26th September 1774.

In addition to technical benefits Duesbury, an astute business man, would have been quick to realise the commercial prestige which might accrue to him by virtue of his acquisition of the Chelsea works. For nearly twenty years Chelsea had had the lion's share of the metropolitan luxury trade in English porcelain, enjoying the patronage of royalty and the high nobility. To much of this Duesbury justifiably hoped to succeed, and to this end in 1773 he opened his London showroom in a building, formerly the Castle Tavern, in Bedford Street, Covent Garden, with William Wood as his agent—succeeded in 1777 by Joseph Lygo. We have noted the visit of the King shortly after the opening of the showroom and, on 23rd July 1776, the Queen

[1] See Appendix V, p. 125.

also visited the premises and William Wood wrote to Duesbury at Derby:

'On Friday last her Majesty accompanied with the Duchess of Ancaster was pleased to honor with her presence Mr. Duesbury's Ware Rooms in Bedford Street, Covent Garden. Condescended to express great approbation at these Beautiful articles of Derby and Chelsea Porcelain and Paintings and Encouraged the same by making some purchases.'

The Queen's visit must have been encouragement indeed for Duesbury, and royal patronage continued from this time for many years. In December 1783, we find Duesbury writing to his son:

'Wee have all the Prince's china well glased ready to begin when the Holadys is over . . . we have the Duk of Ankistor's things all well glased. . . .'

Preserved in the Derby Public Library, much of the correspondence between Joseph Lygo and Duesbury I and II provides many interesting sidelights on the activities of the business at the time; some extracts from these letters are given in Appendix V. It is plain that the London showroom was of invaluable assistance to Duesbury, providing a link between customer and factory. Through the London agent came commissions for important services and decorative wares such as garnitures of vases and, equally important, criticisms and complaints to which any manufacturer would have to attend if he wished to retain such valuable customers. There seems little doubt that it was Heath and Duesbury's careful attention to all sides of the business, balancing that which was technically possible with what was commercially profitable, that enabled the factory to become established on so firm a foundation that Duesbury's son, also William, when he became proprietor on the death of his father in 1786, was able to make the Derby China Works, at least for a short time, the first in the land.

4

CHELSEA–DERBY PERIOD
1770–1784
(ii) FIGURES

The production of figures following the merger of Chelsea with Derby was very markedly a continuation of the Derby tradition rather than that of Chelsea. Indeed, remembering the many large, even spectacular, models produced in the Chelsea factory in the last years of its independent existence, it is remarkable how few were carried over into the Chelsea–Derby period. The most notable exception was the revived production at the Chelsea works of the highly popular 'toys' and seals (Plate 116).[1] Arthur Lane and R. J. Charleston[2] suggest that a few of the moulds from the 'Girl-in-a swing' Factory, as well as a larger number fashioned from models made by Joseph Willems working at Sprimont's Chelsea Factory from 1754 to 1763, were taken over by Duesbury in 1770. From the weekly accounts[3] it is clear that literally thousands of these were turned out in the early years of the Chelsea–Derby period. The following are typical entries from the weekly bills:[4]

'Seals painted by Jinks 33 lambs $1\frac{1}{2}$	$4-1\frac{1}{2}$
Cupid Forgin Harts at 1s 3d	1–3
Overtime painting by Jinks 2 dozen Tomtits at $1\frac{1}{2}$ each	3–0
1 dozen and 6 Cupid as a Doctor	1–9
Smelling bottles of boys catching squirrel at 1s. 3d.	2–6'

It is a remarkable fact that few examples of these Chelsea–Derby

---

[1] 'Toys' are miniature figures, sometimes adapted as scent-bottles, needle cases etc., usually about three inches high; seals are even smaller figures rarely exceeding one inch in height, standing on a mound for mounting on intaglios used to stamp wax seals.

[2] 'Girl-in-a-Swing Porcelain and Chelsea', *E.C.C. Trans.*, 1962, vol. 5, part 3, pp. 131–2.

[3] Jewitt, op. cit., vol. I, pp. 179–186.

[4] Further extracts are quoted in Appendix V, pp. 150–3.

toys have been so identified, perhaps owing to a desire on the part of collectors to label their possessions as of Sprimont's manufacture rather than that of the somewhat less highly regarded Duesbury concern. As for the conventionally sized figures it may be that Duesbury did not feel competent to equal such *tours de force* as, for example, *The Dancing Lesson* by Willems of about 1762[1] and, rather than show himself inferior to Sprimont, he kept to his old Derby models or brought out adaptations from Meissen, Tournai or Sèvres. Certainly there were very few truly original models. The pair of groups *La Bergère des Alpes* and *L'Oracle ou le Noeud de Cravate* derive from Sèvres[2] and the Tournai groups *Minerva crowning Constancy* and *Hercules Killing the Hydra* were almost exactly reproduced in the Derby biscuit groups of 1771, where the figures are represented as cupids or children. The catalogue of the first sale of the united Chelsea and Derby factories in 1771[3] contains the first mention of 'biscuit', in which the porcelain body is fired but not glazed. This branch of the ceramic art was not invented at Derby, but at Sèvres in 1751; it was, however, uniquely developed at Derby although it is remarkable that the finest technical examples, with their unsurpassed ivory-like surface, were not achieved until Michael Kean's managership, by which time Derby's best modellers had been lost. The factory at Tournai was also the inspirational source of a set of figures known as the *French Seasons*. It is perhaps not altogether a coincidence that in 1773 the former Tournai modeller Gauron was engaged by Duesbury to work at Chelsea. He is thought to be Nicholas-François Gauron, who worked as chief modeller at Tournai between 1758 and 1764. Although as Arthur Lane observes,[4] it is unlikely that he actually brought Tournai models with him, nevertheless it is inconceivable that knowledge of the French style gained during his years at Tournai could fail to influence his work and the style of the models he produced at Chelsea. In fact, remembering the popularity of French models in fashionable London at that time, Duesbury may well have engaged him in order to exploit his French expertise. Truth to tell, however, tradition ascribes the above mentioned set *The French Seasons* to Pierre Stephan, who appears to have been the chief modeller for the combined Chelsea and Derby factories at least during the first years following the amalgamation.[5]

A quite considerable number of Derby models produced between

[1] An example may be seen in the London Museum.
[2] Modelled in 1766 by Etienne Falconet after designs by Boucher; Derby copies in the Victoria and Albert Museum, Schreiber Catalogue, I, no. 352.
[3] Nightingale, op. cit., p. 19.
[4] Lane, op. cit., p. 104.
[5] See Biographies, Appendix I, p. 106.

1771 and 1795 have been attributed to Stephan. Amongst these were the statuettes of national heroes; the original signed models of some of these in Dorset clay are in existence, as well as a signed model in Wedgwood basalt from the workshop of Wedgwood and Bentley at Chelsea. This series included *Charles Pratt*, the Lord Chief Justice; *Lord Chatham* (William Pitt); *Mrs. Catherine Macaulay*, the historian; *Lord Howe*; *Admiral Rodney*. The pair of portraits of *John Wilkes* and *General Henry Seymour Conway* (Colour Plate D), which were produced together with the above, were in fact copies of earlier models made at Derby in the 1760s: they were made again between 1772 and 1775, when Wilkes, now released from prison, had become a popular figure and, in 1775, Lord Mayor of London. *General* (afterwards Field Marshal) *Conway* (1721–1795) is shown with a baton in his right hand and his left hand resting on a cannon: at his feet is a cupid supporting a shield with the crest of his family, a Moor's head.

A list is given here of those models which are generally accepted as from Stephan's hand:

Set of the *Elements* (incised nos. 3[1] & 48)
Set of the *French Seasons* (incised no. 123)
Set of the *Senses*
Pastoral Group (incised no. 12) (Plate 97)
Two Virgins awakening Cupid (incised no. 195)
Bacchantes adorning Pan (incised no. 196) (Plate 98), and
Three Graces distressing Cupid (incised no. 235) (Plate 99), after
    paintings by Angelica Kauffman
Group of four *Cupids* (incised no. 234) (Plate 94)

The following may also be examples of Stephan's work:

Hercules slaying the Hydra and *Minerva crowning Constancy* (this
    also listed as a group with a central pyramid) (Plate 95)
Time clipping the wings of Love (Plate 92)
Prudence and Discretion
Cephalus and Procris
Gardener and Companion (Plate 100)

The above are mentioned in the sale catalogue of 1771.

Another artist who worked as a modeller for Duesbury in the years following the acquisition of the Chelsea factory was John Bacon R.A.[2] Many attempts have been made to identify the work of Bacon in

[1] See p. 180, figure no. 3.
[2] See Biographies, Appendix I, p. 75.

D. PORTRAIT FIGURES OF JOHN WILKES AND GENERAL CONWAY
Date 1772–75   Height 12 in.
Victoria and Albert Museum   See page 40

Derby porcelain and to distinguish it from that of Stephan; but in the absence of documentary evidence this is both difficult and uncertain. This is perhaps not surprising when one considers that the resulting figure has to be judged not only after a set of moulds have been taken of the original model (which generally meant cutting the model into pieces) but porcelain casts having been taken from the moulds, these pieces had to be finally assembled by the 'repairers'. The chance that the finer points of the sculptor's individual style should survive all these intermediate processes is remote indeed. This is particularly true in the case of Bacon (and to a similar extent of Stephan after 1773, when he was no longer directly employed by Duesbury), he being responsible only for the sculpting of the original subject, and in a medium other than porcelain (usually modeller's clay or wax), and not at all in any of the succeeding processes. In a much better position to control the appearance of the final product were Planché in earlier, and Spengler in later times (see pp. 49–51). They not only created the original model but, having been trained in the art and practice of potting, had a hand both in the casting in porcelain and in the assembling of the cast pieces.

The following figures have been suggested as being the work of Bacon but it should be stated that such attributions have no documentary support and have been, from time to time, disputed by various writers and connoisseurs: *Shakespeare*; *Milton*; *Virgil*; *Addison*; *Arts and Sciences* (incised nos. 39–45) (Plate 101); *Music and Poetry* (incised nos. 216–217); *David Garrick as Richard III* (incised no. 21); *George III and members of the Royal Family* (at Windsor Castle). These last, which are a set of three pieces, viz., the King himself standing by a pedestal, a group of Queen Charlotte and two young children, and a group of four children, derive from a picture painted by Zoffany in 1770 and may have been personally commissioned by the Queen. This could account for the origin of the tradition that Duesbury was given royal permission to use the crown in his factory mark in 1773. However, these royal family pieces, the *David Garrick* and the *Arts and Sciences* or *Liberal Arts*,[1] may well be models by Stephan. The cherubs in the *Arts and Sciences* group particularly show that modeller's very distinct tendency to give his children disproportionately large heads. This is especially striking in the set of *Seasons* which Stephan modelled for Champion at Bristol as well as for Duesbury at Derby. This idiosyncrasy, if it may be so called, seems only to apply to Stephan's models of children, and if the customary attribution of the three all-round groups *Two Bacchantes adorning*

[1] Copied from almost contemporary models by Acier at Meissen, Lane, op. cit., p. 105.

Pan (incised no. 196), *Two Virgins awakening Cupid* (incised no. 195) and *Three Graces distressing Cupid* (incised no. 235) be accepted as Stephan's, then the *Music and Poetry* figures (incised nos. 216 and 217) might well be his work also. The attribution in one of the Factory Price Lists of the above three all-round groups to Spengler can be discounted by their being included in the sale catalogues of 1778 and 1782, years before Spengler came to England.

Study of the 'Price List of Figures' quoted by Haslem, together with the contemporary sale catalogues (see Appendix VI) makes it clear that there was a considerable production of figures in the Chelsea–Derby period—probably about 250 different models—including perhaps a score or so which, originating in the 1760s, continued to be issued in this period. There were, however, comparatively few subjects or themes and by far the commonest was the class illustrating classical mythology either in the form of statuettes of gods and goddesses: *Juno* and *Jupiter* (Plate 91), *Minerva*, *Calliope* (Plate 93), or groups such as those of *Bacchantes adorning Pan* and *Andromache weeping over the ashes of Hector*. Cupids abounded either as *Eros* the god of Love, or exploiting their appealing and decorative qualities, as cherubs or *putti* (Plates 87, 88, 94). Concerning these last there is evidence in the Lygo correspondence[1] that these were made in hundreds and perhaps thousands, and that there was a thriving export business to France. Popular too was the classical pastoral theme, or rather its romantic eighteenth century French interpretation, in which figures of Shepherds and Shepherdesses were used either singly, sometimes incorporating candleholders, or in pairs as in the charming *Pastoral Group* which is no. 12 in the Factory Price List (Plate 97). New versions of long popular sets of *Seasons* and *Elements* were issued and the new series of national heroes mentioned above.

A pair of models first mentioned in the sale catalogues of 1784 is worthy of note because of its phenomenally long-persisting popularity. These are the famous *Derby Dwarfs*[2] (Plate 133) said by some to derive from the earlier Chelsea models, the latter taking their inspiration from an engraving by Callot. It seems more likely however that the Derby models commemorate the topical dwarfs which stood outside the Mansion House in London. The various advertisements—more than twenty different versions have been identified—on the large hats of the Derby pair refer to the practice of attaching public

---

[1] Joseph Lygo became Duesbury's London agent in 1777. There exists in the Derby Public Library a quantity of letters written between 1777 and 1797 by Lygo to the Duesburys at Derby. In the form of orders, suggestions and requests to his employers, the letters contain a wealth of interesting and often historically important information. A selection is given in Appendix V.

[2] See p. 185 no. 227.

advertisements to the Mansion House figures. Such was their popularity that they continued to be produced into the Bloor period at the
old factory, and in large numbers not only from the King Street
Factory in the latter half of the nineteenth century, but from the
Osmaston Road works of the Royal Crown Derby Porcelain Company
down to the present day. There also exist Continental reproductions
of the earlier models.

Although evolving from the Derby traditions of the 1760s, Chelsea-
Derby figures may be said to possess distinctive styles in both modelling and decoration. Influencing the former, an important contributory
factor was the change in the composition of the paste, in which
calcined bones were an added ingredient giving greater strength.
When the figures were less likely to become mis-shaped in the firing,
modellers became more bold and adventurous and were able to achieve
finer detail, especially in the biscuit figures. The simple 'pad'
or 'bun' bases were superseded by the more elaborate 'rocky bases'
on which the figures or groups are mounted, irregular slabs of porcelain being shaped to simulate natural rock (Plate 89). These latter
are often decorated with accessories appropriate to the subject,
such as shells and sea-weed surrounding the figure of *Neptune* (Plate
96). The rock bases, roughly circular, may be up to three inches
in height. Scroll bases remained in common use; in the later
examples the scroll-work was sometimes pierced so that the base
stands on feet. This is the first time that Derby figures show this
characteristic.

Hitherto the bases of Derby figures, even when the scroll-work was
deeply cut, had remained solid, a characteristic of considerable use
when distinguishing early Derby figures from those made at Bow or
Chelsea. In this period too came the first of the square or rectangular
plinths or pedestals (Plate 90) either with or without chamfered
corners. The edge of the pedestal is sometimes embellished with a
moulded 'Greek key' pattern.

A notable feature at this time, due no doubt to the improved
modelling qualities of the paste or china body, was an increase in the
number of groups made. Three and often four full-length figures
were so arranged as to illustrate the story of some classical myth,
and we find the *Seasons*, hitherto issued as a set of four separate
figures, as a single group (no. 68 in the Factory Price List).

The underside of the bases continue to show 'patch marks' (see
p. 22) and the opening into the inside of the figure had reached
relatively large proportions compared with the 'screw-hole' of early
years. The bases, too, often show evidence of considerable grinding
down to enable the figure to stand firmly. There is little if any glazing

on the base and none in the interior of the figure, this latter characteristic developing only in the nineteenth century.

The enamelled decoration of figures in the Chelsea-Derby period
followed closely the Derby tradition. The most noteworthy improvement was the improved appearance of the very characteristic Derby
turquoise now clear and unsmudged. The pale pastel colours hitherto
in use were augmented by a brick or Indian red, a strong hue which
was new to the Derby palette. Pale yellow and mauve were typical
colours for cloaks etc., and ladies' skirts and bodices and gentlemen's
breeches and waistcoats were frequently decorated with flowers
formally painted in small circular medallions done with great delicacy.
The use of gilding increased through the period, particularly on the
scroll bases, although always with restraint.

5

CHELSEA–DERBY PERIOD
1770–1784
(iii) USEFUL AND DECORATIVE WARES

In contrast to the policy governing the production of figures, after 1769 the output of services and decorative pieces such as vases followed much more closely the styles and techniques used at Chelsea. First there was the introduction of bone-ash into the china body; this was the most important technical improvement since 1756. The very glassy body (with a silica content of over 60%) was all too prone to go out of shape in the firing and proved a very impracticable medium for useful wares which were required to withstand hot water. The addition of up to 40% of bone-ash, which had been the practice at Chelsea since about 1758, and the consequent reduction in the glassy constituent by about half, enabled Duesbury to produce those thinly-potted and for the most part well-shaped, useful wares which he completed by the addition of his charming and elegant neo-classical decoration. The Derby factory was still unable to match the technical excellence, including the heat-resisting properties, of the Worcester paste, which incorporated steatite (soapstone) but no bone-ash. Nor did the Derby glaze fit as smoothly and evenly as that of Worcester; nevertheless its fusible nature readily accepted enamel colours and was particularly sympathetic to the landscape painters working in the style of the English water-colourists, the colours melting to a large extent into the glaze. But landscape painting did not come before the 1780s and throughout almost the whole of the Chelsea-Derby period, painted decoration strongly reflected the neo-classical fashion, which permeated nearly all art forms at this time, its exploitation by Wedgwood being perhaps the most well-known example. The fashion is best exemplified in those designs incorporating classical urns (Plate 105) and bust portraits of classical figures painted in medallions (Plate 106), usually *en grisaille*, and flower-garlanded urns were popular and typical, often accompanied by scattered sprays of flowers and borders with gilt arabesques. Both Chelsea during the gold anchor period, and Worcester also, made much use of the same motif. The habit of scattering the flower decoration into small sprays and even individual flowers, was very characteristic of the period and is in marked contrast to the larger bouquets that were to follow. The globular teapot with gilt dentil rim and sprays of flowers (Plate 108) is a good example of the use of scattered flowers for formal decorative effect. Another very fashionable decoration was that of cupids or *putti*, usually painted amongst clouds in rose *camaieu*, that is to say in different tones of the same colour. Richard Askew is generally regarded as the artist responsible for these endearing cherubs.[1] Over the years Askew must have painted thousands of cupids, *putti* and cherubs, and a notable example is to be found in a set of vases, decorated with applied flowers, from the Hurlbutt Collection now in Derby Museum (Plate 117).

The use of blue for borders was as commonly employed at Derby as elsewhere; yet, perhaps owing to the tendency of the blue to run in the soft body and glaze, Duesbury did not much favour underglaze painting for this purpose. Instead, Derby made great use of an overglaze blue for borders, commonly known as 'Smith's blue' after an employee of that name, Constantine Smith, who was head colour-man in the early 1770s and stayed till about 1790. He had a son, William, apprenticed to him in 1773.[2] Smith's blue was a pleasing saxe blue, much enhanced by gilt designs of geometric shapes or by stylised leaves, fruit and flowers. The gilt geometric patterns are exemplified by a fluted coffee cup and saucer decorated also with typical scattered sprays of flowers in colours beneath the blue and gold border (Plate 119b).

Another favoured form of decoration at this time was the moulded shape, sometimes with straight parallel fluting but, more often, spirally fluted in the form of stylised leaves in long fronds. In some instances the moulded design was filled in with Smith's blue or other colours. A teapot with moulded fronds filled in with the well-known Derby turquoise is a typical example of this form of embellishment. A handsome sucrier and cover (Plate 109) in the Derby Museum has gilt spiral floral panels with alternate white and blue grounds. Sometimes the flutings were picked out with gilding, as in the case of a cup and saucer which not only has displays of charming posies of flowers on both cup and saucer, but also under the rim and even on the base of the saucer. Similar gilt decoration is seen on a handsome ewer (Plate 118) together with bands of Smith's blue and

[1] See Biographies, Appendix I, p. 71.
[2] Derby Public Library, Duesbury MSS. See Appendix V, p. 125.

gilt, and a panel with a figure subject probably painted by Richard Askew. A variation of this decoration is seen in a cup and saucer (Plate 110) where the gilt lines are broken up into small lengths.

The most common form of decoration, however, was the flower-spray, sometimes applied in the French manner in colourful festoons and garlands but more usually in isolated groupings. A typical example is afforded by a teapot (Plate 107) and a bowl, cover and stand (Plate 104). The only flower painter we know by name at this time is Edward Withers[1] and it is likely that he painted most of the important pieces, e.g. the mask jug (Plate 112). Characteristics of flower painting at this time are the hair-like stems of the flowers and the presence of a single flower extended beyond the spray. The effectiveness of this form of decoration springs from the skilful balance between the area covered by the painting and that left in the white. In the early years the necessity of disguising flaws in body or glaze by painted flowers or leaves sometimes tended to destroy the balance of the decoration as a whole, but these technical short-comings grew rarer as knowledge and experience increased.

The Chelsea-Derby period also saw the beginning of a type of pattern which was later to become the factory's best-selling line and, at least in the minds of the general public, be associated with Derby to the exclusion of almost all else: the Japan pattern. This was largely inspired by export Japanese porcelain known as 'brocaded Imari'. Such pieces are frequently marked with an imitation Chinese seal character and the pattern is well illustrated in a saucer dish (Plate 111), no. 3 in the Derby Pattern Book. It should not be confused, however, with a pattern copied from Worcester and found only in Chelsea-Derby times, consisting of vertical panels alternately containing pseudo-Japanese dragons and plants and white rosettes reserved on a blue ground, as in the case of a straight-sided mug or tankard (Plate 113).

There is no doubt that Chelsea-Derby table-wares possess much distinction; they were eminently suited to their purpose, tasteful and dignified and never ostentatious.

The decorative wares throughout the Chelsea-Derby period are no less distinctive and attractive. The sale catalogues (see pp. 161–76) mention an astonishing number and variety of vases and what are described as 'jars'. Many of these are large and obviously important productions on which the best artist-craftsmen must have been employed. The 'classical' shapes are dominant and these often tally closely with pieces made at the Sèvres factory, as for example in the use of Smith's blue to imitate the French *bleu-de-roi*. This is well

---

[1] See Biographies, Appendix I, p. 108.

shown in a vase painted in blue and gilt, the hemispherical body hung with festoons of white drapery in relief on a blue ground,[1] and this should be compared with a Sèvres *vase drapé* in the Wallace Collection, London. Of classical shape too is a pair of vases[2] with short expanding fluted neck, truncated oviform body with urn-shaped foot resting on a square plinth; two scrolled loop handles rise above the rim. The body of each vase is decorated with vertical bands of white and the very usual turquoise blue. There is a vase in the British Museum which is unusual in exhibiting a hybrid style combining the rococo with the classical. A pair of vases in the Victoria and Albert Museum[3] is remarkable in that the bodies are supported by three white caryatid figures terminating in lions' paws, the high domed covers being decorated with gilt pierced rococo scrolls surmounted by a bouquet of flowers. Very attractive also are the ewershaped vases usually decorated in oval reserves with finely painted landscapes and scenes depicting classical myths. A garniture of three was sometimes made up of two vases of this shape flanking a central two-handled 'therm' vase.

A small class of wares which first appeared in Chelsea-Derby times comprises mask-head drinking mugs and cups. Mentioned in the sale catalogues for 1780 (see p. 17) they include a handled drinking mug with a mask of Jupiter (Plate 114) and a Bacchante mask mug modelled with the features of a Greek youth. Others, without handles, take the form of a fox's and a fish's head, and the production of these would seem to have extended into the nineteenth century.

William Duesbury I survived the closure of the Chelsea works by some two years, dying in 1786. He was succeeded by his son, also William, who doubtless had been engaged at the China Works for some years. The productions of the factory under William Duesbury II and his successors have now to be considered.

[1] Example in the Victoria and Albert Museum (Schreiber Collection, I, no. 367).
[2] Example in the Victoria and Albert Museum (Schreiber Collection, I, no. 368).
[3] Schreiber Collection, I, no. 372.

6

THE LATER FIGURES
1786–1848

The most important aspect of figure-making during the proprietorship of Duesbury II would seem to have been the continuation of that collaboration, begun by Duesbury I about 1780, with the Swiss clock-maker Benjamin Vulliamy. Clocks and barometers made by him were elaborate pieces standing on high painted pedestals and supported by allegorical biscuit porcelain figures mounted in marble and ormolu settings. Examples are to be seen in the Victoria and Albert Museum, Syon House and the Bank of England.[1] From the Vulliamy –Lygo–Duesbury correspondence[2] it is obvious that Vulliamy was an exacting client and we find that a number of young London artists who later achieved fame as sculptors were engaged to model under the keen and watchful eye of Vulliamy, who then passed on their work to the Duesburys to be translated into porcelain. Artists so engaged include John Deare (1784), Charles Peart (1787), whom Vulliamy thought 'the most capable', and John Rossi (1788–9). Rossi is said to have made the models for the classical figures of *Aesculapius* and *Hygeia* for Vulliamy's clocks. *Venus*, *Mars* and *Diana* have also been attributed to him, although their numbers in Haslem's 'Price List', namely 114, 115 and 120 respectively, would seem to indicate that these models date from some ten years earlier; indeed in the sale catalogue of May 1779 is mentioned a 'pair of *Aesculapius* and *Hygeia*, in biscuit'.

However, by far the most important discovery in this search for artists was the introduction to Vulliamy in May 1790, by Joseph Lygo, of a new arrival in England. The newcomer was Jean Jacques Spengler (or Spangler as it is sometimes spelt).[3] Vulliamy seems to

[1] L.G.G. Ramsay, 'A Masterpiece of Clock making', *Connoisseur*, CXXXVIII, 1956, p. 250.
[2] In the British Museum, Victoria and Albert Museum and Derby Public Library.
[3] See Biographies, Appendix I, p. 104.

have been impressed by his potentialities and supplied a drawing of a figure symbolising *Astronomy* (Plate 102) from which Spengler produced a model which evidently satisfied Vulliamy's keen scrutiny, since it was passed to Duesbury, who paid Spengler £13. 2s. 6d. for it.[1] Very few figures can be ascribed to Spengler with certainty; the following, however, may be mentioned:

1. *Russian Shepherd* (British Museum)
2. *Blind Beggar and Daughter* (Liverpool Museum)
3. *Palemon and Lavinia*[2]
4. *Figure with a vase, Morning*
   Figure with a vase, Noon
5. *Three Graces*
6. *Pair Burying a Dead Bird*
7. *Mythical Group, Bacchus with the Nymphs of Mt. Ida* (incised no. 376)[3]
8. *Meditation*[4]
9. *Shepherdess* (Lady Lever Art Gallery, British Museum)

No. 4, for which Spengler was paid 7 gns., no. 5 for which he was paid 6 gns.[5] and no. 8, *Meditation*, have not yet been identified. No. 9 was intended to have a companion *Shepherd* (Plate 122) but Spengler absconded from Derby before it was modelled and the work was undertaken by William Coffee.[6] The model for the companion to Spengler's *Shepherdess* (Plate 122) was based on a cast of an antique figure of *Antinous* in the collection of Joseph Wright of Derby. Notwithstanding the low opinion of Coffee's work expressed by both Lygo and Charles King, Duesbury's works manager at Derby, the finished figure is by no means unworthy to stand alongside Spengler's.[7] The following entries in the Factory List quoted by Haslem make it reasonable to conclude that these forty-one items must include quite substantial numbers of models by both Spengler and Coffee which have not been identified:

'335 to 359 Twenty five. Spengler's and Coffee's Figures and Groups.

[1] Jewitt, op. cit., vol. II, p. 95.
[2] Lane, op. cit., p. 110; Bemrose Collection Catalogue, p. 26.
[3] Lane, op, cit., p. 110; illustrated by E. Percival Allan in 'Artist modellers of the old Derby Porcelain Factory', *Connoisseur*, LXXXII, 1928.
[4] Allan, loc. cit.
[5] Jewitt, op. cit., vol. II, p. 95.
[6] See Biographies, Appendix I, p. 86.
[7] Examples in the Victoria and Albert Museum, British Museum, and Derby Museum. The original figure, modelled in Dorset clay and fired, is in the Castle Museum, Nottingham.

373 to 377 five figures names not given
379 to 389 Eleven Figures names not given'

We now know that no. 388 is a large and imposing group of four boys typifying the *Seasons* (Plate 120). No. 389 is a pair, *Girl Dancing* and *Boy Piping*, and no. 384 is a figure of an admiral, probably Lord Howe. Nos. 388 and 389 are models of fine quality and could well be the work of Spengler. The following figures by Coffee have been identified:

'359 *Female figure*
378 *Scotchman and his Lass*
379 *Apollo*
396 *Shepherd* (companion to Spengler's *Shepherdess* No. 395)'

It does not seem possible to calculate with any accuracy the number of different models brought out in the time of either Duesbury II or Michael Kean.[1] Evidence of existing figures would suggest that more were produced in biscuit than were glazed and enamelled. All the known work of Spengler and of Coffee too, is in the biscuit state, and it was during the period of Kean's managership that the unglazed wares attained their highest technical excellence, when the material was deliberately given a beautiful ivory satin sheen by the presence of volatilized glaze in the kiln. This most attractive surface distinguishes the specimens made in the earlier periods; in the later Bloor period the products display a dry chalky appearance.

Compared with the number issued during Chelsea-Derby times, there are surprisingly few enamelled figures which from style of decoration can be attributed to the years 1790–1814. Although the work of the two chief modellers working at Derby within these years (Spengler and Coffee) would seem to be entirely in the biscuit, nevertheless there is a strange dearth of re-issues of models which were in more or less continous production during the 1780s. From a comparison of the models (both enamelled and in biscuit) mentioned in the sale catalogues[2] with the list of groups and figures given by Haslem we may fairly assume that the numbered series of models had reached about no. 300 by 1780. From this we may conclude that some 300 different models had been issued within a space of ten years, for the marking of figures with an incised number does not antedate Duesbury's purchase of the Chelsea works. Yet the fact that the last model done by Spengler before he ran away from Derby for the last time in 1795 was the *Shepherdess*, which bears the incised number 395, compels the conclusion that in the fifteen years after 1780 less

[1] Taken into partnership by Duesbury II in 1795. See below pp. 61 and 94–5.
[2] Nightingale, op. cit.

than one hundred models were issued. The number of new models over any period does not, of course, necessarily govern the overall output of figures from the factory since there might well be a number of older models which retained a high popularity year after year.[1] Nevertheless the sale catalogue of 1785, in which services and pieces such as vases etc. greatly exceeded the figures, seems to support the conclusion that during the proprietorship of Duesbury II the emphasis was on useful and decorative vessels rather than on figures. Much the same seems to have applied throughout the managership of Michael Kean (1797–1809), during which period there is no record of a full-time modeller; Coffee may have supplied some models, but on a free-lance basis, since from about 1798 he was in business on his own. The evidence of the Price List quoted by Haslem would seem to suggest that there was an almost complete cessation in the introduction of new models from about or shortly after the death of Duesbury II until about 1820, when there would seem to have been something of a resurgence in the production of figures, both of new and old models, decorated in colours to suit the fashion of the times. Amongst the few modellers whom we know by name are François Hardenburg, Edward and Samuel Keys and John Whitaker.

Hardenburg, possibly engaged after Coffee had left the works,[2] would seem soon to have left Derby and set up in London, making figures and ornaments in marble and plaster for interior decoration. He is better to be remembered, however, for the part he played in making the Factory List of figures (see pp. 54–55, 180–92).

Edward and Samuel Keys were brothers, the sons of Samuel Keys.[3] Edward succeeded Isaac Farnsworth, the 'repairer' or 'assembler' of models, in 1821 and Haslem[4] attributes to him the models of *Dr. Syntax* (Plate 175) and also portraits of *George IV* and *Napoleon* as well as small figures and animals including the *Monkey Musicians*

[1] We are of the opinion—from the evidence of this Price List together with a study of the sale catalogues given in Nightingale—that the incised numbers found on Derby figures can be a guide to the chronology of the models (perhaps 'subjects' would be a better description in this context) put out by the factory. Thus *Pastoral Group*, incised no. 12, can be said with certainty to have been an earlier model (or subject) than *Two Virgins Awaking Cupid* (no. 195 in the list). But the incised numbers by themselves cannot be used to date any individual piece or specimen since, as we have said, models or subjects may retain their popularity and continue in production over many years.

To date an individual specimen, consideration would have to be given to the styles of decoration and the colours of the enamels used: e.g. turquoise blue/green and a somewhat 'dirty' pink would suggest the Chelsea-Derby period, and maza-rine blue and chrome green the nineteenth century Bloor period.

[2] Haslem, op. cit., p. 158.
[3] See Biographies, Appendix I, p. 95.
[4] Haslem, op. cit., p. 161.

(Plate 132). These last were, of course, derived from Meissen, where such models had been produced for many years.

The white glazed figures, particularly of animals (Plates 126 and 127), produced by the Derby factory about 1830, are sometimes confused with similar subjects modelled by Planché between 1750 and 1756. The following tabulated information may prove useful in distinguishing the two groups:

Planché 1750–56	*Bloor c. 1830*
'Dry-edge' (see p. 10)	Normal glazing
Small 'screw-hole' in base (occasionally no hole at all)	Large hole and glazing visible inside figure
No gilding	Some gilding
Thick glaze often running into pools and tending to spoil the details of modelling	Good quality glazing
No bocage on figures before 1756 and then flowers large and individually made	Bocage almost always present and made of small moulded or stamped flowers and leaves

Samuel Keys junior was employed about the same time as his brother. Haslem states[1] that he was the modeller of *Paul Pry* and a number of other theatrical figures of contemporary fame. He was succeeded in 1830 by John Whitaker[2] who was superintendent of the figure-makers until the close of the factory. The only model which can be attributed to him with certainty is the well known *Peacock among Flowers* (Plate 128). This proved so popular that it was also made over a long period by the King Street Works as well as at the present Royal Crown Derby Porcelain Factory.

A minor artist whose work is associated with the later years of the Derby factory was George Cocker.[3] Cocker left the Derby factory within five years of the completion of his apprenticeship and although he returned to Derby in 1826 it was to start up on his own, and all signed pieces were made at his works in Friar Gate, Derby. Nevertheless, from the statements made by Haslem[4] that he made busts and portrait statuettes of celebrated characters of his day and figures of a rustic character, as well as animals and baskets of flowers, it is possible that some of these came from his hands during his period of direct employment at the Nottingham Road factory.

In the 1830s there were re-issued several models of rather romantic

---

[1] Haslem, op. cit., p. 161.
[2] See Biographies, Appendix I, p. 108.
[3] See Biographies, Appendix I, p. 85.
[4] Haslem, op. cit., p. 159.

and sentimental subjects which had, on the evidence of their serial numbers, been first issued in Chelsea–Derby times. Their occurrence, however, in the form and colouring of the original issues, is extremely rare, but an example of the *Stocking Mender* (no. 77) is in the British Museum collection. Several of the models carry an imitation Meissen mark in blue. These include a pair of small figures, the boy holding a handful of flowers, the girl a bouquet on her lap, each figure standing on a shaped brown and gilt base which carries an incised no. 8; a small figure of a girl playing a guitar and representing *Music* (Plate 130) with the incised no. 11, and a girl seated in a chair on a gilt and pierced base with the incised no. 314, one of a *Pair of Sitting Figures*. There is an example of the companion figure in the Derby Museum, a youth seated and reading a book which he holds in his right hand; it too bears the incised no. 314, but the figure is placed on a floral scrolled base and carries the crown, batons and D mark in red. Perhaps the most frequently encountered subjects of these nineteenth century versions of eighteenth century models are the *Stocking Mender* (incised no. 77), the *Shoemaker* (incised no. 78) (Plate 131), the *Shoeblack* (incised no. 81) and *Hairdresser* (incised no. 84). Examples of nos. 78 and 81 with an imitation Sèvres mark in blue, are to be seen in the Derby Museum; they are mounted on pierced circular bases which are characteristic and distinctive of this period. Other distinguishing features of these late re-issues are: the gilt scroll bases with the pronounced 'side-wing'[1], and the pierced scroll base with similar 'wing' as in the pair *Pipe and Tabor* with incised no. 311; the under-sides of the bases are glazed and the area inside the central hole is also glazed; there are no 'patch marks'; the most characteristic colours are mazarin blue with gilt designs of tiny flowers and leaves in formalised patterns, chrome green instead of the turquoise green of earlier years; and there are a number of other colours such as orange, and ochreous browns, which distinguish nineteenth century Derby figures.

This output of models from an earlier period, although of little importance in the wider story of English ceramics is, nevertheless, of considerable interest in so far as several of them—particularly the *Shoemender* and the *Hairdresser* mentioned above—are so widely known that for the uninitiated they have often served as an introduction to the subject of Derby figures, as have the famous 'Japan' patterns to Derby table-wares.

The number and variety of figures and figure groups produced by the Derby factory was truly prodigious. Haslem gives what he quite straightforwardly calls a 'Price List of Groups and Single Figures'[2] and

[1] There are examples in the Derby Museum collections.
[2] Haslem, op. cit., pp. 67–85, reproduced in Appendix VIII.

although he does not give any indication either of the source or date of his list, it follows closely that given by Bemrose who says that his 'list was made out, and a valuation put thereon, in 1819 by four old workmen named Soar, Longdon, Farnsworth and Hardenberg for the purpose of a Chancery suit, *Duesbury* v. *Kean*'. It purports to list the moulds and models belonging to William Duesbury in 1795. The Bemrose list begins with a numbered list of 397 models; the numerals are presumably meant to refer to the incised numbers found on the bases of the pieces themselves. Haslem's list has 390 models which compare closely but not exactly with the numbered figures in Bemrose's list. These discrepancies are difficult to understand, for if the numbers were taken from those incised on the porcelain figures then there would not seem to be any room for error. Moreover, it is logical to suppose that the numbers on the models denote a chronology of their manufacture, since it is difficult to understand by what other means the numbers could be allotted. It was not the practice to number Derby models before 1770; nevertheless, there are a very small number of figures first issued in the 1760s without numbers which were repeated after the numbering practice had begun and which were then given a number (e.g. *Welch Taylor and Family*, no. 62 (Plates 123 and 124); *Falstaff*, no. 291; *Tithe Pig Group*, no. 293; *Shakespeare*, no. 305, etc.). In addition to the numbered series Haslem gives 16 models of birds and animals as being in the list but not numbered. It seems probable that these refer to models earlier than Chelsea–Derby times as do also 37 figures said to be from Bow and Chelsea models. Finally Haslem gives a list of 73 models by Edward and Samuel Keys, Louis Bradley and John Whitaker. Following the numbered list given by Bemrose there is an Inventory of 318 items but in this there are many models which are mentioned more than once. Nevertheless, from the information given in Haslem's book, which is an itemised list and not an inventory of stock, there was a total of more than 500 different models made at Derby. And this is exclusive of the models made before 1770 and not issued after that date.

USEFUL AND DECORATIVE WARES
1786–1848

Towards the end of the Chelsea–Derby period there developed that very distinctive contribution which the Derby factory made to English porcelain decoration: the landscape in reserves or panels. It was, of course, no Derby invention; but where the German and French factories copied engravings from oil paintings in the 'old master style', Derby adapted the English water-colour tradition. This was a particularly happy choice since the soft glaze absorbed the enamel colours and rendered very truthfully the pale tints so characteristic of eighteenth century water-colour drawings. Moreover, while the Continental landscapes often had an opaque, impasto look, suggesting oil paintings, the delicate wash drawings on Derby pieces were much more appropriate for decoration on such small objects as cups and saucers or even vases and *jardinières*, etc. The scenes too, were in the English topographical tradition and taken in the main from contemporary engravings and illustrated books: an account dated 10 June 1786 was for the purchase by Duesbury of two numbers of Mr. Middiman's *Latest views of Great Britain*. In addition, however, to those copied from engravings there are quite a few scenes from Derby itself and the surrounding country, and the original drawings for these are likely to have been made by the artists on the spot.

The earliest known landscape painter on Derby porcelain was Zachariah Boreman,[1] described as 'the father of landscape painting on china'. A French-shaped cup and *trembleuse* saucer in the Derby Museum with gilding on a mazarin ground in the Sèvres style has landscapes probably by Boreman. From the nature of the paste and potting and the fact that the saucer carries an incised script 'N' and the cup a gold anchor and 'D' these pieces may well represent one of the earliest examples of truly topographical landscape painting on Derby porcelain (Plate 103). The great majority of the painting

---

[1] See Biographies, Appendix I, p. 81.

E. EWER AND BASIN

Date about 1790   Height of ewer 9½ in.   Mark 9 in puce

Victoria and Albert Museum   See page 59

nowadays attributed to Boreman would appear, from the evidence of the paste, glaze and factory mark, to have been done in the years he spent working at Derby between 1783 and 1794. Examples of his work in public collections are a fine cabaret set on pink ground,[1] a plate with circular landscape[2] and a charming coffee can, the title *View from Cheltenham* written on the base (Plate 137). This piece bears the factory mark in blue and the pattern no. 260, which was one of the patterns assigned to him for decoration (see p. 81). There is also a porcelain plaque,[3] signed and dated 1797, indicating that it was done after he left Derby.

Boreman was undoubtedly a prolific worker and was given many important services to decorate. His work for the Duesburys, by whom he was employed for almost a quarter of a century, must amount to many hundreds of pieces. His method[4] was to wash in the subject in a neutral tint, over which he laid the positive colours and these, being transparent, allowed the neutral colour to show through. After these colours had been fixed by passing through the enamelling kiln Boreman hatched and stippled over the foliage and other detailed parts before the second and final firing. His skies often show an ochre tint with neutral tinted clouds, and sometimes the white edges of the clouds and other high lights are wiped out with the pointed wooden end of the brush. Small human figures or animals in the middle distance executed with meticulous care, and often including one or more spots of bright red, are very characteristic features of his landscapes. In his use of green he inclined towards the blue-greens, in contrast to 'Jockey' Hill (see p. 92-3) who favoured yellow-greens. This latter artist, so called from his love of horses and his habit of riding to work on horseback, had a style very similar to that of Boreman. Indeed, they had been fellow workmen at Chelsea between 1779 and 1784.[5] The handsome tea-service (Plate 135) bearing pattern no. 320 is decorated with beautifully executed landscapes more recently attributed[6] to Hill but by Haslem, in the catalogue of his collection, to Boreman. Jockey Hill's landscapes are frequently found on pieces with the 'canary' yellow ground for which Derby was justifiably famous. The astonishing delicacy of his work is well shown in the two-handled cabinet cup, cover and stand (Colour Plate F) in which the crescent-

---

[1] Victoria and Albert Museum, Herbert Allen Collection, no. 161.

[2] Victoria and Albert Museum, Schreiber Collection, I, no. 413.

[3] In the Victoria and Albert Museum. *Connoisseur*, January 1934, Figs. XI and XII.

[4] W. H. Tapp, 'Zachariah Boreman', *Connoisseur*, January 1934.

[5] See Biographies, Appendix I, p. 92.

[6] W. H. Tapp, 'Jockey Hill, Painter of Ceramics', *Connoisseur*, June and Sept. 1936.

shaped panels in the stand are unusual. His fondness for putting small meticulously modelled human figures in the middle distance makes his style particularly difficult to distinguish from that of Boreman, but in addition to his predeliction for yellow-greens it has been suggested[1] that unlike Boreman, Jockey Hill never stipples over his leaves and foliage but 'dentilates over them with sharp minute elongated brush lines'.

Boreman and Hill, as well as Richard Askew and James Banford, who both specialised in figure subjects, were much concerned with the decoration of those distinctive Derby products, the small straight-sided mugs generally termed 'coffee cans'. These seem most likely to have been conceived as cabinet pieces not meant for daily use, displaying, as they do, some of the most exquisite work of the factory's best artists. Developed perhaps from the tall coffee cups of the early years, and dating from about 1785, they are almost equal in height and diameter, which vary from $2\frac{3}{8}$ in. to $2\frac{5}{8}$ in. Good examples, especially those on a 'canary' ground are much sought after by collectors. Typical examples are to be seen in the collections of the Victoria and Albert Museum and Derby Museum (Plate 136).

Although the years of Duesbury II's proprietorship saw the development of landscape painting in reserves, nevertheless flower painting maintained its popularity and there was employed at Derby at this time the best known exponent of this art. William Billingsley was apprenticed at the Derby factory in 1774 and spent a number of years working under Edward Withers until he succeeded the latter in about 1790. However, it was not from Withers that Billingsley learned the style of flower painting which revolutionised this branch of ceramic decoration, but from Boreman. For what is generally known as the 'wiping out' technique, whereby the painter covers the whole flower with the tint required and then wipes out the highlights with an almost dry brush, Billingsley almost certainly learned from his close friend and mentor, who had used a somewhat similar technique in his landscapes painted as described above. The technique was skillfully exploited by Billingsley to achieve a more naturalistic modelling of the flowers and led to a more ambitious and complex grouping of different species of flowers than was ever attempted by Withers. His favourite flower was undoubtedly the rose, but the yellow hollyhock, iris and many other English garden flowers of the time were painted with great skill. The large ewer and basin painted in association with pattern no. 172[2] is almost certainly Billingsley's most important work, and one of the finest examples of ceramic flower

[1] W. H. Tapp, 'Jockey Hill, Painter of Ceramics', *Connoisseur*, June 1936.
[2] From the Hurlbutt Collection and now in the Victoria and Albert Museum.

painting of any factory or period (Colour Plate E). The famous *Prentice Plate* (Plate 141) which Billingsley did specially for the instruction of apprentices at the Derby factory, is now in the Derby Museum. There and at the Victoria and Albert Museum there are excellent examples of his work, which invariably carries the factory mark of crown, batons and 'D' in puce. A good example of his skill in the grouping of flowers is shown in a dish and table centrepiece (Plate 143). The Pattern Book entry '174—fruit and flowers by Bilensley' would seem to justify this attribution of the diamond-shaped dish (Plate 142), which is most beautifully painted.

Other fine and unusual examples of Billingsley's work are to be found on four plates,[1] each carrying the factory mark of crown, crossed batons and script 'D' and the numeral '7' on the footrim in puce (see p. 115). Evidence for this attribution is provided by a statement by Samuel Keys, a gilder at the old factory and apprenticed to Duesbury in 1785[2]: 'When Mr. Duesbury (the second) had been here for a short time an order came for some plates to match a Chelsea plate with a single plant in a curious style from nature. Withers was gone, no one knew where at the time and Billingsley made the attempt with the instructions of Mr. Boreman. He copied any garden or wild flowers that suited and when the order was sent off it gave great satisfaction.' These plates bear a striking similarity to some made at the Chelsea factory which carry the brown anchor mark; the feather-scroll moulding painted in brown and turquoise blue is especially typical. Indeed the Derby plates might well have been made from moulds acquired by Duesbury I when he purchased the Chelsea factory in 1769. Each of the plates is painted with a different selection of species of flowers, and that which depicts a group of roses with open flowers, buds and foliage shows the style and technique particularly attributed to this artist. There seems little doubt that it was the general habit of Billingsley to copy his flowers direct from nature; in these replacement pieces his work contrasts strongly with the flowers painted on the earlier Chelsea wares which appear to have been copied from botanical books. From the free and naturalistic style of his work it would seem unlikely that Billingsley was ever engaged on painting so called 'botanical' plants. It seems probable that Billingsley was responsible for flower painting on the borders of some 'botanical' services, in the same way as Billingsley's flowers embellish services painted, in reserves, by Banford (figure subjects) and Boreman (landscapes) (see

[1] Collection of C. K. Klepser, Seattle, U.S.A. One has been given to Derby Museum (Plate 140).

[2] Quoted by Wallis and Bemrose, *The Pottery and Porcelain of Derbyshire*, 1870, pp. 11, 12.

Plate 138). Services displaying 'botanical' plants usually bear the factory mark and the Latin name of the plant (sometimes with the addition of the common name) painted in blue enamel.[1]

A Derby artist whose work, despite his very long association with both Duesbury I and II, has been very seldom indentified is, George Complin.[2] He would seem to have been a most versatile painter and to have depicted fruit, flowers, birds and animals as well as landscapes, though it is with birds and fruit that his name is most commonly associated (Plate 144). Haslem considered that he painted in a conventional as distinct from a naturalistic manner, using bright and gay colours with a decorative effect. Although his birds are not the exotic species but rather English tomtits, chaffinches etc., nevertheless these he painted in the gayest of colours. Haslem also makes the comment that when Complin introduced small birds and animals into his fruit paintings he did not always observe the proper proportions, 'a squirrel, for instance not being much larger than a mouse, judging by the size of the fruit by which it is surrounded'. Complin's work is today eagerly sought after by collectors.

The period of William Duesbury II, 1786–1797, was undoubtedly the Golden Age of the Derby factory. Inheriting from his father an establishment which, while founded and run on sound commercial grounds, had nevertheless been motivated by high artistic endeavour, Duesbury II was able to bring to full fruition the promise of the earlier years. He succeeded in gathering round him a most remarkable band of artist workmen, including not only skilful artists able to paint subjects of all kinds, but also potters who could consistently produce finely potted pieces to display the work of the artists, and expert gilders whose craftsmanship in the fashioning of elaborate borders and arabesque patterns was of a high order. Despite the refinement of the potting, however, Duesbury's porcelain remained constantly liable to breakage by hot liquids, and in 1790 he advised Lygo to warn Sir John Shaw, one of his customers, 'that his servants should take care to warm up the tureen gradually to avoid damage.' In the same year he issued a general advice 'To prevent Accidents with Tea Pots' (Appendix V, p. 141).

Unfortunately Duesbury's health was not as robust as that of his father and proved unequal to the strains put upon it as proprietor and

[1] In the Derby Museum is a plate with a continuous rose-wreath border decoration contained between two gilt bands while a third runs midway between the roses. The border flowers may be confidently attributed to Billingsley but the centre is painted in a completely different style with a single plant named on the base '*Jasminum officinale*' 'Common Jefsamine'. The factory mark, pattern no. '142' and the plant names are painted in blue enamel (Plate 139).

[2] See Biographies, Appendix I, p. 86.

F. CHOCOLATE CUP, COVER AND STAND
Date about 1795   Diameter of stand 6 in.
Mark 9 and 'View Near Matlock, Derbyshire' in blue
Derby Museum   See page 57

manager of what must by this time have become a factory of no mean size. There are no known complete lists of employees at this time and estimates have varied from 200 to 400. There is little doubt that the maximum, whatever it was, would have been reached during the proprietorship of Duesbury II. In 1795, in an effort to relieve the strain on himself, Duesbury took into partnership Michael Kean, an Irish miniature painter. We shall never know what prompted this choice of partner who, however skilled as a miniature painter, is not known to have had any knowledge or experience of china manufacture. That it was an unhappy choice there is all too much evidence. Duesbury himself died within two years at the, even for those times, very early age of thirty-four and within two years hardly any of the skilled artists craftsmen formerly in Duesbury's employ remained at Derby.[1]

However, Kean was not entirely to blame for this, nor should it be imagined that the factory that had been built up so patiently and skilfully by the Duesburys disintegrated under the managership of Kean. Far from it. Indeed, at first Kean was able to make good the departure of Boreman and Jockey Hill by the enrolment of George Robertson[2] and Robert Brewer, and there was William ('Quaker') Pegg[3] available to succeed Billingsley. These were artists scarcely, if at all, less skilled than their predecessors. Moreover, we find not only a continuation of conventional landscapes but the introduction of the only known examples of seascapes on Derby porcelain. These were undoubtedly inspired by British naval victories in the Napoleonic Wars and might be said to be Derby's contribution to the national hero-worship of Nelson and his fellow admirals. The evidence of the factory marks (see pp. 110–12) would indicate that the great majority of seascape painting on Derby porcelain was done between about 1790 and 1806. There is in the Derby Museum a water-colour signed 'G. Robertson', depicting in meticulous detail a frigate the counterpart of which appears in almost identical shape and position on a teapot with rose-coloured ground[4] and on a cream jug with a pale yellow ground (Plate 156).[5] A good example of Robertson's work appears on

---

[1] Kean married Mrs. Duesbury, the widow, but the marriage was not a success and there ensued a bitter and long-drawn-out lawsuit on the subject of the sharing of the profits and of the ownership of the factory etc., on its lease to Robert Bloor. (See Bemrose papers in the British Museum.) Kean continued until 1811.

[2] Robertson may well have come to Derby in the last months of Duesbury's life (see Biographies, Appendix I, p. 101).

[3] Pegg was first employed during Duesbury's lifetime (see Appendix I, p. 99).

[4] With titles: *A Calm* and *Fresh Breeze*. Factory mark and pattern no. 464 in blue. Collection of Commander G. L. Pendred.

[5] With title: *A Calm*. Factory mark in blue. D. A. Hoyte Collection.

an oval teapot (Plate 155) from a cabaret set with shipping scenes on an apple green ground. The title 'The Anson engazing (sic) La Loire and Kangoroo' (sic), appears on the base of the tray only. Two vases and a *jardinière* with a sky-blue ground (Colour Plate G) in Derby Museum have named seascapes finely painted which also may be reasonably attributed to Robertson.[1] There are eight patterns allotted to Robertson in the Pattern Books and study of the seascape subjects on pieces with these patterns leads to the conclusion that Robertson achieved a finer degree of detail in such subjects than did either of the brothers Brewer. Tapp[2] attempts to describe the technique habitually employed by Robertson in his seascapes; he asserts that pennants and jacks are brilliantly painted and the reflections of the ships distinctly shown; the sailors have either red or blue jerseys. The clouds, he says, are generally portrayed in mauve but where there is a storm they become a blue-black.

As the Pattern Books do not give Christian names it is not possible through them to obtain any clues to enable the work of John Brewer to be distinguished from that of his brother Robert.[3] The evidence of the water-colour drawings[4] provides but little assistance in efforts to differentiate their work. In the realm of seascapes both brothers would seem to have aimed at atmosphere rather than nautical exactitude such as we have noted in the work of Robertson, though perhaps the evidence of the detailed work on the 'botanical' services (see p. 64) which are generally attributed to John would lead to the conclusion that he came nearer to Robertson's meticulous style than did his brother.

There is a small class of military scenes on Derby porcelain dating, it may be presumed, from the same period as the seascapes. Examples may be seen on a pair of vases,[5] similar in shape to the seascape vases in the Derby Museum described above, and the subject also appears on coffee cans (Plate 145). These military subjects have been attributed at different times to both John and Robert Brewer.

Although an interesting facet of Derby decoration, and one which inspires keen searching by present-day collectors, naval and military scenes were but a minor part of the general output of decoration at the factory and of these three artists. The quite considerable output of landscape painting at Derby between 1795 and 1820 was almost certainly the work of Robertson and the brothers Robert and John Brewer. Examination of water-colour drawings by these artists shows

[1] See Biographies, Appendix I, p. 101.
[2] W. H. Tapp, 'George Robertson, painter of Derby China', *Connoisseur*, Nov. 1935.
[3] See Biographies, Appendix I, p. 83.
[4] Derby Museum, Collection.
[5] Victoria and Albert Museum.

that the technique of sharply outlining topographical detail, especially notable in buildings and to a degree in figures of animals and human beings, was more strongly developed in Robertson, whilst Robert Brewer's work had a somewhat solid opaque appearance, more comparable to oil painting.

It is appropriate here to note a change in the composition of the Derby china body which took place in the early years of the nineteenth century caused by the addition of china stone (see Appendix IV). This brought the Derby recipe closer to the formula worked out by Josiah Spode which became the standard for English porcelain during and after the nineteenth century. This change, however, had an unfortunate side-effect: it produced a porcelain requiring a much harder glaze, into which the enamel colours could no longer be absorbed as they had been with such beautiful effect in the case of the earlier, softer porcelain. Moreover, the enamel colours, remaining on the surface of the glaze—the relief or impasto effect can be felt by the tip of the finger—were all too prone to flake away, and subjection to hot water, causing unequal expansion of body and glaze, and other domestic hazards, resulted in the formation of countless minute cracks in the glaze, known as 'crazing'.

The general effect was to bring the decoration much closer to the opacity and density of oil paint than the translucency of water-colours. This is particularly noticeable in the case of landscapes, which nevertheless continued to flourish at Derby in the hands of the artists mentioned above.

Examples of landscape painting by Robertson are plates with square reserves framed by pattern no. 254, which in the Factory Pattern Book (see p. 101) is allotted to this artist, traditionally said to have favoured autumn scenes and to have had an especial fondness for autumnal reds and browns.

Campana-shaped vases (Plate 171) with continuous landscapes and figures have been attributed to John Brewer and the scene on the square dish (Plate 148) may also be by his hand. The best-known example of his landscape painting is on the *Hafod* service (Plate 154),[1] made towards the end of the century for Mr. Johnes for use in his summer estate at Hafod in Wales.[2] This service is decorated from engravings made of the estate in 1792 by the topographical artist John Warwick Smith,[3] and the mention of 'Hafod' in John Brewer's

[1] Examples from this service can be seen in the Victoria and Albert and Derby Museums.

[2] See Elizabeth Inglis Jones, *Peacocks in Paradise*, London, 1950, for an account of this fabulous palace among the wildness of the Welsh mountain scene.

[3] A set of these aquatints is at the National Trust property, Croft Castle, Herefordshire, where Thomas Johnes spent his younger days.

accounts submitted to Duesbury[1] makes it a reasonable assumption that he was in fact the artist who painted the services decorated with scenes from this series of engravings. It is strange that so few landscapes on Derby porcelain have been attributed to this artist, since in the above mentioned accounts, in 1795, the number of landscapes predominates over all other types of decoration by John Brewer.

We have unfortunately no documentary evidence of painting on Derby china by Robert Brewer. Indeed we do not know how much, if any, of his work he himself painted on the china or how much of his output he may have supplied in the form of drawings or paintings to be copied on to china by one of the factory hands, for he, and his brother John, were 'drawing masters' in the town (see p. 83). A beaker with continuous landscapes and figures (Plate 153), and a service at Chatsworth[2] with named landscapes, have both been attributed to Robert Brewer. A bough-pot with figures (Plate 167) has been tentatively attributed to this artist, although it might possibly be from the hand of George Robertson, in whose work the human figure played an important part and whom, it is interesting to note, a Derby Directory of 1830 described as a 'portrait painter'.

After the departure of Robert Brewer (about 1815) and Robertson (about 1820), the chief landscape painter until the close of the factory was Daniel Lucas. His work, painted on the much harder glaze (see p. 121), shows typically the opacity of oil painting (Plates 170, 174) and, with a palette of colours which lacked subtlety, the general effect is one of heaviness and even dullness. Whether from the absence of competent artists or the hardness of the glaze, landscape painting at the Derby factory never again regained the level of excellence which began with Boreman about 1785 and ended with Robertson about 1820. For some reason the change in the composition of the body and glaze mentioned earlier, which brought about a look of heaviness to the landscape painting, did not have the same effect on flower-painting, which maintained in large measure the freshness and quality that had earlier distinguished Derby porcelain. After the departure in 1796 of Billingsley to help John Coke with his new porcelain factory at Pinxton, the flower painting at Derby was shared between William Pegg and John Brewer. The latter, a very versatile artist, in addition to painting bouquets and flower groups after the manner of Billingsley, is usually credited with the painting of 'botanical' services. These, sometimes with a broad coloured border,

---

[1] MS in British Museum, quoted by Jewitt, op. cit., vol. II, p. 107.

[2] Collection of the Duke of Devonshire; illustrated in *E.P.C. Trans.*, no. IV, 1932, p. 75.

depict flowers, leaves, fruit and the root system in such a manner as to suggest a botanical magazine or text-book as their source; and this conclusion is strengthened by the fact that the pieces carry on their base the Latin name of the plant, which is often an exotic species quite alien to Britain. A service executed for the Welby family of Grantham, Lincolnshire, has, in addition to such botanical subjects, the family crest skilfully painted on the borders of the plates by a hand different from that responsible for the flower subjects. This and similar crests were probably executed by an independent enameller, one Anthony Amatt, at Twerton near Bath (Plate 177).[1]

William, usually known as 'Quaker', Pegg[2] was a flower painter second to none, Billingsley himself not excepted. His style was quite his own; his flower studies, hardly ever less than life-size, are flung right across and even over the edge of the piece being decorated, and, unlike some of his contemporaries, he always painted from the life, never copying from botanical drawings, and invariably inscribed the names of his flowers *in English* on the reverse of the porcelain. Pegg worked at Derby during two quite widely separated periods. In the first, from about 1795 to 1800, it is likely that his work would carry the factory mark and name of the flower in blue. It is reasonable to attribute a fine pair of ice-pails (Plate 152) and a large tureen and cover[3] to Pegg during this period. His work in his second period of employment at Derby, from 1813 to 1820, coincided with the factory mark in red and included a number of services painted with a panache which assuredly places him as one of the great flower painters of his own or any other period. Apart from the famous *Thistle Dish* (Colour Plate H), one of the most exquisite flower paintings ever executed on porcelain, there exists no known documented work by him,[4] yet there seems little doubt that a dish in the Derby Museum (Plate 149) with the mark in red, is an example from his second period. His work is nowadays much sought after and commands high prices. Not surprisingly, therefore, a good many pieces are claimed as from his brush which are, in fact, only more or less after his style. His work is found accompanied by only a narrow band of gilding (rarely, it would seem, with rich gilt arabesques) although in his earlier years some of the services he decorated carried a broad band of some pale colour, e.g. beige in the case of the ice-pails mentioned above. Working at about the same time was another flower painter also

[1] See Appendix V, p. 149–50.
[2] See Biographies, Appendix I, p. 99.
[3] In the Victoria and Albert Museum.
[4] That is to say on china; there exists a note book of his sketches in Derby Museum.

named William Pegg.[1] There are some porcelain plaques signed 'Wm. Pegg' and these are more likely to be the work of this artist than of Quaker Pegg.

A painter who modelled his style on Quaker Pegg's and whose work is often mistaken for that of his mentor, was Leonard Lead.[2] He employed a strong palette, particularly favouring yellow, red and magenta and had a passion for including tulips in his flower groupings, which were skilfully drawn and well modelled, lacking only the freshness and spontaneity of the master's (Plate 150).

A contemporary of Quaker Pegg, but following much more in the manner of Billingsley, was Moses Webster,[3] best known as the flower painter of the *Trotter* service (Plate 146). Haslem says that his flowers can be recognised by their dashed and somewhat faded appearance and, compared to the style of Pegg, this is perhaps a fair assessment. The *Trotter* service pattern, with its distinctive bands of chrome green separating the reserves of flowers round the rim of the plates, proved very popular and other flower painters were employed in the production of similar services. These latter had the factory mark in red; the original *Trotter* service was marked in gold. There is a variation of this pattern in which flower reserves by Webster alternate with small landscapes by William Corden[4] (Plate 147).

Other flower painters in the later years of the factory were Edwin and Horatio Steele, sons of Thomas Steele.[5] A plaque, with the initials 'E.S.', by Edwin is in Derby Museum (Plate 151) and examples of the work of Horatio decorate a service made in about 1842 for Queen Victoria.[6] Thomas Steele was famous for his highly coloured fruit painted with much care and skill, on vases,[7] services (Plate 163) and plaques, which latter are today eagerly sought by collectors. They command surprisingly high prices which seem to bear little relation to either their artistic merit or ceramic importance.

Bird painting has a long history at the Derby factory, going back to the first years of the proprietorship of Duesbury I. In the period of Duesbury II and somewhat later, its chief exponent was John Brewer[8] and a pair of bough-pots decorated with birds in a landscape are probably his work (Plate 168). The last artist to be associated with

---

[1] See Biographies, Appendix I, p. 99.
[2] See Biographies, Appendix I, p. 96.
[3] See Biographies, Appendix I, p. 107.
[4] See Biographies, Appendix I, p. 87.
[5] See Biographies, Appendix I, p. 105.
[6] Now in the Victoria and Albert Museum.
[7] In the Victoria and Albert Museum.
[8] Bemrose papers at the British Museum, quoted by Jewitt, op. cit.

this form of decoration at the old Derby works was Richard Dodson.[1] His work, bright and rich in colour, is somewhat heavy though this latter defect, when compared with the work of John Brewer and George Complin, may well have been an inevitable consequence of the change in chemical composition of body and glaze mentioned above (Plate 164).

An interesting example of Derby porcelain decorated with paintings of birds is the mourning service (Plate 165) said to have been ordered by John Pares, of Hopwell Hall, near Derby, on the death of his daughter in 1812. The painting of the birds and the landscapes in which they are set is entirely in black and gold and the subjects were copied from wood engravings by Bewick.[2]

In sharp contrast to bird painting, which seems to have had an unbroken vogue throughout the whole lifetime of the factory, animal subjects on Derby porcelain are but rarely met with. Indeed, apart from a small number of cabinet pieces they would appear to be confined to a few services painted to pattern no. 268 (Plate 157) and probably made between about 1790 and 1800. Recent research indicates at least two types: one painted with British animals (Plate 158), or animals at least long domiciled here,[3] and the other painted with foreign animals almost certainly copied from engravings. The British animal series so far examined carry the factory mark and pattern number in blue and provide a rare example of the mark in this colour unaccompanied by a title or description in script. The foreign animal series is also without script titles but the factory mark and pattern number are in an unusual plum colour.

At least three Derby artists have been suggested for the paintings on these services: Cuthbert Lawton, Jockey Hill and John Brewer. The first of these can be discounted, since Lawton was a nineteenth century painter[4] and these services belong in their style of decoration quite definitely to the eighteenth century,[5] albeit the last decade. The claims of Jockey Hill are advanced[6] because of the alleged close similarity between the hand on the English animal service and a landscape service carrying the previous pattern number, which the author thought might reasonably be attributed to Hill. Although the evidence of the Pattern Book here might be rebutted on grounds of *non sequitur*, nevertheless it could be said that in the background

[1] See Biographies, Appendix I, p. 88.

[2] This service, consisting of 66 pieces was sold by auction at Nottingham in 1890 and fetched £250. The validity of the Pares tradition is uncertain.

[3] G. L. Pendred and D. A. Hoyte, 'Rare subjects on Derby porcelain', *Antique Dealer and Collector's Guide*, Aug. 1967.

[4] Hurlbutt, *Old Derby Porcelain*, Plate 38. See Biographies, Appendix I, p. 96.

[5] In the nineteenth century there were services depicting fox hunting scenes, and Cuthbert Lawton might well have painted some of these.

[6] W. H. Tapp, *Connoisseur*, Sept. 1936.

landscapes to this animal service there are similarities to land-scapes on Derby porcelain which have long been generally attributed to this artist. That these suspected likenesses may reside in the style of the period rather than in that of an individual artist seems possible from the discovery of the service depicting exotic animals. For from what we know of Jockey Hill, the man and the artist,[1] it seems very unlikely that he would have been put to copy from engravings. How-ever, we have documentary evidence[2] that John Brewer was engaged by Duesbury II to paint 'animals, figures, landscapes and flowers'. Since the well-known Derby 'botanical' services with plants copied from engravings and showing their anatomical features are generally attributed to John Brewer, it seems reasonable to advance this artist as the decorator not only of the animal service copied from engravings but perhaps of the other animal subjects also.

Throughout the proprietorship of Duesbury I, and probably most if not all of that of his son, the practice of decorating with gold had been by what is usually termed 'honey gilding'[3]. Gold leaf was ground up in honey, applied with a brush and fired at a relatively low tem-perature. Such gilding had to be put on rather thickly and, while it adhered fairly readily to the soft glazes used at Derby in the eigh-teenth century, it could not be burnished or polished. Hence the distinctive dullness of honey gilding; when used as a single band or border it often had a thickness which is easily detected by the eye or felt by the finger. Nevertheless, this process did lend itself to a con-siderable degree of fine detail. Many examples are to be found on tea-services and especially cabinet pieces, e.g. coffee cans, two-handled cups, covers and stands etc., of beautifully executed patterns. Many of these are in the form of stylised leaves and flowers, others in geo-metric patterns, e.g. ellipses, triangles ('dog-tooth'), small stars etc. etc.

About or shortly before 1800, it was realised that by mixing the gold with mercury, in the manner of the metal gilders, instead of honey, it could be applied more easily and cheaply, and also that, when fired, the residual gold left after the mercury had vaporised could be burnished and polished. This technique opened the way for the elaborate and indeed often highly skilled arabesque patterns found on the best services and decorative pieces. Very distinctive are the series of vases, campana-shaped with ring handles surmounted on mask

[1] See Biographies, Appendix I, p. 92.
[2] Jewitt, op. cit., vol. I, p. 107.
[3] In the period 1750–1756 the application of gold, if used, was probably by some mastic or sizing medium and unfired. This process would have had little or no permanence and may account for the apparent absence of gilding on Planché models.

G. JARDINIÈRE WITH SHIPPING SCENE

Date about 1800   Width 11 in   Mark 10 in blue

Derby Museum   See page 62

heads and urn-shaped with scroll handles. These are decorated with flowers, fruit or landscapes, usually in reserves, accompanied by elaborate arabesque gilding on the vase framing the reserves and also on the supporting plinth (Plates 172 and 173). Many of the services, too, bear complicated designs often based on geometric motifs and executed in a very competent manner (Plates 161 and 162).

Services decorated with family coats of arms are not common on Derby porcelain. In the Derby Museum is a square dish with the crest of the eighth Duke of Hamilton; this piece is also interesting in that it carries the rare painted mark 'Duesbury, London' (see no. 16, p. 113). More widely known is the service made for P. Barry-Barry about 1800. This is decorated with a border of roses on a black ground and a band of mazarin blue and gold; a wreath of oak leaves encircles the arms of the Barry family; the factory mark is in gold (Plate 166).[1]

It was doubtless the improved wearing quality of the gilding obtained by the mercury process which enabled Bloor[2] to exploit with such commercial success the famous 'Japan' patterns. For it was the colour of the gold in association with the Indian red and mazarin blue which gave the rich luxurious appearance. It should be remembered, however, that gilding on Bloor Derby porcelain can only be called durable relative to the earlier honey and size or mastic techniques. It was only later in the century, after the close of the old factory, that more modern gilding processes were developed which give the fair measure of durability we find on porcelain today.

Some writers mention the manufacture at Derby in the Bloor period of incense or pastille burners in the form of a cottage. We can find no firm evidence of this and it seems more likely that such are mistaken attributions of pieces from the Rockingham, Spode, Minton or Worcester factories. The form favoured at Derby for these burners was a vase with a perforated cover. An attractive example with a hunting scene attributed to William Cotton is to be seen in Derby Museum (Plate 169). Other Derby pastille burners are of campana shape standing on lion paw feet, with perforated covers having pine-cone knops.

The last years of the old Derby manufactory make a sad story. The strains first of paying off the £5,000 Bloor had to borrow to lease the factory in 1814 and then of keeping solvent in the face of the

---

[1] According to the Bemrose Sale Catalogue, 1909, this service was sold at auction in Nottingham in 1894 and fetched £496; at the above Bemrose Sale two plates sold for £67. At Sotheby's, on 4th February 1969, a plate from this Service made £300.

[2] Robert Bloor, who succeeded Kean in about 1811.

economically difficult years after the Napoleonic Wars (not to mention meeting the competition of such factories as Worcester, Spode, Coalport and Rockingham) all took their toll of his health. In 1828 Bloor suffered a mental breakdown from which he never recovered and, in the light of the circumstances, one is surprised at the general competency of the factory's products during the last years of its existence before it was finally closed down in 1848.

The date of commencement of the 'Bloor period' has long been the subject of some doubt. A lease of the 'Old China Factory'[1] was granted to Robert Bloor on 24th June 1815,[2] in which he was described as 'China Manufacturer'. He was employed at the factory in 1811 when Michael Kean withdrew from the firm, but was certainly in business on his own account by May 1814, when he advertised a large sale of china (lasting thirty days) 'at the large Warehouse of the Porcelain Manufactory, Derby'.[3] In view of this, the Bloor period cannot be regarded as commencing before 1811 at the earliest, in which year the sale to Bloor of the stock and utensils of the factory was under discussion.[4]

[1] See p. 13.
[2] Derby Public Library MSS.
[3] *Derby Mercury*, 19th May, 1814. Appendix V, p. 158.
[4] Bemrose Papers in the British Museum (a memorandum dated 8th March 1814).

APPENDIX I

BIOGRAPHIES OF WORKPEOPLE
EMPLOYED AT THE FACTORY

ABLOTT, Richard   *Landscape painter*

Said by Haslem to be one of the last Derby apprentices but no dates
are given and none of his work at Derby has been positively identified.
A signed plaque with a view in Scotland was sold at Sotheby's in
December 1966, but this might have been made at one of the Staffordshire factories at which he was employed after leaving Derby. In the
1870 Derby Art Exhibition there was a Coalport dessert service with
views in Derbyshire and Haslem says he was working in 1876 for
Messrs. Davenport.

   Lit: Haslem, op. cit.

ASKEW, Richard (d. 1798)   *Figure painter*

Worked for Sprimont at Chelsea and his work is said to be found on vases
and cups and saucers with yellow ground. Between 1770 and 1772 he
worked for Duesbury at Chelsea and in the latter year went to work at
Derby. He returned to London in 1780 and set up in business as a
'miniature enamel portrait painter'. Between 1785 and 1793 he was
in Dublin and also in Birmingham and in August 1794 signed an
agreement with Duesbury II to work by the piece instead of by the
day.[1] Jewitt[2] gives a list of pieces decorated by Askew, taken from two
bills dated 1794 and October 1795, delivered by Askew to Duesbury,
and these give valuable clues to the identification of Askew's work:

   '*Mr. Wilm. Duesbury, Deptur to Rich^d. Askew, July* 1794.

                                                       £   s. d.
   'a coffe can, with the king of france, one days work 0   5   3
   a coffe can, with the Queen of france, one day 0   5   3

[1] See Appendix V, p. 136.   [2] Jewitt, op. cit., vol. II, pp. 99–100.

	£	s.	d.
a coffe can, with a woman spining, one Day	0	5	3
a coffe can, with the head of the Duke of york, one day ...	0	5	3
2 coffe cans, with cupeds, tow Days & a half	0	13	1
a cadle cup, with a woman & child, tow days	0	10	6
a cadle cup, with a begar-Girl & child, tow days	0	10	6
a coffe can, a woman holding flowers siting, a day & half	0	7	10
a flower Pot, with a woman & child, tow days	0	10	6
a cadle cup, with a woman & a Lion, tow days	0	10	6
2 coffe cans, figuors of fath & hope, to days & a half	0	13	1
a cadle cup, with the fourting-teller, three and a half days	0	18	4
a coffe can, with the head of the Prince of Wails, tow days	0	10	6
a coffe can, with a Girl & bird, one Day & a half	0	7	10
2 coffee cans, with cupids, tow Days and a half	0	13	1
a cadle cup, with a woman siting at Woark, tow days ...	0	10	6
a cadle cup, with Doatage and beauty, three days	0	15	9
a cadle cup, with Age and youth, three Days	0	15	9
2 coffe cans, with cupieds, tow Days and a half	0	13	1
a coffe can, with a man & woman offiring to Cuped, 3 days & a half	0	18	4
a coffe can, with cupied chiding Venus, 3 days & a half...	0	18	4
2 cadle cups, first & scount lasson of love, Eaght Days ...	2	2	0
a Plate, with a head, half a Day	0	2	7
a cup & saucer with landsceps, one Day......................	0	5	3
a coffe can, with a Girl & a Rabbet, tow Days	0	10	6
a coffe can, with hebe & Eagle, tow Days	0	10	6
2 coffe cans, with the Prince of Wails & Dutches of york, 4 days	1	1	0
a coffe can, with maid of Corinth, four Days	1	1	0
a coffe can, with love sleeps, four Days	1	1	0
a coffe can, with sapho & Cuped, 3 Days & a half	0	18	4
a coffe can, with a offering to cuped, 3 Days & a half......	0	18	4
for Drawings, tow Days & a half	0	13	1
a cup & saucer, in brown, half a day	0	2	7
a coffe can, in brown, half a Day..............................	0	2	7
a Plate, with Plamin & lavinea, 3 Days	0	15	9
2 coffe cans, with single figuars, tow Days	0	10	6
a Plate, with a cupied & Emblems, tow Days & half......	0	13	1
12 Tea cups, in brown figuars, three Days & a half	0	18	4
a Plate, with a cupied only, a Day & a half	0	7	10
8 coffe cans, single figuars, Eight Days	2	2	0

	£	s.	d.
2 coffe cans, with figuars, Day & a half Each	1	11	6
4 coffe cans, with the four Elements, 4 Days Each	4	4	0
to three weekes Drawing of cupieds	4	14	6
4 coffe cans, with figuars, a Day & half Each	1	3	7
4 coffe cans, with figuars, a Day & half Each	1	10	6
a coffe can, with the Duke o york, tow Days	0	10	6
a Pair, with figuars, 5 Days.....................................	1	6	3
2 chamber Pots, with cupieds in the inside, 4 days.........	1	1	0
a coffe can, with the Prince of Wails	0	10	6
to Drawing of cupieds, 5 Days	1	6	3
a stand, with cupieds, in Rose couler, Day & half	0	7	10
a cram Pot, in Do, half a Day	0	2	7
a cram Pot, with figuar in brown, half a Day..............	0	2	7
4 coffe cans, with dancing figuars, 5 Days	1	6	3
4 coffe cans, with the Elements, 4 Days	4	4	0
a cadle cup, with a woman & children a brakefarst, 3 Days & half..	0	18	4
a cadle cup in Do, at supper, 3 Days & a half	0	18	4
a stand, a tay Pot, 2 coffe cans, a sugar Bason and cram Pot, work warry heily & neatly finishd by Pertickler Desier, 5 weekes	7	17	6
5 cups, in landskips, 2 Days..................................	0	10	6
	£61	0	4

the subjects on the stand, 3 womans & cupied tyde to a
    tree.
on the coffe cans, to woman offering to Pan & to woman
    awaking of cupied.
on the Tea Pot, maid of Corinth & love sleeps.
on the sugar-Bason, Euphorsnay & cuped.
on the crame Pot, a flying cupied.

Dilevered October the 3, 1795.'

		£	s.	d.
' 1.	2 coffe cans, with the King & Queen of france	0	10	0
2.	1 Do, with the duke of yorke	0	5	0
3.	1 Do, with the spining weele...............................	0	3	0
4.	2 Do, with Cupets	0	10	0
5.	1 cadle cup, with a woman & child.....................	0	7	0
6.	1 Do, with Begar Girl & child	0	7	0
7.	1 coffe cup, with a woman siting........................	0	5	0

		£	s.	d.
8.	a flower Pot, with a woman & cupet	0	9	0
9.	a Cadle cup, with Hosea & a Leon	0	7	0
10.	2 coffe, cans, with hope & fath	0	10	0
11.	a cadle cupe, with the fortin teller	0	14	0
12.	a coffe can, with a head of the Prince of Wales	0	7	6
13.	a coffe can, with a Girl & bird........................	0	5	0
14.	a cadle cup, with a woman siting at work	0	7	0
15.	a cadle cup, with doatage & beauty	0	12	0
16.	Do, with age and youth	0	12	0
17.	2 coffe cans, with cupets	0	10	0
18.	2 cadle cups, first & secont leson of love	1	8	0
19.	2 coffe cans, with venus and cupet & sacrafise to love	1	10	0
20.	a Plate, with hand	0	2	0
21.	a cup & saucer, with Landsceps	0	6	0
22.	2 coffe cans, hebe & the child & rabbet	0	18	0
23.	2 coffe cans, with heads of the Prince of Wales & Dss of York	0	15	0
24.	a coffe can, with the maid of corneth	0	15	0
25.	a coffe can, with love slepes............................	0	15	0
26.	a coffe can, with sappho to Phaon	0	15	0
27.	a coffe can, with offering to cupet	0	15	0
28.	for Drawings	0	12	0

Deliverd. November the 26, 94.   £15 11 6
RICHARD ASKEW.'

Although Askew is most famous for his cupids painted *en camaieu* which he executed throughout the whole of his career as a china painter, it is clear from the bills of work that he was entrusted by Duesbury with a wide variety of figure subjects, many done on those distinctive Derby products, the coffee cans.

In the Derby Pattern Books he is assigned three patterns in the Plate Book, viz:

'177 Cupid on a basket of flowers in the clouds by Askew.
180 Cupid painted by Askew, flowers basket clouds etc., by Billingsley.
181 Palaemon and Lavinia by Askew in colours.'

and five in the Cup and Saucer Book, viz:

'361 Love sleeps by Askew in colours
363 Figure in colours by Askew

370 Panel pattern by Askew
374 Boy on a board by Askew, in colours
389 Venus and Cupid in colours by Askew.'

He died at Bilston, Staffordshire, in 1798.

Lit: Jewitt op. cit., vol. II, pp. 98–100; Haslem, op. cit., p. 46; Hurlbutt, op. cit., pp. 87–93; W. H. Tapp, in *Connoisseur*, June 1934.

ASKEW, Robert

Son of Richard and came to Derby from Chelsea with his father in 1772. He absconded with another young employee, John Laurence, in the same year.[1] Hurlbutt says that Laurence worked at Wedgwood's Decorating Establishment in Chelsea and suggests that Askew junior might have gone with him.

BACON, John, R.A. (b. 1740, d. 1799)   *Sculptor*

The only known authentic information linking this artist with the Derby factory is contained in a letter from Henry Duesbury to John Haslem,[2] dated 27th November 1862, in which he says: '. . . I see by an old mem. book now before me (of my great grandfathers) that he paid Bacon, the first sculptor of the day £75. 7s. 2d. in 1769 for models . . .'. *The British Magazine and Review* for October 1782, in an account of Bacon who was by this time a sculptor with a national reputation, states: 'In the year 1755 he was placed with Mr. Crisp of Bow Church Yard who having a Manufactory of China Lambeth, which Mr. Bacon sometimes attended, he had an opportunity of observing the models of different sculptors which were frequently sent to a pottery in the same premises to be burned. The sight of their models inspired him with an inclination for this art.'[3]

We do not know whether Bacon ever executed models for translating into porcelain figures or whether the above payment by Duesbury was for large figures from Coade's Artificial Stone Manufactory at Lambeth of which Bacon had just become Manager;[4] in the latter case the models would have been intended for the academic instruction of the Derby modellers. Haslem attributes the model of *Garrick as Richard III* to Bacon but this is not now generally accepted. The

[1] Jewitt, op. cit., vol. II, p. 98.
[2] Haslem, op. cit., p. 43.
[3] Toppin, *E.C.C. Trans.*, 1933, vol. 1, p. 38.
[4] Lane, op. cit., p. 93.

APPENDIX I: BIOGRAPHIES

Three Royal Groups after the painting by Zoffany (described by Duesbury in his catalogue, June 1773); nos. 39–45, *Arts and Sciences*; no. 144, *Virgil*; and nos. 216 and 217, *Music and Poetry* have also been rejected or accepted with much doubt. The portrait figures of *Addison, Milton* and *Shakespeare* have been attributed to Bacon.

Lit: Haslem, op. cit.; Jewitt, op. cit.; Toppin, op. cit.; Lane, op. cit.; Savage, *18th Century English Porcelain*, pp. 178–180.

BAKEWELL, Thomas   *Chinaman*

The *List of Voters*, 31st January 1772, and the *Canvas of Freeman*, 5th July 1774, described him as 'Pottman' but in the *Voters List* of 20th January he is designated as 'Chinaman'. Only two or three 'chinamen' are named in these lists, including William Duesbury himself, so Bakewell must have been of some importance in the factory.

Lit: Williamson MSS in Derby Museum.

BANCROFT, Joseph (d. 1857)   *Painter*

Born at Derby and apprenticed at the old works, Bancroft left shortly after completing his time and worked first for Copeland's and then with Minton's where he spent most of his life and did his best work. This was in considerable demand and fetched high prices. He painted flowers, shells and insects etc.

There is a folio of forty drawings in the Bemrose Collection in the Derby Public Library. Although it is doubtful whether he did much painting on Derby porcelain there are in the Derby Museum two plates which, from comparison with the above drawings, might have been executed by him. One of these has tulips in the centre and the other Spanish iris.

Lit: Haslem, op. cit.; Folio of drawings mentioned above.

BANFORD, Bernice   *Painter*

The wife of James Banford. She was employed as a painter at Wedgwood's works in London. Owing to her husband's unreliability she sought work from Duesbury to be done in her home, 'towards the

76

APPENDIX I: BIOGRAPHIES

support of my family and to assist my husband to pay some debts'.[1] Her work has never been identified.

Lit: Jewitt, op. cit.

BANFORD, James (b. 1758, d. 1798)   *Figure painter*

Born at Berkeley, Gloucestershire, and apprenticed to Richard Champion of the Bristol Factory, 19th January 1773. When in 1778 Champion became bankrupt, many of the workmen and apprentices sought work elsewhere. Banford, with his friend Henry Bone, later a well-known miniature painter, went to London, where they appear to have done freelance work. It is thought that Banford did painting for Duesbury during this period and some of the dishes and comports decorated with classical shaped urns and garlands of flowers have been attributed to him.[2] It was doubtless through his friendship with Henry Bone that Banford learned figure painting (Plate 134). In 1789 he came to work at Derby, but was a man of very unstable character, much given to drinking, and seems to have done very little work between 1792 and 1794, relying on his artist wife Bernice (see p. 76). He left in 1795 through dissatisfaction with the wages he received.[3] He seems to have gone to Bilston, where he died in 1798.

If an artist's popularity and skill can be assessed by the number of patterns assigned to him in the Pattern Books then Banford easily heads the list with sixteen (the brothers Brewer have twelve between them, Billingsley nine and Askew and Robertson eight each). The following patterns are assigned to Banford in the Cup and Saucer Book:

220 'Landskip, a tinted drawing by Banford'
229 'Cupid disarmed by Euphrosyne by Banford'
232 'Venus chiding Cupid by Banford'
233 'The genius of modesty preventing love unveiling beauty by Banford'.
239 'Hope in colours, by Banford'
242 'Panels by Banford from lady's paper flower jars'
256 'Romeo and Juliet in colours by Banford'
257 'Griselda in colours by Banford'
258 'Cupid disarmed and bound by Banford'
271 'Two Virgins with flowers from Complins print by Banford'

[1] See Appendix V, p. 135.
[2] W. H. Tapp, *Connoisseur*, Feb. 1937.
[3] See Appendix V, p. 134.

77

275 'Sheltered Lamb by Banford'
332 'Lanskip by Banford, first ground pearl colour'
343 'Cupid with two Doves by Banford'
351 'Ground of coloured flowers by Billingsley filled in with gold and in the panel Cupid disarmed by Banford'
352 'Ground same as 271, Love sleeps, Maid of Corinth by Banford back two Dovedale landskips all in colours'
387 'Coloured group by Banford'.

In addition the following have been attributed to Banford:

215 'Dancing Girl with twinkling cymbals'
216 'Beggar girl with boy'.

It has been noticed[1] that where Askew used fine stippling underneath his wash to produce the low lights, Banford relied on washing on his colour with only a little cross-hatching, and he usually, though not invariably, added wings to his cherubs. In his figure paintings (*Hope* on a coffee can in the Victoria and Albert Museum), the arched, rather high, eyebrows and aquiline nose are said to be distinctive of his style. The landscapes resemble Boreman's but may be distinguished by the sharp contrasts between the principal colours—blue, yellow and green—and the absence of bright colours in the minute human figures.

Banford was certainly one of the most accomplished artists to decorate Derby porcelain. Unfortunately his adult working life cannot have lasted much more than fifteen years and the work indicated in the Pattern Books must have been confined to no more than six (1789–1795), of which two (1792–93) seemed to have been lost through illness brought on by excessive drinking. It does not seem possible to identify with certainty any work he may have done for Duesbury as a free lance.

Lit: Jewitt, op. cit.; Hurlbutt, op. cit.; W. H. Tapp, *Connoisseur*, Feb. and April 1937.

BARLOW, James (Junior)   *Painter of birds and insects*

Worked at the factory in its closing years. He then went to the Potteries and in 1876 was foreman at Messrs. Allerton & Sons, Longton. His father was in the potting department of the Derby factory and foreman from 1837 till his death in 1842.

Lit: Haslem, op. cit.

[1] W. H. Tapp, *Connoisseur*, Feb. and April 1937.

APPENDIX I: BIOGRAPHIES

BILLINGSLEY, William (b. 1758, d. 1828)   *Flower painter*

The eldest son of William and Mary Billingsley was baptised in St. Alkmund's Church, Derby, 12th October 1758. His father had been employed as a flower painter at the Chelsea factory and had come to Derby about 1756, where he worked for Duesbury I until his death in 1770. The widowed mother apprenticed her son to Duesbury in September 1774, for five years, to learn china painting.[1] It was most fortunate for the young Billingsley that in 1783 there arrived from the Chelsea works Zachariah Boreman (see p. 81) and a strong friendship developed between the two. From Boreman, some twenty years the senior and an artist of the first rank Billingsley was able to acquire an invaluable insight into the full craft of painting on china and it was from his mentor that he learned the 'wiping out' process of painting flowers. There is little doubt that during the years 1783 to 1793 Billingsley also learned the art of landscape painting and that the two men worked together in experiments in the composition of the china body. Although the Duesburys allowed him no opportunity to show his skill in either of these arts whilst employed at Derby, nevertheless Billingsley made good use of the former in his work at Mansfield and elsewhere as an independent decorator, and of the latter at Pinxton, Swansea and Nantgarw.

Billingsley's finest work at Derby was done between 1790, when he succeeded Edward Withers as chief flower painter, and 1796, when he ended his association with the Derby factory and began an extraordinary series of wanderings. These took him successively to Pinxton, Mansfield, Torksey (Lincs.), Worcester, Swansea, Nantgarw, back to Swansea and finally to Coalport, where from 1820 he worked until his death in 1828.[2]

Billingsley's name appears ten times in the old Pattern Books.

In the Plate Book:

   53 'Roses and Cornflowers by Billensley'
   135 'Moses (Moss roses?) with some tinging yellow flowers upon a
        feint brown shaded ground'
   144 'Group of coloured flowers'
   172 'Large group with handsome border'
   174 'Cornucopias, fruit and flowers by Bilensley'
   176 'Rich border of roses and lilies of the valley, bell shaped sprigs
        in centre'

[1] See Appendix V, p. 125.
[2] W. D. John, *William Billingsley*, 1968.

180 'Cupid painted by Askew, flowers, baskets clouds etc. painted by Billensley'.

In the Cup and Saucer Book:

246 'Teacup, fawn coloured Vandyke borders: blue-leaved Coronilla plant by Billensley'
326 'Basket of flowers upon pedistall before olive ground'
351 'Mug, ground of flowers by Billensley filled in with gold and "Cupid disarmed by Banford" '.

Lit: Haslem, op. cit.; John, op. cit.; Wallis and Bemrose, op. cit.

BLOOD, John   *Gilder*

Haslem says this man was probably among Duesbury's earliest apprentices and became a clever gilder and painter of arabesque borders. He was married to Elizabeth Clayton at All Saints Church, Derby, on 9th March 1784.

Lit: Haslem, op. cit.

BLORE, Robert (b. 1810, d. 1868) *Modeller and china manufacturer*

Although apprenticed at the old manufactory it would seem that he left almost as soon as he had completed his time, and worked at Minton's. He very shortly returned to Derby but to start in business on his own, having a kiln in Bridge Gate, Derby, in the yard of his father, a monumental mason. Here he modelled small articles and figures (including animals) as well as vases and ewers. His best known work is the *Sleeping Endymion* done in biscuit porcelain from the original figure by Canova at Chatsworth. In Derby Museum are two biscuit figures, *Mary* and *Samuel*. About 1835 he went to Mason's of Lane Delph, Staffordshire, and then to the pottery firm at Middlesboro of Isaac Wilson & Co. He was no relation to Robert Bloor, the proprietor of the Nottingham Road factory from 1814.

BOOT (or Booth), Jonathan   *Repairer*

This name, together with the date 1764 has been noted incised on the base of a 'frill' vase.[1]

[1] See p. 28.

APPENDIX I: BIOGRAPHIES

BOREMAN, Zachariah (b. 1737, d. 1810)   *Landscape painter*

Possibly apprenticed at Chelsea and working for Sprimont in the 1760s, Boreman was employed by Duesbury I from the time he purchased the Chelsea works in 1769 until he closed them down in 1784. From the weekly Bills quoted by Jewitt, Boreman, at a rate of 5s. 3d. a day, was the highest paid workman mentioned until the arrival of the modeller Gauron (see p. 35) in June 1773. Although his name does appear in the lists[1] of men working on the miniature 'toys' etc.—'30 seals painted in Mottows by Boreman and Wollams'— it is known that much of this sort of work was done as 'overtime', and as one of the highest paid craftsman we can be sure that Boreman would be employed on much more important work. No documentary examples of his landscape painting are known during Chelsea and Chelsea-Derby times although the late W. H. Tapp[2] made attributions on what he claimed to be reasonable grounds.

On the closure of the Chelsea works in 1784 Boreman signed an agreement to come to Derby for three years[3] and he seems to have worked for Duesbury until 1794.[4] Whether he worked continuously is open to question, for in a letter to Duesbury dated 9th July 1787 Lygo says: 'sorry to hear Mr. Boreman has decided to leave Derby— I think it may be a try on', and in various lists of artist workmen quoted by Jewitt, Boreman's name is present in some and absent from others where Billingsley's name is present on all. Whatever the truth, Boreman was a prolific worker and was given many important services to decorate.

On leaving Derby Boreman went to the London enamelling and decorating establishment of John Sims and remained there till his death in 1810.

Boreman is mentioned in the Pattern Books as follows:

In the Plate Book:

134 'Black upon Moonlight Landscip'
178 'Landscip near Critch'

In the Cup and Saucer book:

244 'Brown Landscip'
260 'View from Cheltenham'
264 'Coloured Landscip'

[1] Jewitt, op. cit., vol. I, pp. 180–181.
[2] *Connoisseur*, Jan. 1934.
[3] Bemrose, op. cit. pp. 134–6.
[4] See also Appendix V, p. 132 and 152.

330 'Landscip'
336 'Lanskips in colours'.

Lit: Bemrose, op. cit.; Haslem, op. cit.; Jewitt, op. cit.; Tapp, *Connoisseur*, Jan. 1934.

BREWER, John (b. 1764, d. 1816)   *Painter*

Although he did not come to Derby until 1795, John Brewer is said by Jewitt to have been employed by Duesbury as early as 1782, and to have been assured that he should not have less than a guinea and a half for the first year and two guineas afterwards. In 1795 he was to paint figures, animals, landscapes, and flowers by the piece, a schedule of prices being drawn up for that purpose.[1] In February 1808 John Brewer inserted an advertisement in the *Derby Mercury*: 'Mr. Brewer returns his most grateful thanks to the Nobility, Gentry and Public of Derby and its Vicinity for support during the last two years . . . and solicits a continuance of favours'. This would seem to imply that Brewer had left the Derby factory in 1805 or 1806.

There have long been differences of opinion in identifying the porcelain decorated by John Brewer. The Pattern Books make no distinction between the brothers John and Robert. There are a number of drawings and water-colours in existence and Williamson, in manuscript notes made about 1932, and Tapp[2] mention a sketch book in the possession of the family. In Derby Art Gallery are three water-colour drawings by John Brewer and two aquatints after drawings by him. From the evidence of the drawings etc. (the above mentioned sketch book contains a number of very small circular medallions of fruit and flowers, finely executed by John Brewer (Williamson MSS)) it would seem reasonable to attribute to John the porcelain pieces decorated in the water-colour tradition of transparent colours and fine detail. In the British Museum are some accounts presented by John to William Duesbury II for work done, and one for 1795 mentions 7 shipping scenes, 24 plant and flower subjects, 46 landscapes, 10 bird studies, 2 figure subjects and 20 plates 'with rose borders'. The patterns allocated to the Brewers in the Pattern Books are as follows:

299 'One figure with a serpent entwining'
377 'Landskip and ships—colours'
378 'Moonlight landscip'

[1] See Appendix V, p. 136–7.
[2] 'John and Robert Brewer, the Derby Painters', *E.P.C. Trans.*, 1932, no. IV, p. 77.

384 'Lessons of Love and Landskips (coloured)'
391 'Basket of Flowers (in colour)'
393 'Flora and a Muse (In colours)'
414 'A Bacchante (in colours) Adelaide (in colours)'
415 'Love Sleeps (in colours) Maid of Corinth' (see also Banford
    no. 352)
428 'Camp scene (colours)'
432 'Coloured figures, ships in colours all round'
458 'Camp view (colours)'

Assuming that John was painting china for Duesbury from about
1782 and that he left the factory about 1805 the greater part of his
work would carry the factory mark in puce or blue with only a few
pieces in red. The shipping scenes painted in the above-mentioned
water-colour style in somewhat pale colours can be fairly attributed
to John. For although both Robert Brewer and George Robertson
worked in water colours, nevertheless their palettes and technique
seem to come nearer to the strong colours and opacity of nineteenth
century rather than the colour washes of the eighteenth century
artists. In the Victoria and Albert Museum is a beautifully decorated
coffee can with a military camp scene. It would seem reasonable to
agree with Bernard Rackham[1] in ascribing this to John Brewer rather
than to Robert as claimed by W. H. Tapp.[2] An example of one of the
bird studies mentioned in the accounts quoted above may be afforded
by a *jardinière* in Derby Museum; this particular piece probably
dates from about 1805.

Lit: Jewitt, op. cit.; vol. II, p. 107; Haslem, op. cit., pp. 97–98; Hurlbutt,
op. cit.; W. H. Tapp, op. cit.

BREWER, Robert (b. 1775, d. 1857)   *Painter*

Born at Madeley, Shropshire, and thought to have been apprenticed
at the Caughley china factory and then employed at Worcester
before coming on to Derby in about 1797 (Hurlbutt). It seems
fairly certain that he was employed at the Derby factory at least
until the death of his brother in 1816. In that year he inserted an
advertisement in the *Derby Mercury*: 'Mr. Robert Brewer, Drawing Master (Brother of the late Mr. John Brewer deceased). Takes
the liberty to acquaint the liberal and respectable Inhabitants of
Derby that he has undertaken the professional business . . . and as
he purposes that the widow and daughter of his much lamented

[1] *Connoisseur*, Sept. 1927.
[2] *E.P.C. Trans.*, 1932, no. IV, p. 75.

Brother shall derive certain profit therefrom respectfully solicits their kind support'. Whether he severed his connection altogether with the Derby factory at this time or did occasional work we do not know. He inserted several similar advertisements in the *Derby Mercury*; the last would seem to be 19th August 1820.

His work on Derby porcelain must consist very largely of land-scapes. A few seascapes and military camp scenes have been attributed to Robert, though without documentary evidence and it seems much more likely that Robert spent more of his time on landscapes. We can only regret that the Pattern Books make no distinction between the brothers (Plate 153).

Lit: Haslem, op. cit.; Jewitt, op. cit.; Hurlbutt, op. cit.; W. H. Tapp, *E.P.C. Trans.*, 1932, no. IV, p. 75.

BROUGHTON, Joseph (1805–1875)   *Gilder*

Haslem says he first began working at the Derby factory at the age of eleven years and was later apprenticed to japan painting and gilding. He remained at the old works until their closure in 1848 and there-after was employed at the King Street works until his death.

Lit: Haslem, op. cit.

CLARK, James   *Gilder*

Haslem says he was one of Duesbury's early apprentices working at the factory at the end of the eighteenth century and for more than thirty years in the nineteenth century. He was a skilful gilder, especially of arabesque patterns, and is said to have introduced coloured work among the gilding.

Lit: Haslem, op. cit.

CLAVEY, Philip   *Flower painter*

Haslem states that he was apprenticed at the end of the eighteenth century and learned flower painting at the Derby works. He is said to have specialised in the painting of single plants, and numerous dessert services were decorated by him in that manner.

Lit: Haslem, op. cit.

COCKER, George (b. 1794, d. 1868)   *Modeller*

Apprenticed to figure modelling about 1808 and left in 1817 to go to
Coalport. After an unsuccessful attempt to start a small manufactory
at Jackfield he went to Worcester before returning to Derby in 1821.
In 1826 he set up a small establishment in Friar Gate, Derby. In the
advertisement (quoted by Jewitt[1]) it states: 'DERBY NEW CHINA
WORKS for the manufacture of porcelain figures, ornaments etc., . . .
also a variety of tea and dessert services . . .'. The porcelain figures
were in biscuit as were the ornaments which took the form of raised
flowers for brooches etc.; the services would have been bought in the
white from other factories and merely decorated at Cocker's factory.
The factory in Friar Gate continued until 1840 or 1841 when
Cocker moved to 8 Chenies Street, Bedford Square, London, and some
figures carry this address incised. In 1853 Cocker gave up manufacturing and went to Minton's at Stoke-on-Trent, where he remained until
his death. All the figures of Cocker which have been identified were
made at his own factory, either in Derby or London, and nothing is
known of his work at the Nottingham Road factory.

Signed works as follows:

Roman Matron 'Cocker Derby'
Boy with hurdy-gurdy and monkey 'G. Cocker'
Dying Drunkard 'G. Cocker Derby'
Girl with a lamb under her arm 'D Cocker Derby' (D. Cocker,
     probably a son)
Queen Victoria seated 'D. Cocker 8 Chenies Street Bedford
Square'

The following figures have also been attributed to him:

Hannah More, Minton's factory
Duke of Wellington
Boy with a bird cage
Boy at a well
Rape of the Sabines⎱ Exhibited by Cocker at the Derby Mech-
The Queen   ⎰ anics Institute Exhibition, 1839

Three figures representing stages of *Drinking* as a warning
against excess, modelled for Dr. Douglas Fox of Derby (Specimens
in the Brighton Museum).

Lit: Haslem, op. cit.; Williamson MSS in Derby Museum; Jewitt, op. cit.

[1] Op. cit., vol. II, p. 108.

COFFEE, William T. *Modeller*

Came to Derby in 1791 from Coade's Artificial Stone Manufactory, Lambeth, London and in 1794 entered into an agreement with Duesbury to be paid either 3s. 6d. a day for each day of 10 hours 'or at the rate of 7s. for any single human figure of 6 inches high whether standing or in any other action which if standing would be 6 inches high; and that all figures shall be roughed out naked in correct proportions before draped' and an extra threepence was paid for each half inch additional height. Duesbury raised his wages in 1795 hoping that Coffee would prove a successor to Spengler, who had again absconded from his employment at Derby. However, Coffee himself did not stay for long (just long enough to complete what was to prove his magnum opus, the *Shepherd* to partner Spengler's *Shepherdess* (see p. 50) before leaving to work at Sir Nigel Gresley's newly opened china works at Church Gresley, near Burton on Trent. Within twelve months he returned to Derby and seems to have started up a small rival porcelain factory in partnership with one William Duesbury (a workman relative of the proprietor of the Derby factory). After some months Duesbury (now in partnership with Michael Kean) persuaded his relative to come back to him and Coffee carried on alone, making terracotta figures and garden ornaments presumably in the style of Coade's Lambeth factory at which he had been trained. Coffee was still in Derby in 1810, when he was described as a modeller and sculptor.[1] Although not directly employed at the Derby China Factory, Coffee may well have continued to supply models to Kean between about 1798 and 1810 or even later. Hurlbutt says, quoting no authority, that Coffee eventually left Derby for London, where he opened a shop and then went to America, where he spent the rest of his life.

Lit: Haslem, op. cit.; Hurlbutt, op. cit.

COMPLIN, George *Painter*

Perhaps brought from France to Chelsea by Sprimont about 1755, Complin may have come to Derby about 1758, when the Chelsea factory was in difficulties due to Sprimont's illness. He is thought to have painted fruit, flowers, birds, animals and landscapes. Of his work before about 1785 nothing has been identified. He seems to have worked at Derby until about 1795 when he may either have returned to France or died.

[1] *Derby Mercury*, 27th Sept. 1810.

136 'Fruit by Complin: upon landscape background'
138 'Fruit by Complin'
140 'Fruit by Complin'
150 'Birds and landscapes by Complin'
236 'Fruit and birds by Complin'
237 'Fruit and birds by Complin'
245 'Fruit by Complin, with tomtit and bullfinch before dark landscip'
254 'Fruit and birds'
259 'Fruit and birds'
262 'Fruit and birds'
325 'Fruit and flowers'

Lit: Haslem, op. cit.; Hurlbutt, op. cit.

COOPER, William   *Painter*

Jewitt says: 'a clever flower painter 1770–1776'.

Lit: Jewitt, op. cit.

CORDEN, William (b. 1797, d. 1867)   *Painter*

Apprenticed in 1811 and worked at Derby until 1820. Shortly before he left the china works it is said that he painted the greater part of a dessert service with subjects copied from Thurston's illustrations to Tegg's edition of Shakespeare's plays, 1812. He painted on some of the largest pieces of the famous Rockingham service made for William IV.[1] He also painted china plaques.

Corden went to London and practised as a portrait painter and was patronised by Queen Victoria and the Prince Consort.

There are in Derby Museum four plates painted with landscapes by him and with flowers by John Keys (q.v.).

COTTON, William   *Landscape painter*

Haslem says he worked at Derby for a few years before going to the Potteries in 1821. In the Derby Museum collection there is an incense burner variously said to be by this artist or by Cuthbert Lawton (q.v.).

Lit: Haslem, op. cit.

[1] At Windsor Castle.

DEARE, John (b. 1759, d. 1798) *Modeller*

In 1784 he was engaged by Duesbury to model various groups and figures. However, in 1785 he was elected a travelling student of the Academy and went to Rome where he remained until his death.

DEXTER, William (b. 1818, d. 1860) *Painter*

One of the later apprentices at the old Derby works, Haslem says he painted fruit, flowers and birds but 'excelled more particularly in the superior Chinese and Oriental style of decoration'. It would seem that he did not stay long after his apprenticeship and worked in London, Paris and Nottingham as a painter in oils and water-colours as well as an enameller on china, before going to Australia in 1852.

Lit: Haslem, op. cit.; Williamson MSS.

DIXON, William *Painter*

Haslem says he worked at Derby between 1820 and 1823 and painted figures, subjects chiefly of a grotesque or ludicrous character. The source of some of these would appear to have been a series of engravings *Human Passions Delineated* by Tim Bobbins published in Manchester at the end of the seventeenth century (see Plate 159).

Lit: Haslem, op. cit.

DODSON, Richard *Bird painter*

Apprenticed at the Derby works and left in 1820, when he set up a small enamelling establishment on the Nottingham Road. Haslem says he usually painted birds with a landscape background and comments that although rich they are rather heavy in colour and carelessly drawn. Dessert services (with gilt scroll borders by Thomas Till) and small vases and ornaments are said by Haslem to have been decorated by him.

Lit: Haslem, op. cit.

APPENDIX I: BIOGRAPHIES

DODSON, William   *Painter*

Father of Richard, the bird painter (q.v.). Haslem says he succeeded Thomas Soar as foreman over the painters and died about 1820.

Lit: Haslem, op. cit.

DUVIVIER, Fidèle (b. 1740, d. 1837)   *Painter*

Under an agreement dated 31st October 1769 Duvivier promised 'for four years from that date . . . to employ himself in the art of painting china or porcelain ware', for a weekly wage of 24s. Jewitt says he remained some years and was the principal flower painter. Major Tapp[1] believes that Duvivier painted figure subjects and attributed a Chelsea–Derby vase mentioned in a sale catalogue of 1771 to this artist.

In 1790 Duvivier wrote to Duesbury II from New Hall, where he had either been employed or was working independently, asking to be taken on at Derby, but whether Duesbury gave him work we do not know. His signed work appears on Worcester, New Hall and Caughley/Coalport porcelains, probably executed as an independent decorator.

Lit: Jewitt, op. cit.; Tapp, op. cit.; Margaret Foden, 'Fidèle Duvivier: Ceramic Artist', *Antique Dealer and Collector's Guide*, July 1968, p. 56.

EDLIN, Thomas   *Painter*

Described as a 'china-painter', Edlin was married at St. Alkmund's Church, Derby, 5th July 1767. Jewitt mentions a Thomas Elin (sic) as a painter and gilder at the factory 1786–1795.

Lit: Jewitt, op. cit.; Williamson MSS.

FARNSWORTH, Isaac (d. 1821)   *Repairer*

Would appear to have been employed as a repairer of figures from about 1756 until his death in 1821. He marked the pieces he 're-paired', i.e., built up from the cast portions, with an incised star. His work is also found on vases, *jardinières* etc.

Lit: Haslem, op. cit.; Williamson MSS in Derby Museum.

[1] *Connoisseur*, March 1932.

FARNSWORTH, James   *Flower painter*

The only mention of this artist is by Haslem who says that he was one of four flower painters and one landscape artist discharged by Bloor in 1821, presumably through slackness in trade.

Lit: Haslem, op. cit.

FROST, John   *Painter*

In 1770 apprenticed to Edward Philips 'china or porcelain painter' and in 1771 was transferred by fresh indenture to William Duesbury.

Lit: Jewitt, op. cit.

GADSBY, William

Apprenticed at Derby in 1772 for four years 'in the art of making models'.

GAURON, Nicholas-François (b. 1736)   *Modeller*

Born in Paris and came to London about 1750 as apprentice to his uncle, Jacob, a silversmith. He was employed as a porcelain modeller at the French factories at Mennecy and was chief modeller at Tournai from 1758–1764, where he may well have worked on figures and groups done in biscuit.[1] In a list of workmen at Chelsea in 1773 there is mentioned a highly paid modeller or 'repairer' named Gauron.[2]

GOADSBY, James   *Modeller*

Mentioned by Haslem as 'among the clever modellers and clever potters who learnt the art at Derby'. Said to have been at Swansea about 1817.

Lit: Haslem, op. cit.

HALL, William (b. 1800, d. 1861)   *Flower Painter*

Haslem mentions him as one of the artists discharged by Bloor in

---

[1] Lane, op. cit., p. 104.
[2] Jewitt, op. cit., vol. I, p. 186.

1821. In the Derby Exhibition of 1839 he exhibited *Basket of Flowers* in biscuit china. A Coalport plate painted by him is included in the Haslem Sale Catalogue (1884) signed 'W.H. 1822'.

Lit: Haslem, op. cit.; Williamson MSS in Derby Museum.

HANCOCK, George (d. 1850 or 1851)   *Painter and ground layer*

Son of John Hancock, Senior (1757–1847), worked at Derby 1819 to 1835. He was engaged to superintend the new method of laying ground colours on china. The old method with a brush often resulted in unevenness, the new was to lay powdered colours, the reserves to be left white for later decoration, being covered with a protective stencil. Haslem states that George was also a flower painter and is said to have painted in the Billingsley style (for whom he had worked at Mansfield c. 1803–1806). It seems likely that a number of plaques painted with flowers were from his hand. In Derby Museum is a collection of water-colour drawings by him of flowers and also insects and shells.

Lit: Haslem, op. cit.; Jewitt, op. cit.

HANCOCK, John (Senior) (b. 1757, d. 1847) *Painter and Colour Maker*

Apprenticed at Derby 29th September 1769[1] but shortly left, first to work at Swansea and then to the Potteries. To him, c. 1800, has been attributed the invention of the modern method of gilding, in which, instead of gold leaf being mixed in honey as hitherto, the gold was mixed with mercury and, after firing which drove off the mercury as vapour, the gold was burnished.[2] Hancock spent the rest of his working days in the Potteries, and at Spode's was the first to put into practice the gold and silver lustres.

Lit: Haslem, op cit.; Jewitt, op. cit.

HANCOCK, John (b. 1777, d. 1840)   *Painter and ground layer*

Came to Derby in 1820, where he worked under the supervision of his brother George (q.v.) in making colours and applying the new method of ground laying. Haslem says he was also a clever painter particularly of birds, which he imitated in the old Sèvres style. He worked at

---

[1] See Appendix V, p. 124.
[2] The application of the technique of mercury gilding to porcelain seems, however, likely to have been suggested by the methods of the metal gilders.

Derby until his death. Perhaps the John Hancock of 'Hancock's China Body'.[1]

Note: The above had a son who seems to have been known as 'John Hancock Junior', born 1804, died 1839. He is said to have worked at Derby between about 1823 and 1836 painting birds, fruit, flowers, figures and armorial bearings.

Lit: Haslem, op. cit.

HASLEM, John (b. 1818, d. 1884) *Painter*

Apprenticed in 1831 to learn flower painting, he left Derby in 1835. Later learned portrait painting and painted portraits on china. The author of *The Old Derby China Manufactory* published in 1876.

HILL, James (b. 1791, d. 1854) *Flower painter*

Apprenticed at the old factory and worked there till it closed in 1848, when he was one of the six founder members of the King Street factory. He painted flowers. Haslem describes a pattern known as 'Hill's flowers' which he painted in large quantities: it consisted of one group (formed of one large rose and a few small sprigs of different colours) with several sprigs scattered about. He is also said to have modelled some small animals which sold well.

Lit: Haslem, op. cit.

HILL, Joseph *Repairer*

Probably one of the earliest apprentices of Duesbury I and seems to have spent the whole of his working life at the Derby factory. On the figures he built up, from pieces cast in moulds, he is said to have used an incised triangle as his mark.

Lit: Haslem, op. cit.

HILL, Thomas ('Jockey') (b. 1753, d. 1827) *Landscape painter*

W. H. Tapp[2] states that Hill first worked for Duesbury I at Chelsea in 1779; he did not come to Derby at the closure of the Chelsea works but in 1794 received an invitation from Duesbury II to come to Derby and

[1] See page 121.
[2] *Connoisseur*, June 1936.

take the place of Boreman, who had recently left. His style is very similar to that of Boreman (with whom he had worked at Chelsea) putting small meticulously executed human figures in the middle foreground. He had however a great love of yellow and yellow-greens and Tapp says that unlike Boreman he never stipples over his leaves and foliage but 'dentilates them with sharp minute elongated brushed lines'. He left Derby in 1799 or 1800.

There are four patterns bearing his name:

262   Dessert plate with scalloped edge having $\frac{7}{8}''$ mazarin blue band . . . centre panel enclosed blue and gold lines and geometrical gold border.
'Coloured landskips by Hill $4\frac{1}{2}''$'.

269   'Same as 262 only done smaller'.

413A   Tea cup with gold border on white band 'Coloured Landskip by Hill'.

413B   Same description: 'lettered Landskip painted with 1365 by Hill'.

459   Tea cup with yellow ground and white and gold border. Oval panel opposite handle lettered 'Landskip in colours by Hill'.

A circular plaque given by the artist to Mr. Horsley, with whom he lived while he worked at Derby, was given to Derby Museum by Haslem in 1884.

HOLDSHIP, Richard   *China manufacturer*

In 1764 Holdship, formerly one of the proprietors of the Worcester China Manufactory, bound himself to Duesbury and Heath to make and print china ware. He also undertook to teach his process of china making and to 'supply soapy rock' (steatite). It is not known how long the engagement lasted but he was still in Derby in 1769. The somewhat rare examples of Derby blue-printed wares are generally attributed to him.[1]

Lit: Barrett, op. cit.; Jewitt, op. cit.; Toppin, op. cit.; Watney, op. cit.

HOLMES, Charles   *'Chinaman'*

On 24th December 1765 a Charles Holmes, described as 'china man',

[1] Aubrey J. Toppin, 'A Ceramic Miscellany', *E.C.C. Trans.*, 1951, vol. 3, part I, pp. 68–69.

was married at St. Alkmund's Church, Derby. But nothing is known of his work and he is not mentioned by Haslem or Jewitt.

HOLMES, Charles   *Modeller*

Haslem states that he was apprenticed at Derby late in the eighteenth century and was a modeller of sheep and other small animals, as well as a set of *Seasons* as seated figures. His period of employment must have been much later than that of the preceding man of the same name.

Lit: Haslem, op. cit.

HOLMES, George   *Repairer*

There is a figure of a youth (*Shepherd?*) in the Leverhulme Collection inscribed on the base 'George Holmes did this figer (sic) 1765'. Nothing is known of the man or the extent of his work at Derby; he was presumably the 'repairer' or assembler of the above figure. In 1775, a George Holmes applied to Wedgwood for employment, saying that he had worked at Derby for twenty-eight years.[1]

Lit: Tapp, *Apollo*, August 1933; Lane, op. cit.

HOPKINSON, Edward (b. 1788, d. 1868)   *Gilder*

Apprenticed as a gilder and appears to have worked there until the close of the factory, when he and his sons, Edward and William, went to the Potteries.

Lit: Haslem, op. cit.

KEAN, Michael (d. 1823)   *Proprietor*

Born in Dublin, intended to be a sculptor but took to miniature painting. Awarded the Society of Fine Arts Medal 1779 and exhibited at the Royal Academy from 1786–1790. There is no record that he painted on porcelain but the fact that he was a miniature painter must have influenced Duesbury II who took him into partnership in 1795. On Duesbury's death in October 1796, Kean continued to manage the factory and in August 1798 married Duesbury's widow.

[1] Wedgwood Archives at Keele University, Staffordshire; and see pp. 4 and 125.

The marriage was not successful and bitter family quarrels ending in law suits caused Kean to withdraw from the business in November 1811.[1] When he died in 1823 the *Derby Reporter* records his death: 'a few days ago in London after a short illness Mr. Kean formerly proprietor of the porcelain manufactory in this town: he was much respected by all who knew him'.

Lit: Haslem, op. cit.

KEYS, Edward   *Modeller*

Son of Samuel Keys (q.v.). Haslem states that he was the modeller of the fourteen figures illustrating the adventures of Dr. Syntax, the character created by William Coombe. He left Derby for the Potteries in 1826.

Lit: Haslem, op. cit.

KEYS, John (b. 1798, d. 1825)   *Flower painter*

Eldest son of Samuel Keys (q.v.) apprenticed at the Derby works and worked there until about 1821, when he left and taught flower painting in the town. His work on china was said to be in the manner between Billingsley and the more florid style practised later. In the Derby Museum collections are four plates said, on the authority of Moses Webster (q.v.), to have been painted by him.

KEYS, Samuel (b. 1771, d. 1850)   *Gilder*

Apprenticed to Duesbury I in 1785. One of the best gilders of his day excelling in gold arabesque ornamentation, in which he sometimes introduced coloured scrolls (the 'purple scroll' pattern is attributed to him). He also decorated many of the Derby figures, c. 1825–35, done in the Dresden style. Left Derby some years before the close of the factory and went to Minton's.

Lit: Haslem, op. cit.

[1] Bemrose MSS in the British Museum.

KEYS, Samuel (Junior)   *Modeller*

Son of Samuel Keys (q.v.) worked at Derby between 1820 and 1830. Haslem lists several figures as being modelled by him (see p. 53).

Lit: Haslem, op. cit.

LAURENCE, John   *Repairer*

The scroll base of a candlestick figure (one of a pair of *Shepherd* and *Shepherdess*) is incised 'John Laurence'.[1] He was working for Thomas Turner, the Salopian China Manufactory at Caughley, on April 11th 1790, when he wrote to William Duesbury at Derby.

LAWTON, Cuthbert   *Painter*

Worked at Derby in the early years of the nineteenth century. Haslem says that like John Brewer he painted landscapes, hunting subjects and figures; his hunting pieces are painted with great spirit and are pure in colour, and there is an agreeable freshness and a look of nature in his landscapes. His work on Derby china is scarce as he was not employed at the factory for many years. His name occurs with one of the patterns without a number: 'One bird on tree with landscape, $4\frac{1}{2}$ in.'.

In the Derby Museum is a pastille burner[2] with a finely painted continuous hunting scene variously attributed to this artist and to William Cotton (q.v.).

Lit: Haslem, op. cit.; Hurlbutt, op. cit.

LEAD, Leonard (b. 1787, d. 1869)   *Flower painter*

Probably apprenticed at Derby about 1800 and was employed for over forty years. Haslem says that his work is to be found more often on products of the last years of the factory than that of any other flower painter. He was a competent artist whose palette, though somewhat exuberant by modern standards, was rich and decorative (Plate 150). His father (also Leonard) had been a charcoal burner at Derby and moved to Pinxton as a 'Woodcutter'.

Lit: Haslem, op. cit.; Williamson MSS in Derby Museum.

[1] Sotheby Catalogue, 20th May 1969, Lot 243.
[2] Hurlbutt, op. cit., Plate 53.

Longdon, William (Senior)   *Painter*

Jewitt states that he was a flower painter of considerable note, and Haslem that, 'one of the oldest of the hands', he was a good deal employed on the *Chantilly* pattern. The period of his employment is unknown; he was married at All Saints Church, Derby on 11th November 1775.

   Lit: Haslem, op. cit.; Jewitt, op. cit.

Lovegrove, John (b. 1795, d. 1873)   *Gilder*

Apprenticed to William Smith, one of Duesbury I's earliest apprentices, who had set up in Derby as a china painter on his own account. Lovegrove came to work at the Derby factory in 1815 and stayed till the close of the works.

   Lit: Haslem, op. cit.; Jewitt, op. cit.

Lucas, Daniel (Senior) (b. 1788, d. 1867)   *Landscape painter*

Came to Derby about 1825 from Messrs. Davenport of Longport, Staffordshire and was the principal landscape painter until the closure of the works. His work has the opaque appearance of oil painting and lacked character or variety. He was also a painter of public house signs in Derby. He had three sons, John, William and Daniel, all of whom were apprenticed at the Derby works.

   Lit: Haslem, op. cit.

McLacklan   *Landscape painter*

Haslem states that he worked at Derby early in the nineteenth century: his work was of slight character, sometimes in one colour only, in imitation of sepia drawings. Although none of his work has been positively identified Haslem mentions plates with landscapes in black as probably by this artist. Haslem's observations seem to have had the unfortunate result that almost any Derby piece decorated in monochrome, whatever its style or period, is nowadays attributed to this artist.

   Lit: Haslem, op. cit.

APPENDIX I: BIOGRAPHIES

MELLOR, George   *Flower and insect painter*

Apprenticed at Derby but left to go to Pinxton; after subsequent employment at Coalport and in Staffordshire he returned to Derby about 1815 and remained until about 1830. He painted in a delicate yet decorative style and his best work is keenly sought amongst collectors.

Jewitt says he had a son, George, who was a gilder and painter.

Lit: Haslem, op. cit.; Jewitt, op. cit.

MOUNTFORD, Jesse (b. circa 1799)   *Landscape painter*

Haslem says that he was apprenticed at Derby and was one of the painters discharged by Bloor in 1821 through slackness in trade. There is a cup and saucer attributed to him in The Haslem Collection in Derby Museum (Plate 160). He went to Coalport in 1821 for fifteen years and was later at Davenport's.

Lit: Haslem, op. cit.

MOUNTFORD, John (b. 1816)   *Modeller*

At Derby during the last years of the old factory. After the close he was employed by Messrs. Copeland and while trying to rediscover the old biscuit porcelain recipe is said to have accidentally discovered the Parian body. This was disputed by Thomas Battam but, while the latter may have been the first to make use of the new body, to Mountford should go the merit of its first discovery. Actually 'parian' porcelain is a much harder body than Duesbury's biscuit body.

Lit: Haslem, op. cit.

PARDOE, Thomas (b. 1770, d. 1823)   *Painter*

Son of William, china painter at Derby and probably apprenticed at Derby. He would seem however to have left after only a short time and his highly skilled and important contributions to the art of flower painting on china are to be found on that of Swansea, Nantgarw, Caughley, Coalport and other factories, executed whilst an independent decorator of porcelain in Bristol.

H. THISTLE DISH
Date about 1800   8½ in. square
Derby Museum   See pages 65, 99

PEGG, Thomas   *Gilder*

Brother of William 'The Quaker', he seems to have spent his working life as a gilder at Derby.

Lit: Haslem, op. cit.; Jewitt, op. cit.

PEGG, William ('The Quaker') (b. 1775, d. 1851)   *Flower painter*

Born near Newcastle-under-Lyme, Staffordshire, the son of Thomas Pegg, a gardener at Etwall, near Derby. First worked in the Potteries and was apprenticed to china painting in 1790. In 1796 he signed an agreement for five years to come to Derby and, although John and Robert Brewer were also working at Derby at that time, Pegg succeeded Billingsley as chief flower painter when the latter left for Pinxton in October 1796. (Colour Plate H.)

Pegg had very strong religious views and, brought up a Calvinist, he turned Baptist and then in 1800 joined the Society of Friends. Indeed he seems to have been afflicted from this time with a sort of religious melancholia and believing that painting was sinful he gave it up in 1801. From that time until 1813 he worked as a stocking knitter in Derby and elsewhere. In 1813 he returned to The Derby China Works and there did some of his finest work, until the same scruples compelled him to leave once again in 1820. In that year he opened a small general dealer's shop not far from the factory and remained there until his death in 1851.

Lit: Haslem, op. cit.

PEGG, William (b. 1795, d. 1867)   *Flower painter*

Not related to Pegg 'The Quaker', this artist, too, painted flowers until he left about 1819. He is said to have painted with great neatness and taste but none of his work has been identified. It may well be that the plaques with flowers, some signed, which fetch high prices on the presumed belief that they are the work of Quaker Pegg, are the work of this artist; for, remembering his intense religious convictions, it seems extremely unlikely that Quaker Pegg would indulge in such purely decorative articles as plaques and still less likely that he would sign them.

Lit: Haslem, op. cit.

PERKINS, John   *Modeller*

Haslem mentions him amongst a number of 'clever modellers and ornamental potters' who learned the art at Derby. He was married at St. Werbergh's, Derby, 9th May 1825.

Lit: Haslem, op. cit.

PHILIPS, Edward   *Gilder and painter*

Entered into an agreement with Wm. Duesbury to work at Derby for 25s. per week. Haslem says he was a clever gilder and arabesque border painter. He left Derby and went to Pinxton in December 1798 and afterwards into the Potteries.

Lit: Haslem, op. cit.; Jewitt, op. cit.

PLANCHÉ, André (Andrew) (b. 1728, d. 1805)   *Modeller*

The son of Paul and Marie Planché, born in London and in 1740 apprenticed to a goldsmith in the city. Exactly when he came to Derby is unknown but he had a son baptised at St. Alkmund's Church, Derby, on 21st September 1751. The last mention of him is in the baptismal register in the same church 3rd July 1756. He was one of the three persons mentioned in the agreement dated 1st January 1756 between John Heath, banker of Derby and William Duesbury, enameller and Planché, china maker.

It seems certain that he left Derby shortly after 1756 and nothing further is heard of him until 1800, when he was living at Bath, where he died in 1805.

Lit: Jewitt, op. cit.; MacAlister, 'The Early Works of Planché and Duesbury', *E.P.C. Trans.*, 1929, no. II, pp. 45–61.

PRATT, Henry Lark (b. 1805, d. 1873)   *Landscape painter*

Apprenticed at Derby works and employed there until he left for the Potteries about 1830. He seems to have done landscapes on plaques during his time at Derby. He later painted in oils but Haslem says his painting on china was warmer and more agreeable in colour than that in oils.

Lit: Haslem, op. cit.

APPENDIX I: BIOGRAPHIES

PRINCE, Edward   *Landscape painter*

One of the last batch of apprentices at Derby and remained at the factory until its close. His work is said to be recognisable by the warm brown tints. A pair of large bottle shaped vases by him were exhibited at Nottingham in 1872.

Lit: Haslem, op. cit.

ROBERTSON, George (b. 1776, d. 1835)   *Painter*

Born in London and came to Derby about 1796. He painted landscapes and seems to have been fond of bright autumn tints and seascapes, usually either naval engagements or stormy scenes. The seascapes would almost certainly have been copied from marine paintings or engravings. He is thought to have left the factory in 1820, when he set up as a teacher of drawing in Derby.

There is a collection of signed water-colour drawings (including one seascape) in Derby Museum and it has been claimed that there is a distinctive vertical hatching in the tree-tops and a dentillation of the foliage in these drawings which can be used in making attributions of his work on china.

Pattern numbers allocated to Robertson:

In the Cup and Saucer Book:

- 406   'Landskips'
- 416   'Landskips in colours in square panels'
- 417   'In every respect same as 416 but yellow instead of green'
- 418   'Same as 416, except brown instead of yellow'

In the Plate Book:

- 222   'Ships in colour, full 5 in.'
- 245   '3 in. square panel containing coloured shipping *Sailing before the wind*'
- 254   'Coloured shipping, 3 in. square'
- 280   'Landskip 3 in. hexagonal panel'.

Lit: Haslem, op. cit.; Tapp, *Connoisseur*, Nov. 1935.

ROSSI, John Charles, R.A. (b. 1762, d. 1839)   *Modeller*

Lane[1] says that Rossi began working for Derby in 1788 and that the biscuit figures from his models were used by Vulliamy for his clocks.

[1] Lane, op. cit., p. 109.

101

Subjects are said to include *Aesculapius and Hygeia*, a female 'sacrificing figure' and her companion, and some draped figures of boys. These latter would appear to have proved very popular; they are characterised by their fat cheeks and legs. We do not know for how long Rossi supplied models for Derby nor their number or variety but Savage[1] suggests that, in addition to the above mentioned, the following might possibly be attributed to Rossi:

114–115	*Venus and Mars*
120	*The New Diana*
358	*Venus and Cupid*

ROUSE (or ROWSE) James (d. 1888)   *Flower painter*

Apprenticed at the old factory where he worked for some years before leaving to work in the Potteries and at Coalport. He also painted portraits in oil. He was employed at the Osmaston Road china works from their inception in 1877 till his death, and examples of his later work are in Derby Museum.

SIMPSON, Mundy   *Gilder and painter*

Haslem says he was apprenticed at Derby and spent the greater part of his working life at the factory as a gilder and japan painter. Two of his sons were also apprenticed at Derby to the same work; the eldest, John, left Derby in 1836.

Lit: Haslem, op. cit.

SLATER, William   *Gilder and painter*

Apprenticed at Pinxton, at the closure of the factory in 1813 he came to Derby where he remained until the closure of that factory. Haslem says he was a good general hand, painting fruit, insects and armorial bearings, but excelling as a gilder and gold chaser.

Two of his sons, William and Joseph, were also apprenticed at Derby as gilders and painters and both worked in the Potteries after the closure of the Derby works.

Lit: Haslem, op. cit.

[1] Savage, *18th Century English Porcelain*, p. 181.

APPENDIX I: BIOGRAPHIES

SMITH, Constantine   *Colour-man*

This man gave his name to the well known 'Smith's blue' which Duesbury developed in preference to underglaze blue so favoured at Worcester, Liverpool and elsewhere. The period of his employment at Derby is unknown but he was a signatory to an agreement made between Duesbury and Pierre Stephan (q.v.) in 1769, and in October 1773 his son William was apprenticed to him to learn 'the art of preparing colours and Painting and Enamelling Porcelain'. He was married at All Saints, Derby, 11th July 1757 and may have been amongst Duesbury's earliest workmen.

Lit: Jewitt, op. cit.; Williamson MSS in Derby Museum.

SMITH, William   *Colour-man*

Apprenticed to his father, Constantine (q.v.) in 1773. Williamson[1] thinks his father must have been working independently, otherwise William would have been apprenticed to Duesbury. Jewitt says that in 1790 William agreed with Mr. Duesbury, with whom he had 'finished his time' and been since employed, to employ himself 'in preparing enamel colours painting china or otherwise at the discretion of Mr. Duesbury'. On signing this agreement his wages were raised from 21s. to 25s. per week. Haslem states that William left the old works and commenced enamelling china on his own account, but when the same writer asserts that he was the maker of a dark blue enamel which went by his name, surely he is confusing father and son. For 'Smith's blue' is to be found on Chelsea-Derby pieces which must have been made in the earliest years of William's apprenticeship.

Lit: Duesbury MSS in Derby Public Library; Gilhespy, op. cit.; Haslem, op. cit.; Jewitt, op. cit.; Williamson MSS.

SOAR, Thomas   *Gilder and painter*

He was probably one of Duesbury's earliest apprentices and from about 1790 until 1810 was foreman of the painters. He is no. 1 in the list of painters and gilders. Jewitt states that he was a clever gilder and arabesque painter and set up as an enameller in a small business on his own account. An advertisement in the *Derby Mercury*, 5th April

[1] Williamson MSS in Derby Museum.

1810, says, '. . . this long experience in the Derby Porcelain Manufactory encourages him to look with confidence for support which it will be his study to deserve and his pride to acknowledge . . .'. He also announced 'Ladies instructed to Paint china at their own apartments'.

Lit: Haslem, op. cit.; Jewitt, op. cit.

SPENGLER, Jean Jacques (b. 1752) *Modeller*

Learned the art of modelling from his father, who had been one of the chief workmen at the Höchst factory in Germany and was later the director of the Zurich porcelain factory. Letters from Lygo to Duesbury[1] show that Spengler came to London in 1790 and signed an agreement to work for Duesbury at Derby. However, Spengler found the experience of fixed employment irksome and he caused Duesbury much trouble and embarrassment by returning to London. In 1792 he was committed to prison for some unnamed offence, but was released on bail. In 1795 a new agreement was signed and Spengler returned to Derby, but it was not long before he disappeared altogether and nothing is known of his subsequent career; it is almost certain that he returned to the Continent. His departure was a great loss to ceramic modelling in general and to the Derby factory in particular. For despite his wayward temperament and apparent inability to accept any kind of discipline he was a highly skilled modeller and most sensitive towards his medium. Presumably through his early training with his father he conceived his creations in terms of porcelain modelling and not as pieces of sculpture in marble or wood or metal which might be copied in porcelain. Although some of his models (e.g. *Palemon and Lavinia; Belisarius and his Daughter*) are taken from classical mythology, his style was romantic rather than classical and anticipates the nineteenth rather than continues the eighteenth century. Derby never again found anyone remotely to equal him.

Lit: E. Percival Allan, *Connoisseur*, LXXXII, 1928; Haslem, op. cit.; Jewitt, op. cit.; Lane, op. cit.

STABLES, Joseph (or Josiah) *Gilder*

Mentioned by Haslem as one of Duesbury's earliest apprentices and skilled as a painter of arabesque borders. His name appears in the

[1] At the Victoria and Albert Museum.

document dated 1788 relating to the keeping of men employed on one part of the works from entering any other.

Lit: Haslem, op. cit.; Jewitt, op. cit.

STANESBY, John (b. 1786, d. 1864)   *Painter*

Apprenticed at the Derby factory but left about 1808 to practice as a portrait painter. Haslem says he excelled in the painting of roses and executed many beautiful specimens of china painting even after he had moved to London. He also painted on glass and in partnership with a man named Beekler did some ambitious projects in the form of windows for public buildings.

Lit: Haslem, op. cit.

STEELE, Thomas (b. 1772, d. 1850)   *Painter*

A native of the Staffordshire Potteries, where he first learned his art, he worked at the Derby factory from about 1815 until its closing years. Haslem says that his fruit painting on china has never been surpassed, commenting that his colour is remarkably pleasing, rich yet transparent, the grouping is harmonious and the light and shade well managed, each fruit well rounded, its outline softened and blended into the next. Haslem adds that many of Steele's effects were produced by carefully dabbing on the colour, while wet, with his finger, blending the various tints into one another giving softness and delicacy and an appearance of high finish. This artist also painted plaques, some of large size.

In addition Steele painted flowers and insects;[2] his roses have been criticised for having been left too white in the lights, the outline thereby cutting too hard against a dark background.

Three of his sons were apprenticed at the Derby works: Edwin and Horatio were flower painters while Thomas, the youngest, according to Haslem showed promise as a landscape painter but died at an early age.

Lit: Haslem, op. cit.

[1] See Appendix V, p. 128.
[2] See also Bancroft, Joseph p. 76.

APPENDIX I: BIOGRAPHIES

STEPHAN, Pierre   *Modeller*

A Swiss from one of the French speaking cantons. Hurlbutt[1] says that he worked for Sprimont at Chelsea. He does not however give any authority for this statement and the first documentary evidence we have of Stephan is the agreement he signed with Duesbury, dated 17th September 1770[2] in which he binds himself for three years 'to employ himself in that art of Modelling and Repairing China or Porcelain Ware' at £2. 12s. 6d. a week. At the termination it seems probable that he left Derby and worked for a time at the porcelain factory at Wirksworth[3] and afterwards joined Wedgwood's in Staffordshire. Nevertheless there seems little doubt that he continued to work freelance for Derby (and for Wedgwood and for Champion at Bristol too) at least until 1795.

Stephan appears to have been a steady hardworking artist. Although his output is of uneven quality and many of his figures of children have been criticised for their over-large heads, yet at his best (e.g. the set of *Elements*, no. 48) he showed a commendable power of expression and delicacy of execution which shows best in the biscuit figures.

Lit: Hurlbutt, op. cit.; Jewitt, op. cit.

STRONG, Thomas   *Painter*

Described as 'china painter' when he married at All Saints Church, Derby, 22nd December 1765.

TATLOW, Joseph and Thomas   *Gilders and painters*

Haslem states that Joseph and his brother Thomas were apprenticed at the Derby works at the end of the eighteenth century and that Joseph excelled in arabesque borders and other kinds of ornamentation in gold and in colours. Thomas also painted flowers and shells. Joseph left Derby to assist Billingsley at Mansfield and then removed to London where he worked for china enamellers. Jewitt notes that the brothers 'were late apprentices and became clever painters'.

Lit: Haslem, op. cit.; Jewitt, op. cit.

[1] Hurlbutt, op. cit., p. 29.
[2] Jewitt, op. cit., vol. II, p. 97.
[3] Letter to Wedgwood in Wedgwood Museum archives.

TAYLOR, William   *Painter*

Jewitt says he was at first a 'blue painter' and afterwards became a clever arabesque and Indian pattern painter. Said to have painted a service for a Dr. Digby in 1784.

Lit: Jewitt, op. cit., vol. II, p. 113.

WATSON, William   *Gilder and painter*

Worked at the factory for a few years about 1830. Haslem remarks of this eccentric artist that his productions were slight figures usually on vases or other ornaments done in gold, sometimes on a light ground, more often on a dark blue. There are indications of landscapes also in gold such as mountains, trees, houses and churches, the latter perched on the tops of trees or in other impossible places. He went to work at Burton-on-Trent in 1835 and thence to the Potteries.

Lit: Haslem, op. cit.

WEBSTER, Moses (b. 1792, d. 1870)   *Painter*

Apprenticed at Derby but moved to London in about 1817, where he is believed to have decorated Nantgarw porcelain at the establishment of Robins and Randall, and then to Worcester. He returned to Derby in 1821 and worked for Bloor. It is said that he left in 1825 to take up a practice as drawing master in Derby on the death of John Keys. On porcelain he was a painter of flowers (although he was also a topographical artist in water-colours and lithography) and his best known work is the *Trotter* service. Haslem claims that his flowers can be identified by their 'somewhat dashed and faded appearance as if they had been kept in water too long'. This is perhaps rather an unfair assessment for his flower groups are tastefully arranged and he shows considerable freedom of execution. He was one of the best of the later Derby painters.

Lit: Haslem, op. cit.

WHITAKER, John   *Gilder and painter*

A gilder and painter of borders. A partner with George Cocker in his independent establishment in Derby in 1826.

WHITAKER, John   *Modeller*

Grandson of Richard Whitaker (q.v.) he began work at the factory
in 1818 learning modelling and figure making. In 1830 he became
manager of the ornamental department and subsequently of the
whole potting department. Haslem quotes a list of eighteen figures
made between 1830 and 1847, and mentions a graceful peacock as
being the most successful. The striking *Mazeppa* (Plate 176) also may
have been the work of this modeller.

Haslem says he went to Minton's on the closure of the Derby
factory.

   Lit: Haslem, op. cit.

WHITAKER, Richard   *Modeller*

Haslem states that in the early years the three principal figure makers
were Joseph Hill (q.v.), Stephen Lawrence and Richard Whitaker,
all of whom 'had been employed at the works from their commencement'.

   Lit: Haslem, op. cit.

WITHERS, Edward   *Painter*

Although the first painter employed at the factory of whom there is
any reliable account, only one piece is known which can be attributed
to him with certainty, the *Rodney Jug* dated 1782. He excelled as a
painter of flowers in the conventional style then practised; the highlights were left, as in painting in water-colour on paper, and not swept
out with a dry brush as done by Billingsley and all later painters.

Samuel Keys says that there was not enough flower painting to
keep Withers employed and that he left Derby for the Potteries,
Birmingham, where he painted japan ware, and then London.
Jewitt quotes an agreement with Duesbury II, dated 8th May 1789,
in which Withers 'of London porcelain or china painter' undertakes
to work for Duesbury for three years at the rate of 3s. 6d. a day.

   Lit: Haslem, op. cit.; Jewitt, op. cit.

WRIGHT, Joseph, A.R.A. (b. 1734, d. 1797)   *Painter*

Commonly known as 'Wright of Derby' this painter was, like Reynolds, a pupil of Thomas Hudson. Although apprenticed as a portrait painter he is nowadays best known for his pictures of scientific and industrial subjects as well as those depicting moonlight, candlelight and volcanic eruptions etc.

Jewitt[1] says he 'lent his powerful aid on some occasions in supplying drawings and giving advice'. This author also refers to correspondence which shows that Wright advised on the design, arrangement and pose of the figure of *Lord Howe*, modelled by Coffee. Jewitt's reference to a letter, relating to a service made for the Duchess of Northumberland in 1795, which says that the six comports were put into Wright's hands, was mistaken. The Wright named in the letter was a painter at the factory.[2]

Lit: Jewitt, op. cit.

YATES, John (d. 1821)   *Gilder and painter*

A gilder and decorator of china figures in the style of those of Dresden (Haslem). The *Derby Mercury*, in his obituary notice, mentions the Porcelain manufactory '. . . where he exercised his profession for upwards of half a century'. Jewitt states that he was said to have excelled in hunting subjects and flowers.

Lit: Haslem, op. cit.; Jewitt, op. cit.

[1] Op. cit., vol. II, p. 94.
[2] See Appendix V, p. 146.

APPENDIX II

FACTORY MARKS AND WORKMEN'S MARKS

The Derby factory had no factory mark, or indeed any distinguishing symbol, for almost the first quarter century of its existence. The reason for this is hard to understand for, as early as 1757, Duesbury was proudly announcing his wares as 'the Second Dresden' yet unlike a number of other English factories at this time, he never pirated the Meissen crossed swords mark (the use of this mark on Derby figures is confined to the 1830s). The circumstances have been recounted (p. 33) which made it imperative for Duesbury to adopt a factory mark for his Derby wares and the suggestion made that he celebrated the gaining of royal patronage (not to be confused with the later legal granting of Royal Warrant) by the choice of the symbol of a crown, then added the letter 'D' which might equally refer to the initial letter of Duesbury or Derby (nos. 5–8 below). We do not know when the concurrently used anchor and 'D' (nos. 2–4) in gold was first adopted; it probably dates from the early months after the merger with Chelsea, since it is clearly only a modification of the already existing gold anchor mark used in the last years of the Chelsea works.

1782 is usually given as the year in which the crossed batons and dots were inserted between the crown and 'D' (no. 9 below) from the fact that the earliest known piece on which it appears is the *Rodney Jug* which commemorates the admiral's naval victory in that year. There is no evidence to associate the crossed batons with the crossed swords marks of Meissen, but that such a connection might exist is possible.

The use of marks nos. 9 and 10 painted in puce enamel would appear to be concurrent with their use in blue enamel. The latter would seem to be confined to those pieces which were decorated with a named landscape (or seascape) or flower or plant, whilst the mark in puce would seem to have been used on pieces without names or titles.[1]

[1] An exception to this is a small class of pieces decorated with figures of animals. These are usually found with the mark in blue but without any title. There are some pieces and services decorated in blue only, and on these the mark is, not surprisingly, in this colour.

APPENDIX II: MARKS

There is unfortunately no documentary evidence which enables us to say with certainty when the standard mark (nos. 9 and 10) came to be painted in red.[1] Moore Binns[2] says that on the arrival of Kean in 1795 a new mark was adopted (no. 17) which was used along with the usual mark in red until the adoption of the printed marks (nos. 23–25). In these statements Binns would appear to be following Chaffers[3] but neither writer produces the slightest evidence and their dogmatic assertions are for the most part unsubstantiated. In the first place mark no. 17 is an excessively rare mark: a large mug painted in a very untypical Derby style with a landscape and rainbow[4] being the only known example; secondly, the authors have yet to see a piece carrying the factory mark in red earlier than about 1805 and certainly not as early as 1795. Examination of many dozens of pieces does not lead to the conclusion that the red mark was used concurrently with the blue and puce. On the contrary it would seem rather that the change to the factory mark in red denoted a significant event in the history of the works, probably the important change in chemical composition of paste and glaze. Here again it is unfortunate that there are no factory records to give a clue as to the time when this change was made but the circumstantial evidence of artists' styles would lead us to conclude that it was about 1805. The greater part of the decoration attributed to John Brewer (who is generally thought to have left the factory to set up as a drawing master in 1806) is to be found on pieces carrying the mark in blue. There is however a pair of *jardinières* in the Derby Museum with the mark in red, painted with birds, which has been reasonably attributed[5] to this artist. There is also a service painted with landscapes attributed to Robert Brewer[6] which is known to have been purchased by the sixth Duke of Devonshire, but the date of his purchase has not been discovered and can only be estimated between 1811 and 1815.[7] This service has the painted factory mark in red.

There are, apart from and outside the Chelsea–Derby period, a small number of pieces carrying the painted mark in gold. This is generally thought to denote a special commission, as for example the *Trotter* service (see p. 66). However, the mark in gold is sometimes

[1] Not to be confused with the carmine colour used concurrently on a small number of pieces.

[2] W. Moore Binns, *The First Century of English Porcelain*, 1906, pp. 137–8.

[3] W. Chaffers, *Marks and Monograms on European and Oriental Pottery and Porcelain*.

[4] Now in the Victoria and Albert Museum.

[5] W. H. Tapp, *E.P.C. Trans.*, 1932, no. IV, Plate XXII.

[6] *Ibid.*, p. 85.

[7] The sixth Duke succeeded to the title in 1811 (died 1858).

found on quite ordinary pieces and this can perhaps only be explained by a lapse of discipline on the part of the foremen.

There are almost a score and a half of different factory marks used at the Derby manufactory and, in the absence of any documentary evidence in the form of factory papers etc., it is not possible to be positive about the nature and periods of their use. The statements made here are based on the examination of many hundreds of specimens taking into account also the circumstantial evidence afforded by paste and glaze, decoration and gilding etc.

A. TABLE OF FACTORY MARKS

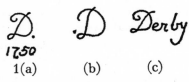

1(a)   (b)   (c)

These marks are incised on the bases of three small cream jugs (see p. 4).

2   3   4

Chelsea-Derby. Perhaps as early as 1770 but not likely to be later than 1782. In gold, no. 3 is the commonest.

5   6   7   8

Chelsea-Derby. Not thought to be earlier than 1773 nor later than 1782. No. 5, in gold, known also without the crown but with script N, is very rare. Nos. 6–8

are most commonly in blue, but occasionally in puce. These latter probably date from the time immediately preceding the adoption of the succeeding marks.

9   10

The standard factory mark between c.1782 and c.1820. Often with a pattern number under the 'D'. In puce and blue, also variations in carmine and 'plum', until perhaps about 1805, then in red. Special services or pieces marked in gold. Carefully drawn in earlier years, more carelessly in later years.

11   12

Examples of the more carelessly drawn marks. The numerals are pattern numbers.

13

Incised mark used on some figures after 1782 (mostly on biscuit figures). The factory mark was not commonly used on figures (except perhaps after c.1825) but rather the serial number from the List of Figures and Groups described by Haslem, as a 'Price List' (see p. 180). This series of numbers would appear, from comparison with the early auction sales catalogues (see pp. 159–177), to have begun in 1771.

14   15

17

The monogram of Duesbury and Kean; therefore may have only been used between 1795 and

1797 although the Duesbury family had a controlling interest throughout the period of Kean's managership. An excessively rare mark, known only on a large mug now in the Victoria and Albert Museum.

18   19   20

Painted marks occasionally found in red on pieces c.1815–1820. Haslem says they probably derive 'from the whim or caprice of the workman rather than from any instruction he might have received'.

21   22

These are also painted marks which may be termed 'personal variations', in this case by William Slater (Senior). Haslem, who worked at the same bench as Slater, records that the latter painted these variations in blue or red or gold between 1825 and 1830.

Resentment by the workmen against the time it took to put on the painted mark naturally resulted in progressively more slipshod versions. After complaints from customers it was decided to use transfer printed marks. The mark was transferred from a

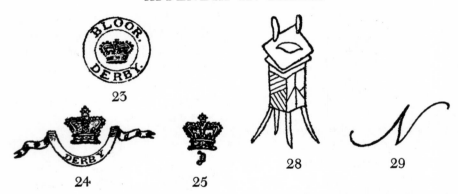

23

24   25

26   27

28   29

copper plate by means of a leather boss, but to save time again the workmen often used their thumbs with the result that there are many imperfect impressions of these marks also. In common use from c.1820 until the close of the factory in 1848.

In spite of Duesbury's claim as early as 1757 for Derby as 'the Second Dresden', the imitation Meissen mark is rare on Derby porcelain wares. It would, however, appear to have been used more frequently on enamelled figures c.1825–1835. The imitation Sèvres mark (with or without the addition of the small crown) is also a rare mark on domestic wares but somewhat more frequent on enamelled figures c.1830.

Although Haslem states that he had come across this mark (no. 28) only on hard-paste porcelain of evident Oriental origin it does seem that it was used on a very small number of pieces made at the Derby factory. In the Derby Museum are two pieces, a tureen and a bough-pot marked with this so-called 'Chinese potter's table'. There seems little doubt that both of these are from the same moulds as similar pieces bearing a standard factory mark. The tureen has an Oriental decoration and could have been made as a replacement to an Oriental service.

The script '$\mathcal{N}$' is a mark whose origin is unknown; generally incised, sometimes painted, usually in blue enamel,[1] the incised version has been thought to date from c.1765. The painted versions however would seem to belong to the Chelsea-Derby period and is sometimes found in association with both the anchor and conjoined 'D', and the crown and 'D' mark in blue enamel. It does not seem to have been used after the

---

[1] Some Longton Hall porcelain has this mark in *underglaze* blue.

Chelsea-Derby period.

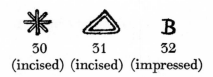

30   31   32
(incised) (incised) (impressed)

These are not factory marks, but workmen's marks. No. 30 was that of Isaac Farnsworth, No. 31 that of Joseph Hill. These marks were incised on the base. No. 32 is found as an impressed Roman capital letter approximately $\frac{3}{16}$ in. high; about a dozen different letters are known and it is thought that they may have been used to distinguish batches of wares as they passed through the kilns. There is documentary evidence of the use of similar letters at the Pinxton china works.[1]

B. GILDERS' MARKS

In addition to the pattern numbers described above, numerals are to be found on certain Derby pieces, either on the inside of the footrim or on the base closely adjacent. These are usually called gilders' numbers.[2] Jewitt quotes a draft order in his possession, which he says is in William Duesbury's own handwriting, thus:

'Every Painter to mark underneath each Article he may finish the number corresponding to his name, and any other mark which may be required in such a manner as he may be directed (viz):

Thos. Soar	1	Wm. Longdon	8
Jos. Stables	2	Wm. Smith	9
Wm. Cooper	3	Jno. Blood	10
Wm. Yates	4	Wm. Taylor (except	
Jno. Yates	5	on blue and white)	11
	6	Jno. Duesbury	12
William Billingsley	7	Jos. Dodd	13'

Contrary to Haslem's assertion that 'most if not the whole of the above, with the exception of Billingsley, were gilders' we find that at least seven (nos. 3, 5, 7, 8, 9, 10 and 11) were painters, therefore the description 'Gilders List' first used by Haslem and followed by almost all subsequent writers is not strictly correct. The above list is in some respects more interesting in respect of the names that are missing. If Duesbury was issuing directions to his painters as well as his gilders why do we not find the names of Banford, Boreman, Complin and Jockey Hill? Could the instruction, by some strange coincidence, have

[1] C. L. Exley, *The Pinxton China Factory*, Derby, 1963, p. 31.
[2] Haslem, op. cit., p. 230; Jewitt, op. cit., vol. II. p. 103.

been issued at a moment when the first three had just left and the last named had not arrived? This could perhaps have conceivably been the case in 1794. For if any of these important artists had been in Duesbury's employ at the time he issued these orders, is it likely that they would have been left out, whilst Billingsley was included?

It is very tempting to use the footrim numerals to identify the gilders or painters mentioned in the above list. But unless from other evidence the pieces can be dated about 1794, this should be resisted since we do not know to whom, on the departure of any of these persons from the factory (e.g. Billingsley to go to Pinxton in 1796), the numeral was allotted as a successor. Indeed Haslem[1] gives a second list which he dates 'about 1820' as under:

Samuel Keys	1	John Moscrop	18
James Clark	2	Munday Simpson	19
— Torkington	7	James Hill	21
John Beard	8	George Mellor	27
Jos Brock	14	Thomas Till	33
Jos Broughton	16	John Whittaker	37

Haslem continues

'the numbers used by many others might be given[2] but would not possess much interest as . . . they could not now be depended upon for identifying the work of any particular man unless with a knowledge . . . of the time the man was employed, as on the removal or death of one workman another succeeded to his number as a comparison of the two lists will show.'

In view of the fact that a number of pieces carry two numbers (sometimes in different coloured enamels) on or under the footrim, we may conclude that one of these relates to the person who executed the formal pattern, i.e. the gilder, whilst the other presumably refers to the artist who decorated the panels or reserves. Unlike the pattern numbers, the footrim numbers are occasionally found on pieces carrying the printed marks of the Bloor period. Only a relatively small proportion of Derby wares bear these workmen's marks and whilst they have a certain historical interest these series of numerals should not be used as an aid to attributions of artists' and gilders' work unless substantiated by a weight of other documentary or circumstantial evidence, which would render their slight assistance unnecessary.

[1] Haslem, op. cit., p. 230.
[2] Numerals as high as 78 are known on pieces with the painted red mark.

APPENDIX III

THE PATTERN BOOKS

There exist (now in the Dyson Perrins Museum at Worcester) two sets of coloured drawings of designs for services made at Derby.[1] These are undated but since on the wares themselves the pattern number is found associated with the painted crown, crossed batons and 'D' mark only, and never on pieces with the earlier or later marks, it would appear that they refer to a period from about 1782 to about 1820. The patterns are serially numbered and probably represent a broad chronological sequence, though some of the low-numbered patterns are not known on the surviving wares made during the earlier years of the period, whilst a few of the patterns bearing higher numbers are known upon earlier wares. The numbers refer only to the formal borders and not to any painted subjects in reserves. Adjacent to some of the drawings is a pencilled interpolation of the name of an artist, which presumably signifies that on pieces carrying that specific pattern number the named artist did the painting in the reserves at least on some occasions. For example, pattern no. 258 shows a blue and gold stylised leaf pattern and an oval reserve framed by 'pearls' on a beige ground; in the reserve is written 'Cupid disarmed and bound by Banford'. But it cannot be concluded from this that all pieces bearing the pattern no. 258 had reserves painted by Banford. For in a document written by Duesbury II[2] painters are instructed to add identification numbers to their work (see p. 115); this would have been unnecessary had the same workmen always painted on the same designs.

One of the books contains patterns of breakfast and tea-services, chocolate cups etc., to the number of 770, while the other displays rather more than 400 dinner and dessert services. This gives a grand total of almost 1200 designs. Although it is, of course, quite impossible to take a comprehensive census of all Derby pieces carrying a pattern number, it would nevertheless be reasonable to suppose, from evidence

[1] A coloured photostat copy of these can now be seen at Derby Museum.
[2] Jewitt, op. cit., vol. II, p. 103.

available amongst all the wares made in the years covered by the Pattern Books, that not more than about half carry a pattern number. On the other hand there are instances of patterns in the books which can be matched with wares thus decorated but which do not carry a pattern number with the factory mark. For example, in the Derby Museum collections are two plates and a dish each decorated with a design which appears identical with pattern no. 3 in the Plate Book; yet not one of these pieces carries this, or any, pattern number. Study of the Pattern Books and especially of the higher serial numbers over 500 leads to the conclusion that either a large number of the patterns delineated in the books were never used on actual wares or only a fraction of the Derby output has survived. And to make the confusion worse, the evidence of a number of low serial numbers on Bloor period pieces with the factory mark in red makes it virtually certain that there must be at least one other Pattern Book which has never been located, for the above mentioned low serial numbers in no way match up to their corresponding numbers in the two existing Pattern Books.

The pattern number on the vast majority of pieces is placed immediately below the 'D' of the factory mark. In a few instances it is found at the side of the factory mark and, rarely, close to the footrim. In the Derby Museum collections are pieces from the *Hafod* service where the pattern number, 67,[1] is thus placed, and wares decorated with patterns 66[2] and 69[2] have these numerals, prefixed by a script 'N', under the footrim.

For some reason unknown, pattern numbers ceased to be put on wares after the painted mark was superseded by the printed mark (see p. 113). If, as one must suppose, the purpose of a pattern number is to facilitate ordering or re-ordering of patterns favoured by customers and potential customers, then surely their usefulness would have been equally great when the factory had adopted a printed mark. The Pattern Books themselves may well represent an attempt at a later date to bring together a mass of scattered drawings which were originally produced as day to day instructions to the artist-craftsmen concerned. The naming of particular painters against some of the drawings was almost certainly done at the later time when the Pattern Books were being put together; for they are written in the form of comments or opinions rather than instructions to be carried out.

[1] In the Plate Pattern Book.
[2] In the Cup and Saucer Pattern Book.

APPENDIX IV

PHYSICAL CHARACTERISTICS AND CHEMICAL COMPOSITION

These factors can be grouped into four periods:

(i) 1750–1756

Chemical composition (*Lady with a Lute*, Victoria and Albert Museum, 679–1925):[1]

	%
Silica	70·4
Lime	20·6
Alumina	5·4
Oxide of lead	2·1
Magnesia	1·3
	99·8

This is a non-phosphatic paste; the high proportion of silica gave a glassy as well as a heavy body.[2]
Glaze uneven with patches left uncovered.
Appearance by reflected light: creamy white.
As there are no pieces of flat-ware known in this period the appearance by transmitted light cannot readily be tested.

(ii) 1756–1770

Chemical composition substantially as (i) above.
Paste: glassy.
Appearance by reflected light: bluish white.
Translucency: poor to medium, due to the fact that it was

[1] Honey, *Old English Porcelain*, 1948 ed., p. 108.
[2] The characteristics are well set out in J. L. Dixon, *18th Century English Porcelain*, pp. 52–55.

APPENDIX IV: CHEMICAL COMPOSITION

impossible to achieve thin potting with a non-phosphatic soft-paste porcelain of this chemical composition. The evidence from the examination of both flat-ware pieces (saucers, plates etc.) and figures shows that the Derby factory must have experienced great difficulty not merely in preventing the wares from going out of shape (which they rarely succeeded in doing at this period) but in preventing them from becoming so mis-shapen as to be unsaleable.

(iii) 1770–c.1810

Chemical composition[1] (a plate painted with flowers; mark Crown and D in puce):

	%
Silica	41·94
Oxide of lead	0·36
Alumina	15·97
Lime	24·28
Phosphoric acid	14·96
Soda	1·06
Potash	0·90
Magnesia	0·20
	99·67

This is a phosphatic paste; calcined bones had been used at Chelsea since about 1758 and the change in composition had doubtless been introduced in the Derby Factory by workmen from the Chelsea works who remained in the employ of Duesbury after the merger in 1770. 14·96% Phosphoric acid represents about 45% bone-ash.

Glaze: clear and smooth. The dark brown spots known as 'sanding' became much less common and by the 1790s virtually disappeared.

Translucency: fair to very good. In Chelsea-Derby times the potting (except for small things like saucers, tea-bowls etc.) tended to be rather thick, inevitably inhibiting translucency. In the periods of Duesbury II and Michael Kean the potting was generally delightfully thin and the translucency correspondingly improved. Appearance by transmitted light: cream in the earlier (and thicker) pieces; greenish after about 1786.

[1] Herbert Eccles and Bernard Rackham, *Analysed Specimens of English Porcelain*, 1922, p. 31.

APPENDIX IV: CHEMICAL COMPOSITION

(iv) c.1810–1848

At some date not precisely known, but probably early in the Bloor period the Derby factory changed the composition of the china body and glaze in an effort, no doubt, not to be outdone by the considerable improvements conferred by the new recipe invented by Josiah Spode in the closing years of the eighteenth century. This was a hybrid of the Oriental or hard-paste recipe, in so far as it made use of china stone, china clay and bone-ash. So successful was Spode's formula that both his porcelain and his name 'Bone China' have remained practically unchanged down to the present day. The new Derby body was of a similar nature, with a harder glaze to which the enamel colours sometimes failed to adhere.

The following hitherto unpublished recipes are a selection from a manuscript notebook in the possession of a descendant of Robert Blore and give some idea of the variety of recipes in use at the Derby factory during the last thirty years of its existence:

'Hancock's China Body

Frit[1]

(China) stone	20 parts
flint glass	20
flint	20
pearl ash	16
common salt	12
borax	4
nitre	2
china clay	2

Body:

bone	140 parts
china clay	100
china stone	70
frit	100 (?)'

'John Hancock's "New Body" Sept. 5th 1836

bone ashes	176 parts
(china) stone	120
(china) clay	112
flint	16
barytes	16'

[1] Frit is fired in the kiln, then pounded into a powder and mixed with water, and then added to the other body ingredients.

APPENDIX IV: CHEMICAL COMPOSITION

The following is given for a 'body china' (undated):

'bone ashes	140 lbs
flint	56
(china) stone	84
china clay	120
pipe clay	30
smallts[1]	5 ozs.'

It will be noticed that these recipes contain china (or 'Cornwall') stone, which is the petuntse of Oriental hard-paste porcelain but which is invariably absent from English eighteenth century soft-paste china. The high proportion of bone-ash will also be noted.

The following recipes for 'fritt' body and 'fritt' glaze which give information about method as well as ingredients are worthy of record:

'china Fritt Body (Sept. 1837)

For the Fritt	
ground Cornwall stone	160 lbs.
ground bone ashes	160
fine pounded cullitt[2]	40
Lynn sand	40

The cullit should be the best flint glass, well washed and picked; the Lynn sand should be well washed till the water stands quite clear upon it and well picked free from bits of stone.

Mix the above in a dry state, pass the whole thro' a fine wire sieve into a tub, dissolve 20 lbs of pot ashes into as much water as will make the above into large round balls, about the size of sugar bowls, the above should be as stiff as saggar clay, so that the balls will stick together; put them into clean saggars, free from flint in the biscuit oven, care and cleanness must be particularly attended to when the above is fritted, pound it and subject it to the same process as cornwall stone ground very fine and dried in kiln.

For the Body:	
take of the fritt in dry state	280 lbs.
china clay	80
best blue clay	40
stain with half oz of blue smallts'	

---

[1] Cobalt oxide in dilute form, a blue colorant used to take the yellow colour out of the china body.

[2] Broken glass.

APPENDIX IV: CHEMICAL COMPOSITION

Lead would seem to have been an invariable ingredient in the glaze used on English soft-paste porcelains in the eighteenth century and continued in use into the nineteenth. The following, dated 1837, may perhaps be taken as typical:

'Frit for the glaze:

ground Cornwall stone	100 lbs.
borax	70
soda	30
dry flint	5
china clay	25'

The above mixed together were passed through a fine wire sieve and then fired. The resulting frit was pounded moderately fine and used as follows to make the glaze:

'Frit as above	140 lbs.
Cornwall stone	28
dry flint	28
white lead	30
pearl ashes	5'

The use of lead as an ingredient constituted a serious hazard to the health not only of the workers at the factory but also to those living nearby and in 1820 John Rose, proprietor of the Coalport China Works, was awarded the Gold Medal of the Society of Arts for a leadless glaze. Since there is in the MS a recipe for what is termed 'Coalport Glaze' it seems probable that it was used at some period at the Derby works:

'Felspar	27 lbs.
Lynn sand	4
Borax	10
Soda	3
nitre	3
Cornwall clay	3

frit this in the biskit kiln, then add 3lb of calcined borax and grind for use.'

Although so desirable in the interests of the health of employees and others, John Rose's 'felspathic glaze' as it was called was considered inferior to glazes containing lead and its use was not generally adopted.

APPENDIX V

EXTRACTS FROM CONTEMPORARY MANUSCRIPTS

A. THE DUESBURY COLLECTION OF MANUSCRIPTS IN THE DERBY PUBLIC LIBRARY

There are some 2,000 manuscript documents in the collection, and many are of a personal nature not concerned with the China Factory. Only a selection can be reproduced or summarised here:

1. INDENTURES OF APPRENTICESHIP

10th March 1765	George Bradbury—'Repairing China or Porcelain Ware'; 7 years.
23rd September 1765	Joseph Bullock—'Painting on China or Porcelain'; 7 years.
6th June 1766	John Winrow—'Painting upon Porcelain or China Ware'; 7 years.
29th September 1769	John Hancock, son of George Hancock—'Painting on Porcelain or China Ware'; 7 years. John Hancock made his mark 'X'. The Indenture signed by Wm. Duesbury and John Steer.
16th April 1770	John Frost apprenticed to Edward Phillips to learn painting on porcelain; 7 years. This Indenture was assigned to Wm. Duesbury on 25th February 1771 for a consideration of one shilling.

Edward Phillips was a china painter in Derby, apparently self-employed who, on 2nd September 1772, was negotiating an Agreement to serve Duesbury 'as his servant to the best and utmost of his skill and knowledge, exercise and employ himself in the art of painting China or Porcelain Ware for the said Wm. Duesbury'. The copy

Agreement is not signed and the period left blank. It appears, however, that there was a long association between Phillips and the Derby China Works, for on 9th February 1795 Phillips was writing to Duesbury regarding colours supplied to the factory.

25th December 1772   Thomas Southall—'Painting on China or Porcelain Ware'; 7 years.

28th October 1773   Wm. Smith apprenticed to his father, Constantine Smith of Derby, preparer of colours and porcelain painter and enameller, 'in that same art or mistery of preparing colours, painting and enamelling Porcelain'.

This William Smith is often credited with the invention of the Derby overglaze 'Smith's blue', so much used for borders etc., on Derby porcelain during Duesbury II's proprietorship but it is more probable that the invention was that of his father, Constantine. Gilhespy[1] states that he later left the factory and set up in business in Derby as a maker of enamel colours. It is to be noted that he was apprenticed to his father, not to Duesbury, but since the Indenture has survived with the other Duesbury papers it is evident that Duesbury took it over. Constantine Smith was working at Derby in 1775 when he and George Holmes wrote to Josiah Wedgwood seeking employment.[2]

On 23rd November 1778, the same William Smith entered into an agreement with Duesbury to make colours for him for painting upon china. In the Agreement he undertook to support his mother, suggesting that his father had died.

26th September 1774   William Billingsley 'to learn the art of painting upon China'; 5 years.
                          He was to be paid five shillings per week throughout the term of his apprenticeship. It is interesting that Billingsley's apprenticeship was for five years only, whereas the other painter apprentices were required to serve seven years. This may have been because Billingsley was sixteen years of age when first apprenticed and he would normally expect to be out of his apprenticeship by the age of twenty-one.

[1] Gilhespy, op. cit., p. 10.
[2] Tapp, *E.C.C. Trans.* 1939, vol. 2, no. 6, p. 60, and the Wedgwood archives at Keele University.

1st January 1777	Wm. Cooper—'Painting on China or Porcelain Ware'. Cooper's name appeared on a notice in 1788.
7th April 1777	John Porter—'Painting on China or Porcelain Ware'.
21st August 1777	John Morlidge—'Repairing of China or Porcelain Ware'.
16th September 1783	Benjamin Brocklesby—'Painting Porcelain or China Ware'; 7 years. A note attached to Brocklesby's Indenture records that he absented himself 'on Friday August 24th 1787 and has not been seen since'. He was eventually arrested on 6th December 1792 on a charge of deserting his Master's service. He appears to have returned to Duesbury's employment since his name appears with those of other employees on a document dated 1794.
5th July 1790	Wm. Longdon—'Painting Porcelain and China Ware'.

2. VARIOUS AGREEMENTS ETC. WITH WORKPEOPLE

2nd September 1772	An Agreement by David Hoon, Joseph Hale, Jacob Spooner, Robert Woodward, Thomas Wardle, Samuel Weaver, Wm. Whitehall, John Butler and William Yates to work for Duesbury in the glazing and burning of Porcelain for three years at six shillings per week. Jacob Spooner accompanied Billingsley to Pinxton in 1796. The marriage of 'Wm. Whitehall labourer at the China House' was registered at St. Werbergh's Church, Derby, on 3rd June 1754.
2nd September 1772	Wm. Gadsby, 'Mold Maker', agreed to serve Duesbury in 'Making molds' . . and 'repair' for four years at ten shillings per week. He was also entitled to receive a wagon of coal at the end of every year.

APPENDIX V: MANUSCRIPT DOCUMENTS

2nd September 1772

Thomas Mason, 'China or Porcelain repairer' agreed to serve Duesbury for four years 'to employ himself in the art of repairing China or Porcelain Ware'. One guinea per week. Duesbury also undertook to make Mason additionally a present each year of five guineas.

The job of 'repairer' was a highly skilled and important one in a factory a large part of whose output consisted of figures.

8th May 1789

Edward Withers agreed to serve Duesbury as a China Painter for three years from 27th September 1789. Withers had earlier been a flower painter at Derby.

20th May 1790

Leonard Lead, Wood Collier of Belper, agreed to make charcoal exclusively for Duesbury.

In a letter dated April 1795, Lead states 'this last seven years back I have coald for Mr. Wm. Duesbury, but . . . he has quite left off using Charcole'.

22nd September 1792

Thomas Mason, timekeeper, solemnly pledged himself 'to use my utmost caution at all times to prevent the knowledge transpiring that I am imploy'd to use a stop watch to make observations of work done in Mr. Duesbury's manufactory and to take such observations with the utmost truth and accuracy in my powers and give the results faithfully to Mr. Duesbury'.

This is interesting as a very early instance of 'Time Study' in this country.

2nd January 1796

John Musgrove Kiln Man undertook as follows:

'I John Musgrove labourer and Kiln man of the Parish of St. Alkmund's Derby now in the service of Messrs. Duesbury and Kean at the Porcelain Manufactory in Derby aforesaid do engage . . . not to disclose—directly or indirectly—at this or any other time whatever whether in the Service of

127

the said Gentlemen, my present employer or not the secret communicated to me this day respecting the Tryals of the Biscuit Kiln (as described on the back of this obligation) or anything relating thereto—and more especially I engage in like manner not to disclose that I have any way of getting out my Tryals successfully besides extreme care and the personal assistance of either Mr. Duesbury or Mr. Kean under the penalty of £100'.

On the reverse of the document the 'secret' alluded to is shown to be the use of smoked glass 'to enable the person who draws the Tryals to distinguish them in the midst of the heat be it never so intense and for the want of which . . . the kiln men were always obliged to let the air rush in and cool the tryals . . . to the very great danger of having the tryals less burned than the ware . . . and by that means the ware was in danger of being either melted or not fired enough'.

24th September 1788   Works Notice:

'In November last notice was given that persons of one branch of the Manufactory were not to go into the premises of the other unless they had real business there relative to their particular occupation, notwithstanding which the practice is still by some individuals continued. Notice is hereby *finally* given that if any person in future (having received this Notice) shall intrude themselves contrary to this injunction they will positively be fined 5 shillings'.

The following appended their names to the Notice as acknowledging that they had read the same:

Boreman	Joseph Doe	Key
Billingsley	Longdon	Hogg
Soare	Blood	Barton

128

Stables	Taylor	Clarke
Cooper	Smith	Dickenson
John Yates	Buttler	T. Simes
Wm. Yates		Webster

M. Mason
Shirley Arth.

The Barton whose name appears above may well have been Richard Barton who was for a time in charge at Chelsea.

24th November 1790   An undertaking by Jacob Spooner, Kiln Man, that he would not disclose the secret of a 'machine' invented by Mr. Duesbury 'intended to exhibit the contraction of earthen body's when in the Fire'.

Undated, but probably 1796

Draft Heads of Agreement as to the employment of Painters at the Factory:

1. Term to be for so long as William Duesbury requires the assistance of the painters. William Duesbury to give six months notice of termination 'Except any of the Painters shall at any time be disposed to decline . . . Painting on *China or Earthenware* . . . shall give the said William Duesbury . . . six lunar months notice'. Painters leaving William Duesbury's service not to serve with any one else as painter without first re-offering his services to William Duesbury.

2. A ten and a half hour day prescribed.

3. Wages 3s. 6d. per day.

4. A 63 hour week.

5. Painters to employ themselves to their utmost for William Duesbury.

6. Painters not to work in enamel for themselves or anyone else.

7. When work is so circumstanced as to be capable of being enamelled or gilt by the piece each of the said Painters . . . to do the said work by the piece.

K

129

The names subscribed were:
Stables, Taylor, W. Yates, Brocklesby, Rogue, Clarke, 'M.M.', Barton, Sims, T. Soar.

A similar draft (without names) is dated March 1794, but the above would appear to be later since, for example, Billingsley's name is not appended, he having left in 1796.

3. DOCUMENTS RELATING TO INDIVIDUAL WORKMEN

Billingsley Apprenticeship Deed 26th September 1774.

25th December 1790 Letter from Billingsley to Duesbury:

'Sir,

I am much obliged to you for yr. favour of yr. Carriage of ye Box of Pencils. Agreeable to yr. request I will deliver to Mr. Spengler. He is just gone, but, and Sir I have nearly concluded every necessary alteration and Dont Doubt But I shall be able to attend to your Business and make it the First Object of my Study.

Yr. Humble Ser$^{t.}$
Wm. Billingsley.'

23rd September 1793 Account from Billingsley to Duesbury for work done:

'1792 To an Account Deliver^d to Sept. 29 1792   £7 4s. 0d.
   To 36 weeks, one day and $\frac{3}{4}$ Due September 21st 1793   57 3s. 2d.
                                                      ─────────
                                                      64 7s. 2d.
In Nov^m 1792 Receiv^d of Mr. Duesbury a Draft Thirty pounds   30 0s. 0d.
                                                      ─────────
                   The Balance   £34 7s. 2d.

'Sir,

I have lost some little time which in some degree differs from our agreement. But it as been necessity not Choice, and as

130

I shall in the course of a fortnight Quit the Public Business I shall shortly bee capable of making up the time so lost.'

The 'Public Business' referred to the Public House in Bridge Gate, Derby, where Billingsley lived.

20th March 1795

Billingsley's Account for eight weeks, three days and two quarters work:

£13 10s. 4½d.

1st August 1795

Joseph Lygo to Duesbury:

'. . . I hope you will be able to make a bargain with Billingsley for him to continue with you for it will be a great loss to lose such a hand and not only that but his going into another Factory will put them in the way of doing flowers in the same way which they are at present entirely ignorant in.'

This related to Billingsley's imminent departure for Pinxton where he was to set up a China Manufactory financed by John Coke.

14th October 1796

Billingsley to Duesbury:

'Sir,

From the circumstances that occurd when I was last in Conversation with you, I am induc'd to take this mode of informing you of my opinion of the subject then in question. My opinion is, that I have fulfill'd the warning I gave . . . But as I am inform'd that you believe I have some further time to work for you before the Warning is fulfill'd—namely to make up the time I lost in the six months I was under Warning, and as it is my wish to leave no grounds for dissatisfaction . . . I am willing to come and Work that time. . . .'

It does not appear that Duesbury accepted the offer for Billingsley was at Pinxton by the end of the month.

131

Zachariah Boreman   Undated document:

'Whereas heads of an Agreement intended to be enter^d into between Zachariah Boreman and William Duesbury were this day agreed upon and signed this is further to signify that wherever the words "Three shillings and 6d per day" occur in the aforesaid agreement the words "seven shillings per day" shall be inserted in Zachariah Boreman's agreement . . . and also it is further agreed upon between the said Zachariah Boreman and William Duesbury, that in consideration of Zachariah Boreman employing himself in painting in the best manner in his power for the interests of William Duesbury . . . and contributing all in him lays to improve the Enamel Colours etc. etc. used by the said William Duesbury . . . the said William Duesbury agreed . . . to allow the said Zachariah Boreman (*blank*) hours in every week (of six days) for his recreation and for the benefit of the health of the said Zachariah Boreman upon this express condition; that he the said Zachariah Boreman do not disclose to anyone whatsoever . . . that he has had such indulgence (the said Zachariah Boreman having for some time past contented himself with working from 4 to 5 days only in each week) which might make some others discontented that are at present happy.'

The figure of 3s. 6d. per day is that quoted in the draft Agreement with the Derby painters in general in March 1794 and this agreement with Boreman would therefore appear to be of similar date. Evidently Duesbury so valued Boreman's work that he was willing to grant such (for those days) preferential conditions. An earlier agreement with Boreman, dated 26th August 1783 is with the Bemrose papers in the British Museum Department of British and Mediaeval Antiquities.

30th January 1795

Joseph Lygo wrote to Duesbury saying that he had asked Boreman if he wished to return to Derby; he said 'No' as he had not the least intention of doing landscapes at 1s. 6d. each.

James Banford

27th July 1789

Lygo sent Duesbury a specimen of flower painting done by James Banford (recommended by Withers) an apprentice at the Bristol factory, who had since been with Brown, an 'enameller'.

18th August 1789

In a letter to Joseph Lygo, Banford says he has made up his mind to go to Derby but must leave his money with his family to keep them because he will be unable to remit to them for two or three weeks; he asks Duesbury to advance him two guineas.

Undated

Banford to Charles King (Manager at Derby):

'Sir,

Mr. Deakin inform'd me he had seen you and that Mr. Duesbury was angry because I did not call Mr. D. when he told me to make out a bill . . . I am very willing to work for him (Duesbury) as I used to do by the week and will do him justice or else not have his money, but, I never will work by the piece and have just what he pleases to give me for it.'

18th June 1792

Banford to Duesbury:

'Dear Sir,

The manner of your conduct towards me last week has awakened some sensations of the Dignity of Human Nature (which I am sorry to say has been for some time dormant in me) and has held up a mirror which reflects how wretched and

133

abject a man may become by deviating from the path of rectitude—for had I pursued the Ideas which was early inculcated in me I should not now have been *Dependant* no man perhaps feels more pleasure in his sober moments in pursuing the laudable and Social Occupations of life than myself and no-one more wretched after a deviation from them.'

Banford continues at some length in this strain and concludes:

'I do not blame you, Sir, for withholding your friendship for by the message sent by Mr. King you must have thought that if I was lent a little money for a good purpose I should dissipate it . . . but it would not have been so . . .'

Your humble Servt.
J. Banford.'

18th September 1792   Banford wrote to Duesbury saying he owed rent to Mr. Deakin and asked Duesbury to pay it 'as usual' and he will repay at five shillings a week.

1st February 1794   Banford to Duesbury:

'Sir,
As 'tis my intention not to stay in Derby beg leave (according to Agreement) to give you six months notice of leaving you . . . I cannot help informing you that I have been Dissatisfied some time at the Difference of Wages between Mr. Boreman and self. I am not conceited of my Work but every man knows what he is capable of doing and in my line of painting China except Landscapes I have the advantage of Mr. Boreman—cannot help observing that in the Landscape line when there is anything minute or requires neatness my optic nerves are to be strained for eighteen shillings a week less . . . Wherever I go I do not expect to find a

better Master but expect to find more encouragement or I'll drop the pencil for ever.'

13th March 1795

Banford to Duesbury:

'Sir,

I am sorry to inform you that I shall be oblig^d to leave Derby and that soon as 'tis impossible for me to exist on the money I receive, how can you think five people can live seven days on eleven shillings . . . as I owe . . . a good deal of money and through Complin and Withers being so much in debt people is more pressing with me therefore have resolved to leave the place as there is no probability of paying them . . .'

In order to assist the Banford family Duesbury allowed Banford's wife Bernice to do 'outwork' in the way of painting wares at home. A letter from her to Duesbury (undated) reads:

'. . . Return you thanks for allowing me some work I have only painted 4 dozen and 3 Plates at 3d each—Mr. John Duesbury would have sent me more work but Mr. Banford declin'd it till your return as all the men (Mr. Bilinsley and Mr. Complin excepted) treated him in a very unbecoming manner and even threatened him if the work was continued to me.'

Richard Askew

2nd August 1794

Askew agreed to work for Duesbury as a China Painter. He is described as 'Richard Askew, late of Birmingham', and undertook to paint 'in quantity and effect equal to the Cupids on Two Flower Potts by James Banford having Richard Askew's name written upon them (to prevent a mistake in alluding to them)'.

135

Askew was paid 'by the piece' and presented bills to Duesbury from time to time; some have survived:

'Feb—Aug. 1795

    3 Coffee Cans in figuars
    A Coffee Can with the Duke of Yorke
    A Vase with Nymphs waking Cupid
    2 Chamber Potts in Cupids
    A Coffee Can with the Prince of Wales
    4 Coffee Cans with the Four 'Alliments'   £4 0s. 0d.
    2 'Cadle' Cups with Birds.'

Most of Askew's career as a painter was as an independent decorator of china and enamels.

John Brewer

17th April 1793

Nicholas Edwards (brother-in-law of Duesbury II) wrote to Duesbury from London to say that Brewer would be coming to Derby 'tomorrow week' to take up painting on porcelain. Brewer, he said, was a water-colourist 'and had never applied his art to porcelain painting'. Brewer stipulated that he be given time to become acquainted with the process before his rate of pay became fixed; he goes on '. . . . were you in Brewer's case you would not be willing to tie yourself down to the execution of work in colours you are a stranger to as the same terms that you could venture to agree to with those that were familiar to you . . . I showed him the plate with the hand and dagger, I asked the time he would require for that, his answer was "Twenty minutes, I should think would be amply sufficient".'

Undated

An undated document setting out a list of prices to be paid for his work:

'No. 1. An adult of 4 inches high
                    6 shillings

> A Child in proportion   3 shillings
> 3. For a figure of 3 inches in colours
>   4 shillings
>   For a child   2 shillings
> 4. For an adult figure of 2 inches in
>   colours   2s. 8d.
>   etc. etc.

'Background to fill up the compartment if oval to be included—if a circle one 18th part more to be allowed—if a square one twelfth part if besides the background be a plain stippled surface one twelfth more will be allowed over and above.

'If 30 or any number of whole figures be introduced into one piece each figure being of the proportions of no. 1—the price to be multiplied by the figure abating sixpence each figure for background and so through every number.

'If three-fourths of a figure be introduced two-thirds of a whole will be allowed.

'If half a figure three fifths

'If quarter of a figure one fourth

'(The reason of these three last articles being thus calculated is that in general the part of second figures that are introduced are the most difficult such as heads, hands and feet)

'Animals to be half the price of adult figures'.

Then follows on a similar list of views according to size, and flowers were to be valued by *quantity*, not size.

Such was the commercial evaluation of applied art.

4. DOCUMENTS RELATING TO DAY-TO-DAY RUNNING OF THE FACTORY

The following communications relate to the general management of the factory. Some are reproduced in full but in other cases the purport of the document is given, the letters themselves being somewhat lengthy.

23rd June 1776   A letter from William Wood, London, to William Duesbury at Derby enclosing the following notice for the newspapers:

'On Friday last Her Majesty accompanied with the Duchess of Ancaster was pleased to Honor with her prescence Mr. Duesbury's Ware Rooms in Bedford Street Covent Garden. Condescended to express great approbation at these Beautiful articles of Derby and Chelsea Porcelain and Patronise and Encourage the Same by making some purchases.'

20th August 1776 and
13th October 1778   Two documents relating to Duesbury's ownership of a lead mine in Derbyshire known as the 'Sucstone' mine. The terms used in these documents are those peculiar to the lead mining industry, which had been carried on in Derbyshire since Roman times.

'Brassington Liberty, August 20th 1776.

'. . . Then Thomas Slack for the use of Mr. William Duesbury of Derby freed a Founder Meare of ground for old and gave one Dish of ore and called it by the name Sucstans (SUCSTONE). Ranging North and South being in a piece or parcel of Land belonging Mrs. Newton of Ashbourne . . . .

        Jro. and Edwd. Ashton, Barrmaster.'

The second document confirms in more detail Duesbury's ownership of this mine. It has been shown that some of these Derbyshire lead mines, including Sucstone, yielded also a white clay which is said to have been used by Duesbury in the china manufacture.[1]

An important bowl of Derby Porcelain (Plates 85 and 86) bears, in the interior, the inscription 'Success to the Mine Innocent'

[1] J. A. Pilkington, *A View of the Present State of Derbyshire*, 1789.

in the form of words issuing from the mouth of a smoker,[1] referring to another Derbyshire lead mine, also yielding white clay, and perhaps also owned by Duesbury though it has not proved possible to confirm this.[1]

19th August 1786

Lygo wrote from London to Duesbury regarding 'the Great Stock of enamelled figures in the Warehouse, these must be sold first owing to the body being altered and the new figures of different size'.

This reference to a change in the Derby body is obscure. A bone-ash body had been introduced on the amalgamation with Chelsea; there is a record of bone-ash 'sent to Derby' in 1770. It would appear, therefore, that some other change took place. George Savage records that he has tested Derby porcelain of 1780 or later and found some specimens to be non-phosphatic. He suggests that the pre-1770 receipt may have been used, but possibly there were other changes. On the other hand, Lygo may have had in stock figures manufactured from the old formula before 1770.

10th September 1788

Letter from J. Stables to Duesbury in London:

'Yesterday evening late came two gentlemen, one I fancy is a Lord, he told me that the Dutchess of Devonshire would be here to-day, how to receive her I am at a loss and fear I cant give her every information she will expect . . . I think it will be all right to let her see all round the new work, this is finished, therefore shall call Jno Duesbury to bring and set them in order and hope she will give a large order. The supposed Lord seems to be a French man

[1] F. A. Barrett, 'Duesbury and Lead Mining. An unusual Derby Punch Bowl' *The Antique Collector*, August 1955. Also Dr. T. D. Ford, 'The Occurrence of Halloysite in Derbyshire', *Clay/Minerals Bulletin*, vol. 5, no. 30, 1963.

and says the set of China should have a socket (in) the saucer to hold the cup fast and that the French China that is (?) are all made so.'

A postscript adds:

'I find upon inspection there is no China Finished worth the Dutchess's notice but a cup or two of the Duke of Bedford's with no mark upon them!'

Joseph Stables is listed by Jewitt as a gilder, but at this time he was manager of the Derby factory in Duesbury's absence.

29th April 1789

J. Stables to William Duesbury:

'16 Pedestals goes into the Biscuit Kiln this week . . . Lord Cremore's mug will be sent to-morrow—Wardle says nothing's arrived nor wont before Monday—Smith informs me Mr. Boreman wants Lavender Isle of Spike the fatest and thickest Bot. at the Cross Mr. Jones's Covent Garden—Mason says the slip will do to make the Vause.'

Followed by another letter:

'Ld Cremore's mug will not be sent before Thursday it must go thro' another Fire.'

13th April 1787

Lygo told Duesbury that Vulliamy, the clock maker, was complaining about the biscuit figures supplied, which, he said, were 'too small for the brass work got ready'.

25th December 1788

Lygo wrote to Duesbury complaining that the gilder's number was very often omitted from the ware.

21st May 1789

Lygo thinks William Duesbury received his Royal Appointment in 1775. Also he did not think that any figures of the Royal family had been purchased by themselves. This is a reference to the figures of Royalty modelled in biscuit after a painting by Zoffany.

140

18th March 1790	Lygo wrote complaining of the quality of the Derby figures, describing them as 'the best imitations to match the Staffordshire I ever see'.

At about this time Duesbury was receiving complaints that vessels intended to contain hot liquids, such as teapots and tureens, would not stand up to such use. On 17th December 1790 he wrote to Lygo concerning one such complaint from Sir John Shaw and suggesting that Sir John be warned that his servants should take care to warm up the tureens etc. gradually to avoid damage. Duesbury said he intended to make a body 'that would withstand sudden heat better' for tureens, teapots etc.

Duesbury also caused to be prepared instructions to his customers to avoid breakages through hot water as follows:

'To prevent Accidents with Tea Pots— Let about a Tea Cupful of Cold Water be sent up in the Tea Pot, and just before you wish to make Tea pour about 2 Tea Cupfulls of boiling water to the cold in the pot and give it a shake round. This will gradually expand the Pot and prepare it for the Reception of boiling water to make Tea. It being the expansion of Tea Pots etc. by means of boiling water suddenly thrown in that rends them.'

8th November 1790	Extract from a letter written by Duesbury to Lord Rawdon regarding a service being made at Worcester for the Duke of Clarence:

'A Lady has just informed me they are making at Worcester for his Royal Highness the Duke of Clarence a Table Service of 40 Dishes 14 Doz^n plates and other pieces in proportion embellished with Gold . . . If your Lordship could direct me in which channel to apply for the Commission of making the Dessert it would be doing me the greatest Service . . . His Royal Highness the Prince of Wales I am confident would recommend it to his Brother immediately was it but hinted to him.'

141

In the above letter the following passage is deleted:

'I understand the Composition is a blue ground with a figure of Hope on each piece in different attitudes.'

24th February 1791   Copy of letter from William Duesbury to Lord Rawdon:

'My Lord,

For your generous attention to my small present I cannot express my gratitude and thanks—the uncommon interest you pleased to take in the success of my Manufactory induces me to take the liberty of troubling you . . . I believe it may be about thirty years since my Father was appointed "China Manufacturer to the King," paying the customary fees after his death I succeeded him—paying the fees again—and we have neither of us been supplanted in his service (tho' of late years very little encouraged) till the King's journey thro' Worcester at which time his Majesty left liberal commissions which was no-more than encouraging one Manufactory without doing it at the expense of another—but they also directed the Worcester Manufactory to use their Arms and they call themselves "Worcester China Manufactory to the King"—since that time we have not received the least mark of attention from their Majesties but on the contrary they have been making at Worcester as a present to the Duke of Clarence a very extensive Service to the amount of between six and eight hundred pound. This Commission has made a great noise in the Country and we have heard of it from a number of persons who have called at the Works at Derby from whom I have discover^d the unmerited injury my Manufactory must suffer—those who had not seen the Worcester China and jug'd no doubt by the King's decided preference it was easy to discover were prejudiced with the idea that the Worcester Manufactory had of late surpassed the Derby—one Gent^m in particular whom Mr. Stubbs attended lamented very much that the blue of the Derby China could not equal the Worcester and tho' the reverse is exactly the fact Mr. Stubbs could not induce him to believe it—it is but justice to myself to remark that the Worcester Manufactory are behind us not only in some but in every part (as far as I have seen)—as they are not at the expense to imploy the best artists. . . . Before I heard of this expensive Service making at Worcester I had encouraged the hope of getting appointed China Manufacturer to the Duke of Clarence which would have given me an opportunity of doing myself justice with the Publick, as the China *of each* could have been seen together. . . .'

13th July 1791

Letter from William Beard at Bath to Duesbury:

'You do not say whether your very pretty vase has been introduced to his Grace of Clarence or not, nor whether you have seen the Worcester crockery. . . . The Things are glareing and fine enough at the first glance and there is great merit in varying the figure's Attitude so often, but there is not One Single piece in the whole set that is perfect either in shape or colour.'

The service referred to in the above letters is the well-known *Hope* service made by Flight's of Worcester, of which specimens can be seen at the Victoria and Albert Museum and elsewhere. Unfortunately for Duesbury his protestations had little effect, but Derby did subsequently receive its share of orders for royalty.

20th November 1791

Note on an order for the Prince of Wales:

'A Cab(inet) Cup to match that left with gold sprigs

1 Pr. ditto (Solid Gilt . . .) from Mr.
Wright's Cup except the Sprigs and G^d
Starrs as numerous as on the above Cab.
Cup and the blue and G^d—exchanged
for that on Yellow and (?) Plate marked A.

A Desert abt. 25gs (Guineas) value, and an
addition of Icepails dec. for common use
Plants—before the following Service
which must be concluded when I have
shown his R.H. the Plates now in hand.

A Desert (the price not yet determined) 7
plates of a patt^n—all the shapes alike—
(*Peacock plates* all *bad*)

2.A blue and G^d rich Brown and Yellow
and *countrey* pattern.

2.B with outer border made half as broad
again and on blue—the yellow ground
from thence (the same breadth as
before) the same border (not increased)
but on blue no light scrolls—but the
landscape kept the original size ($3\frac{1}{2}$ inch)
so that the yellow must make all up.

2.C Diam. 1 Patt^n—47/8 Landscape pale
ground

2 with Bister landscape views of Chatsworth but with the Gold—as Mr.
Mundys.

2 Do. Quakers Patt. Drab border—$3\frac{1}{4}$
Cumb^d hock moonlight

2.E Lady H's Yellow and Group of flowers
on brown ground A Plate same as his
Cab. cups—smaller sprigs and much
more numerous than No. 100—Landscapes coloured.

An—Gold Cornucopia with some col. in
the Cornice.

A ditto—Group of large featured flowers
(not too numerous) on a *still* French
Grey ground to occupy all the flatt part
—the rem^{dr} rich.'

Some parts of the above are not decipherable and the quotation is
not fully understandable, but the details given may enable any
surviving pieces to be recognised.

5th July 1792	Lygo sent to Derby nineteen copies of a Botanical Magazine 'to copy the flowers'.
5th August 1792	A Letter from Jno. Hancock (Hanley) to Duesbury:

'I have sent you 20lb. of White Enamel' writes Hancock and asks that if more is required he be given sufficient time to make it 'as it is obliged to go into the oven several times'. The price was to be 1/- per lb. 'I have sent you a bit of the yellow I mentioned to you when I was at Derby and hope it will answer. There is two sorts, please to trigh them both they will either of them make a very fine yellow if properly fluxd which I have no doubt Mr. Smith can manage very well'.

Several members of the Hancock family were engaged in the pottery trade as colour makers and painters. John Hancock was apprenticed for seven years at Derby on 29th September 1769 and, according to Jewitt, was settled in Hanley in 1786/7 and was working in Staffordshire for many years. He died in 1847 in his 90th year. This would make him but twelve years of age when apprenticed in 1769.

Duesbury in 1793 was having difficulty in meeting delivery dates of some important orders.

On 23rd May 1793 the firm of Green and Ward of London wrote to Duesbury urging delivery of a set of China for 'the Margrave'.

On 12th July Green and Ward again wrote:

'We are extremely sorry to be again troublesome on the subject of our China but indeed there is an absolute necessity. We are just informed that the Margrave gives a Dinner at Brandenburg House to a very large Party on the 21st inst. and (as) the Gilt Plate is left here for the Summer they will be greatly at a loss without the China.'

To which Duesbury replied, giving excuses:

'. . . all the profit I should have looked for (on this commission) is already sunk in the train of inevitable accidents.'

Green and Ward were still pressing Duesbury for delivery on September 8th; how the Margrave's Dinner fared is not recorded.

8th December 1794	Charles King wrote from Derby to Duesbury in London (King was Duesbury's manager at Derby):

'Sir,

I found 7 more of the Prince's plates which are sent in this box. Banford has not been at work since Saturday at Dinner Time. Mason has had some conversation with me about Coffee's work, he thinks it so very imperfect as not to answer your purpose however low it may come. . . . I should think, Sir, that you might purchase some printed portraits of popular characters that would do for Askew to copy. . . .'

26 March 1795	Charles King (Derby) to Duesbury:

'. . . please inform us how you would wish to have Mr. Egan's Chamber pots finished. . . . Withers came to work on Tuesday morning.'

25th June 1795	Letter from John Duesbury (overseer at Derby) presumably to William Duesbury:

'The Duchess of Northumberland's order I put the last 6 Comportes into Wright's hand (a painter) on Tuesday last; Mrs. Butless wants two largeish size dishes and Hearts Comports Bisquiting, all the rest in hand. Mr. Nelthorpe wants the two largest Size dishes and Sauce Tureens bisquiting, all the rest is in hand, Lady Camdens will be in hand to-day except the Icepails and a few Plates to replace damaged ones in the blue kiln have 2 Ice Pails towards four in the White, there are more bisquiting this week, but it will be three weeks before they are glazed. Should have had the same Tureens Bisq^{td} this week but Matthews has not been to get them ready, all the Dishes and the Comports will be bisq^{td} next week in a Sagar kiln . . . we have

146

delivered a good deal of goods in the Country lately, but the greatest loss in so little being sent to London is in your not having burnishers . . . we have at this upwards of two months work for them . . . please to recollect there are eleven hands at gilding and only eight burnishers . . . I think taking the Patterns in general one Gilder will fully employ one burnisher. . . .'

John Duesbury's report provides an insight into the problems of running a China factory in the late eighteenth century.

12th August 1795   Charles King to Duesbury:

'. . . Wedgwood has written to you saying he had forewarded a sample of their Cornish Clay and Stone to try. The Biscuit Kiln opened yesterday promises well—it is too soon to draw it yet.'

Also, on the same date:

'. . . Sir R. Lawley has written for the figures, sent the patt. (a French plate with a Sweet-Pea Blossom round the brim) for his Ice Pails, but has not determined on the Table Service. We have had another Glaze Kiln and are very good of Bist. Ware . . . We shall have another Bist. Kiln (all useful) fired off on Sunday morning. In Musgrove's Department they are busy preparing for another Glaze K.'

All these letters indicate great activity at the Derby Manufactory.

Derby porcelain is frequently found painted with plants in botanical, rather than purely decorative, fashion, and a list of such plants was prepared for use at Derby. The names of the plants were inscribed, usually in blue, on the piece, giving both the Latin and English names. Much of this painting is attributed to the brush of John Brewer. The list is as follows:

'No.
1. *Chlora perfoliata*   Yellow centaury
2. *Borago officinalis*   Borage
3. *Verbascum nigrum*   Moth Mullen (sic)
4. *Daphne laureola*   Sparge Laurel (sic)
5. *Myosotis scorpioides*   Mouse ear scorpion grass
6. *Stellaria nermosa*   Wood stitch-wort

| 7. *Isatis tinctoria* | Dyers Woad |
| 8. *Astec Tripolium* | Starr of Tripoly (sic)' |

5. EGAN AT BATH

Richard Egan was brother-in-law of William Duesbury II, husband of Anna Duesbury. In 1779 Egan was a Linen Draper of the firm of Egan and Brookes, King Street, Covent Garden. He was still there in 1789. In October 1792 he became a china, earthenware and glass dealer in Bath Street, Bath, where he acted as Agent for the Derby China Factory, and also sold the products of other manufacturers.[1] Duesbury's London Agent, Joseph Lygo, was instrumental in establishing Egan at Bath, and on 30th November 1792 Richard Egan was able to write to his brother-in-law: 'I am now open^d and have been this Week, but cannot brag of any Business worth mentioning yet, the few genteel People that have by accident found me out seem quite pleased and promise great things. . . .'

20th December 1792   Richard Egan to Duesbury:

'I have sold two of the Coffee Cans you sent me from Derby, the same Lady that purchased them has given me an order for another, a green ground exactly like one I have, but that is all plain without any landscape or print—this I want is to have a Brown Landscape done very soft the Brown the same as the best Desert Service—she likewise desires the Saucer may not be so deep by a quarter of an Inch as when the Cup is in the Saucer it hides the Beauty of the Painting. The Landscape is to be in a Square the same as the Beggar Girl is—if I had another Beggar Girl and Child like the last I think it would soon go.'

It is surprising to find that the factory was apparently prepared to pay attention to such individual requirements as would, one would think, prove quite uneconomical.

[1] Among them Thomas Turner (Caughley) 1794–1796; Rose, Blakeway and Rose (Coalport) 1796–1797; Minton's (Stoke-on-Trent) 1798; Spode 1792–1797; Ephraim Booth (Stoke-on-Trent) 1792. The dates given are those for which actual bills have survived and do not exclude the likelihood of business in other years.

23rd January 1793   Egan to Duesbury:

'Sir Richd Clayton wants to know the price of a Tea Set with a yellow ground the same as the set I have but instead of the landscape his arms within a similar Ring to what the landscapes are in . . . he wants to know the price of a White and Gold Desert with his Arms in a Ring and a Gold Border similar to the Border to the 60 guinea Desert.'

To which Duesbury replied on 31st January:

'I should suppose Sr Richd Clayton's Arms enamell^d on a yellow ground tea-set would be about 25 guineas—. . . the Desert same pattern about 70 Gs. but cannot speak positively without seeing the Arms (if there are any *human* figures they require a superior artist) the size would also make a difference . . . if Sir R. pleases we can get a good vellum painting from London (which will not be useless when done with here) and when I see that I will send a sketch of each pattern on paper (or enamel a plate of each) for his inspection.'

15th July 1794   Egan to Duesbury:

'I cannot help saying that your letter has made me very unhappy in the first place it informs me that the best and only friend I have is uneasy in his mind and in the next place it implies that he thinks I do not expedite the Business. . . . We have a pretty many Orders in Hand in the Enamelled Table Sets and when they are finished hope the Money will drop in. *We have a man that lives 1 mile and a half out of Bath that formerly work^d at Cockpit Hill who enamels for me.*' (Authors' italics.)

There has survived a number of Bills which show that the man referred to was one Anthony Amatt of Twerton, near Bath. The surviving Bills set out Amatt's charges to Egan for painting Coats of

Arms and borders on Table Wares in 1794 and 1795. Jewitt states that Amatt was 'a thrower and meritorious painter, who died in 1851, aged 92. He is said to have been born at Derby in 1759, and to have been apprenticed to a thrower who worked at Champions and to have worked there till their close'.[1] Since the Cockpit Hill (Derby) Pot Works ceased to exist in 1779 on John Heath's bankruptcy, and Champion's factory at Bristol ceased to manufacture in 1778, Amatt's stay at Cockpit Hill could only have been a brief one. An example of his presumed work is the border and the crest of the Welby family of Denton Manor, Grantham, in Lincolnshire, on a plate having the Derby mark in blue (Plate 177). It is to be noted that both border and crest are by a hand different from that of the artist (perhaps John Brewer) who painted the botanical flowers on the service, and that the word *Ignem* is mis-spelt *Igrem*.

Lygo lent assistance to Egan by providing gold for decorating ware sent to Bath in the unfinished state:

30th August 1794 Lygo to Egan:

'Inclosed is $\frac{1}{2}$ oz. Grain gold and have sent you a burnisher—which I had from Derby some time since. I do not know where they are to be got here—We have no three Guinea Groups at present in biscuit. I have not been able to find an Imaged B. and B. plate, they are a very scarce article to be found.'

(In an earlier letter Egan had asked Lygo to get him 'Imaged B. and B. plates' to match a customer's set.)

Perhaps the reference is to the blue-and-white Bow pattern known as the 'image pattern' and so described in the Bowcock papers now in the British Museum. (The pattern is one of a tall Chinaman followed by a boy carrying a bundle of Bamboo shoots.) Or perhaps it refers simply to plates painted with figures.

6. BILLS ETC. AT CHELSEA[2]

24–31 March 1770 'Barton and Boyer
6 Large Ornement Pedestals for the Grand

---

[1] Jewitt, op. cit., vol. I, p. 396, in which Jewitt appears to follow Hugh Owen, *Two Centuries of Ceramic Art in Bristol*, 1873, p. 289. W. J. Pountney, *The Old Bristol Potteries*, 1920, disagreed with the view of Amatt's having been at Bristol with Champion.

[2] A small extract from these bills appears in Jewitt, op. cit., vol. II, pp. 71–72.

Popore (i.e. pot-pourri)
5 Large Popore Perfume Pots to ditto
1 Square Perfume Pot deckarted with the heads of the four Seasons
Inglefield pounding of the glass
3 dozen Seals of Lambs
3 dozen of Lyons'

14–21 April   'Seals made 5 dozen Swallows
                                1 dozen Tomtits
Work done this week by Barton and Boyer
2 Antike Perfume Vases with 3 goats hedes
24 Strawberry Compotiers made with the Derby Clay
24 Ditto Royhal pattern
24 Quilted pattern plates'

21–28 April   'Seals   2 dozen Tom Tits
                                3 dozen Owls nests
                                2 dozen Indian boys with hand screen
48 Compotiers made with Derby Clay
24 Ornement Plates made with Derby Clay'

12–19 May   'Barton 6 days at 3/6d.
Boyer 6 days at 3/6d.
Seals made Overtime   6 Cocks
3 dozen Cupid Crying by an Urn
1 dozen and six fine Gentlemen with a Muff
1 dozen and six Shephard Shearing of Sheep
6 Arlequin
Mending the 2 large Quarters of the World'

2–9 June   'Seals made Overtime
1 dozen and six Chineas men a-smoking
3 dozen Cupids as a Letter Carrier
1 dozen and six Cupids with a net'

16–23 June   'Making of Pidgeon House Perfume Pot[1]
and glazing of the work for the Glaze Kiln'

4–11 August   'Inglefield Cleaning of the Bisket Work to be Glas^d'

[1] Colour Plate B.

11–18 August	'Barton 6 days at 3/6d. Boyer 6 days at 3/6d. A Cask from on Board of Ships Boyer Laying of Sapher (Zaphre) Roberts setting of the Glass Kiln'
8–10 September	'Barton making 1 Jar with a Dog and Rabits and flowering of them'
15–22 September	'Making of 2 Antike Vauses 2 Ornement Vauses with Chineas Figuars 2 Ornement Seasons Vauses'
16–23 March 1771	'Chasing and Polishing 2 double handle cups and covers 3 double handle cups and covers 2 Four Scallopᵈ Jars 3 Large Pieces of the Crimson Service at 2/3d. each.
	Polishing only
	4 Row Waggons at 9d. each 2 small perfume pots 1/6d. each 2 Jonquill Jars 1/9d. each 1 Egg Shape Jar 2/- 1 small Jar 4d.'
30 April	Receipt from Richard Askew for £2. 2s. 0d. for '2 Perfume Pots in figuars and 2 Row Wagon in figuars'.
24–31 August	'96 Thimbles Painted Overtime by Boarman 12/-'
14–21 December	'72 Seals painted Overtime'
22–29 February 1772	Receipt by Richard Barton on behalf of

Receipt by Richard Barton on behalf of

'Boreman	7¾ days at 5s. 3d.
Wollams	6½ days at 4s. 6d.
Jenks	8 days at 3s. 6d.
Snowdon	8 days at 3s. 6d.
Boyer	8 days at 3s. 6d.
Barton	6 days at 3s. 6d.
Roberts	2 days at 2s. 6d.'

6–13 January 1773	'Boreman, Wollams, Jenks, Snowdon, Boyer, Barton and Roberts 24 Double Doves Snuff Boxes painted overtime at 1/2d. each'
19–26 June	'Gauron 5¾ days at 8/9d.

      (also Boreman and others as above)

Bottles Smell

    2 Boys catching a Squirrel at 1/3d.

    2 Birds nest at 1/- each

    1 Double Dove

Mottoeing 60 Seals at 1¼d. each.'

7. DUESBURY (DERBY) ACCOUNT BOOKS

Day Book

1787

April 16	2 Asparagus Servers blue	1s.	0d.
19	4 Tomtits	4s.	0d.
	4 Goldfinches	4s.	0d.
	1 Season Groupe	16s.	0d.
24	4 Small Tritons	12s.	0d.
	4 Sea Nymphs	12s.	0d.
	4 Syrons with Shells	12s.	0d.
	4 Boys riding on a Sea Lion	16s.	0d.
	4 Boys riding on Dolphins	14s.	0d.
	4 Boys riding on Swans	14s.	0d.
	2 Boys riding on Seahorses	9s.	0d.
27	Sold Mr. James Duesbury—6 Neptunes' heads	£1. 16s.	0d.
May 3	1 pair duck Sauce boats white and gold	6s.	0d.
9	6 Squirels	6s.	0d.
15	10 Knife handles enamelled Green Leafage and Gilt	£1. 0s.	0d.
	Paid The Duke of Bedford 1 years' Rent due at Christmas	£68. 3s.	3d.
	1 pair Monteths enamelled blue and gold	£4. 14s.	0d.
16	6 Ice Cream Cups enamelled blue and gold	£1. 10s.	0d.
	Paid Mr. Boyce— Land Tax 1 year	£26. 5s.	0d.

Window Tax 1 year	£6. 7s. 0d.
House Tax 1 year	£7. 10s. 0d.
Commutation 1 year	£7. 10s. 0d.
Shop 1 year	£15. 0s. 0d.
Female Servant	2s. 6d.
	£62. 14s. 6d.

17	1 Asparagus Server blue and white	8d.
18	*The Prince of Wales*...Mending 2 Ice Pails	3s. 0d.
18	A Pint Mug with Glass Bottom	8s. 0d.
21	Sold Lady Fordyce—	
	1 white slop basin⎫ A panel of colours⎭	3s. 0d.
	12 Egg Spoons blue and white	8s. 0d.
	6 Hartichoke Cups blue and white	3s. 0d.
	1 pair potting pots blue and white	6s. 0d.
23	1 Sugar box blue and gold pattern 69	10s. 0d.
	1 pair of Butter Tubs Covers and Stands	12s. 0d.
	6 Egg Cups blue and white	6s. 0d.
29	Sold Lord Grey de Wilton—	
	6 Cups and Saucers of the Salopian Ware blue and white	£1. 0s. 0d.
31	1 pair of Groups—	
	Cephalus and Procis⎫ Rinaldo and Armida⎭	£2. 2s. 0d.
	Tythe Pig Groupe	15s. 0d.
	6 Birds	6s. 0d.
June 4	1 Pair large Duck boats white and gold	6s. 0d.
	1 Pair Neptunes Heads	12s. 0d.
	1 Pair Foxes Heads	10s. 0d.
4	2 Small Muffiners white and gold	3s. 0d.
	2 Eggs in biscuit	2s. 0d.
	3 Pint basins blue and white	3s. 6d.
	3 Half Pint basins blue and white	2s. 6d.
	2 Small jugs enamelled fine blue and white	£1. 4s. 0d.

	1 Slop basin enamelled fine blue and white	3s. 6d.
	1 Fish head	5s. 0d.
July 25	6 Old Cabbage Leaves blue and gold	£2. 2s. 0d.
16	Returned to Derby—	
	50 dozen Seals	£15. 0s. 0d.
	40 dozen Trinkets	£12. 0s. 0d.
27	*Credit* Messrs. Flight and Co. For 12 Worcester Coffee Cups Enamd. fine blue and gold to match	£1. 16s. 0d.
30	*Sold* Lord Aylesbury 12 Coffee Cups—Enamd. fine blue and gold to match the pattern returned (Worcester ware)	£2. 8s. 0d.
August 2	4 Large Size Egg Spoons white and gold	14s. 0d.
December 10	Toy Cream Jug blue and white	3d.
	6 Cups and Saucers Pattern No. 18 blue and white	18s. 0d.
	4 Small pickle leaves blue and white	1s. 8d.
	2 Large pickle leaves blue and white	1s. 6d.

1788

January 19	1 dozen small patty pans blue and white	6s. 0d.
	4 Egg Spoons blue and white	2s. 0d.
	2 blue and white saucers	1s. 0d.
	2 small vine leaves blue and white	10d.

1794

June 27	Received of Mr. Lygo Four pounds for Salopian China Bought at Public Sale for Thos. Turner	£ 4. 0s. 0d.

(signed) James Shaw[1]

[1] James Shaw was in charge of Thomas Turner's London Warehouse in Portugal Street. It was called The Salopian China Warehouse and was opened by Thomas Turner, proprietor of the China factory at Caughley, in Shropshire, in 1783. The premises later passed to Spode & Copeland.

1795

March 28   Bill from Grace and Freeman, Indigo Makers, Aldermanbury, Postern London for Smalts

1788

December 22   Joseph Doe for lost time in his apprenticeship   £3. 8s. 1d.

Goods Sent from Derby[1]

1788	£5689
1789	£5863
1790	£5737
1791	£5012
1792	£5383
1793	£5740

Gold Purchased

1781	72 ozs.	
1782	66 ozs.	
1783	66 ozs.	
1784	68 ozs.	
1785	90 ozs.	
1786	125 ozs.	
1787	156 ozs.	
1788	156 ozs.	£686. 8s. 0d.
1789	150 ozs.	
1790	156 ozs.	£686. 8s. 0d.
1791	156 ozs.	£686. 8s. 0d.
1792	192 ozs.	£844. 16s. 0d.
1793	222 ozs.	£976. 16s. 0d.

8. LONDON ACCOUNT BOOKS

10 June 1786   'Paid Mr. Middiman for 2 numbers of the latest Views of Great Britain[2]   8s. 0d.'

27th September 1786   'Sold Mr. McCarty, Cork A Large Center Vause No. 86 enam[d] with a subject of Cupid disam[d] by Euphrosine to a landscape in Compartments richly ornamented with fine blue and gold

[1] Presumably goods sent to London.
[2] *Middiman's Views* provided the source of some landscape decoration on Derby porcelain.

Stripes etc. 1 pair of Side pieces to Correspond Enam^d in Compartments with a figure of Flora and a Muse and Landscapes. £30. 9s. 0d.'

17th February 1787 'Sold Lord Scarsdale

1 pair Vauses No. 67 Enam^d with figures Flora and a Muse a View in Kedleston Park of the front and back part, of the House and richly ornamented with fine Chas^d and Burnished Gold Stripes etc.'

27th February 1787 'Paid Mr. Hattam for Yellow Enamel £2. 2s. 10d.'

7th July 1786 'Sold Thos. Johnes Esq., Haford near Hereford, to be left at the Castle Inn, Landovey 4 Dozen Table Plates white and gold £14. 14s. 0d.'

5th January 1787 'Mr. Vulliamy

3 Large Timepiece figures richly gilt.'

B. THE BEMROSE COLLECTION OF DOCUMENTS AT THE BRITISH MUSEUM

Apart from the large collection of manuscripts at the Derby Public Library there is also a large quantity at the British Museum, Department of Mediaeval and Later Antiquities, formerly in the Bemrose Collection. It includes a number of old deeds which were invaluable in establishing the site of the first manufacture of porcelain at Derby, seventeen Account Books, from 1795 to 1819, and a great number of documents dealing with the disputes and troubles that beset the factory after the death of William Duesbury II, in particular that between the Duesbury family and Michael Kean as to the ownership of certain assets.[1] These papers also throw further light on Robert Bloor's acquisition of the works, of especial interest being a 'List of Models purchased by Robert Bloor which belonged to the Estate of the late Mr. Duesbury and which have not been used since his death'; this list is certified by Francis Hardenburg who was employed at the factory.

[1] Much of the content of these papers was included in Barrett, 'The Derby China Factory Sites on Nottingham Road', *E.C.C. Trans.*, 1959, vol. 4, part 5, pp. 26–44. See also p. 55.

APPENDIX V: MANUSCRIPT DOCUMENTS

C. VICTORIA AND ALBERT MUSEUM DOCUMENTS RELATING TO THE DERBY CHINA FACTORY

Further letters of Joseph Lygo, London Agent, some of which have been referred to in the text, are also in the Victoria and Albert Museum Collections.

D. ADVERTISEMENT DERBY MERCURY MAY 19TH 1814

VALUABLE CHINA

To be sold by Auction By Mr. Cross.

In the large Warehouse at the Porcelain Manufactory, Derby, on Monday May 23rd, 1814 and Thirty following Days. (Sundays excepted).

THE FIRST PART

of the extensive STOCK of Messrs. Robert Bloore and Co. of the above Manufactory.

Consisting of Dinner, Dessert, Breakfast, Tea and Coffee Services, Cabinet and Chimney Ornaments &c. &c. superbly decorated in flowers, figures, landscapes &c. Groups and Single Figures in biscuit, together with Five Thousand Sets of White China in useful and ornamental Articles, some large Plaster figures and Casts &c. &c. which will positively be sold without the least Reserve.

APPENDIX VI

CHELSEA—DERBY SALE CATALOGUES

In 1881 J. E. Nightingale, F.S.A., published his unique *Contributions towards the History of Early English Porcelain from Contemporary Sources*, a large part of which consists of the reprinting of a series of sale notices and sale catalogues relating to the products of the chief English manufactories, including those of Derby, mainly of the Chelsea-Derby period. Although the *Contributions* is perhaps not readily obtainable today, considerations of space do not permit, however desirable, the reproduction here of all the details relating to Derby. However, a summary is given .

1. Advertisements of the early sales, that is prior to the Chelsea-Derby period, have already been quoted and commented upon. The first of a long series of sales of 'Chelsea and Derby' porcelain recorded by Nightingale was that which commenced on 17th April 1771 and continued during the three following days. The catalogue together with the price of each lot, is reprinted by Nightingale *in toto*, but it is not possible, particularly in the case of wares other than figures, to be sure which were of Duesbury's manufacture and which were from the old Chelsea stock. Eighty-five Lots were sold on each of the four days, 340 Lots in all; many of the figures and groups were in biscuit porcelain, and it is of interest to note that several figures are described as 'Finely finished with lace'. The representation of lace in porcelain became very popular in later years and was effected by dipping actual lace in the 'slip' and attaching the same to the figure prior to firing; the lace burns away in the kiln, leaving in porcelain a facsimile of its texture.

Amongst the items in this sale may be noted the following:

	Possible identification in Haslem Price List
Description in Sale Catalogue	
'Group of the Virtues, with Minerva crowning Constancy with a garland of flowers and Hercules killing the Hydra.'	1

	Possible identification in Haslem Price List
Description in Sale Catalogue	

Note: This group, together with a variation 'with a pyramid in the middle' occurs no fewer than 17 times (14 in biscuit); the amounts fetched vary between £5 and £7.

'Set of Antique Seasons on pedestals.'   5

Note: This model or set of models is also mentioned 17 times; twice enamelled in colours the rest in biscuit.

'Set of Small French Seasons.'   6 (or 35?)

'Pair of figures, Gardener and Companion.'   7

'A gentleman playing on the flute and a lady singing, most curiously finished with lace in biscuit.'   9

'Pair of sitting figures, elegantly decorated with fruit and flowers and most curiously worked with lace.'   8 (or 20?)

'Two pair Bacchus and Cupid riding on a goat and panther on pedestal.'   13

Note: Mentioned many times in the early catalogues.

'Two curious figures, Prudence and Discretion with antique urns on pedestals.'

Note: Mentioned 'in biscuit' and 'in festoons of chased gold and highly finished in burnish'd gold.'   15

'Dresden Shepherd richly enamelled in flowers and elegantly finished in burnish'd gold.'   55

Note: Mentioned 8 times, all in colours and gilt, and in two sizes, 'large' and 'small'. There is also a similar subject described 'Dresden Shepherd, small, with lamb and dog'.

Description in Sale Catalogue	Possible identification in Haslem Price List
'Welch Taylor and family riding on goats, elegantly finished in flowers and burnish'd gold.'	
Note: A copy of a Meissen model (see p. 55), this is presumably a re-issue from earlier moulds. It does not appear to have been offered in biscuit.	
'Pair of Sitting figures, gentleman reading and lady knotting, most curiously ornamented with lace.'	
Note: This may be the original version of the well-known and common nineteenth century figures mounted on circular pierced base.	314(?)
'Cupid and Flora chandeliers richly finished in colours and burnished gold.'	
'Two figures with an altar piece.'	

Among the services and decorative pieces offered at this sale were a number of large and lavishly ornamented items and it is surprising that so few of these are known today.[1] The following selection is given here in the hope that it will encourage collectors to look out for them and help in their indentification. The most numerous group, and from the prices fetched the most sought after, were described as 'jars'. Lest it should be concluded that these are what we should now call 'vases', it should be stated that the latter term was used concurrently, so that it is logical to infer a distinction. The former may well have been used to refer to the basically cylindrical forms (however elaborately embellished and decorated) while the latter denoted the more elaborate shapes.

'Set three pieces, of fluted jars enamel'd in flowers, fine seagreen ground, handles richly ornamented in gold and a gold dentil edge.'

---

[1] In case it may be concluded that the specimens described, with their fine coloured grounds, must necessarily be of Chelsea origin rather than Derby, note the similar productions in the London Warehouse Catalogue of 1774 (p. 166); see also *English Porcelain*, Plate 7B, already referred to (p. 34).

'Fine antique jar, with the much admired mazarine blue ground, and compartments enamel'd, most elegantly finished with burnish'd and chas'd gold.'

Note: This fetched £11. 0s. 6d. which may be compared to a complete tea and coffee equipage, 49 pieces, which went for 7 gns.

'A large antique jar with fine blue celeste and pompadour ground, most superbly finish'd with burnish'd and chased gold and embossed festoons.' (£12. 1s. 6d.)

'A curious egg-shaped jar, finely enamelled with a matron feeding her children, richly ornamented with festoons of chased gold flowers and highly finished in burnish'd gold.' (£26. 5s. 0d.)

'A large egg-shape jar painted in compartment with a woman learning her boy to play on the cymbal, a fine pea-green ground and richly ornamented in gold.'

'A fine rich fluted bottle with a fine mazarine blue ground and highly finished in burnish'd gold.'

'A pair of large scallop'd jars with curious handles enriched with burnish'd gold and finely enamelled in compartments with Aeneas and Dido and richly ornamented with a chas'd gold frame of bullrushes.'

'Two curious small perfume pots of the fine pompadour ground enamel'd in compartment in figures with the story of Circe poisoning the water and Glaucus and Sylla on the other, finely decorated with burnished gold.'

'A pair of Chelsea jars, with a fine pea-green ground, curiously enamell'd in compartments, with the story of Jupiter and Leda and elegantly finished with burnish'd gold.'

'A pair of antique jars with goats heads, a fine pea-green ground highly finished with burnished gold, on pedestals.'

'Two curious square jars, for perfume, with the heads of the four seasons, finely enamel'd with pastoral figures and flowers, in compartments, a fine claret colour ground and richly finished with burnished gold.'

'Two large antique jars in compartments painted in Cupids after Busha (sic) and fine pompadour ground, most superbly finished in burnished and chased gold.' (£44)

'Pair of small heart shape jars, enamel'd in flowers and richly ornamented with burnished and chased gold.'

'Fine oval jar, with a fine crimson ground, in compartments enamel'd with figures of Venus and Adonis, gold flowers chased and richly ornamented with burnished gold.'

'Two small perfume vases finely enriched with burnish'd gold, most curiously painted in Cupids and flowers and a fine mosaic ground.'

'Two curious antique beakers of the fine mazarin blue ground, elegantly painted, the triumph of Bacchus, highly finish'd with burnished and chased gold.' (£21)

'Two small jars for perfume of the much admired mazarine blue and gold finely painted in figures, with the nymph Hysperia flying from her lover treads on a serpent and is stung to death; the other Thetis and Proteus.'

'Two curious antique jars with a fine crimson ground, embost festoons with green and gold curtains, superbly finish'd with burnish'd and chased gold.' (£36)

Note: Two similar described 'with the head of a river god.'

'A curious large egg-shape jar enamell'd with the story of Circe poisoning the water that Celia had bathed in, most curiously chased with festoons of gold flowers on a crimson ground.'

'Curious antique jar, with the story of Vertumnus and Pomona from Ovid's Metamorphoses, with a curious gold gadroon frame and entwined with ribbands and garlands of chased gold flowers on a crimson ground.'

'Two Junquil jars, with crimson ground, in two compartments curiously painted with figures, after, Tenier, finely ornamented with burnish'd and chas'd gold.'

'A capital and superb pot pouret and pedestal, curiously enamell'd in figures of a Dutch family after Tenier with landscapes and figures in six compartments, elegantly fine, enriched with chased gold flowers and highly finished in burnish'd gold.' (£63)

'A most grand and magnificent large essence jar finely enamel'd with the story of AENEAS sacrificing to Apollo at Cuma, with landscape and figures highly finished and most curiously chased with festoons of gold flowers enriched with burnished gold, on the much admired crimson ground—a remarkable fine piece.'

Note: This, bought by a Mr. Jones for £85, was the highest price reached in the four days' sale which included complete services.

2. In the next and subsequent sales, Nightingale does not print the whole catalogue, but extracts only are given. The sale 'of last year's Produce of the Derby and Chelsea Porcelaine Manufactories' in 1773 was conducted in two parts, the first on 8th and 10th February the second on 29th, 30th and 31st March. Among the items offered were the following:

Description in Sale Catalogue	Possible identification in Haslem Price List
'Two groups of the elements, Earth and Air, finely modelled in biscuit.'	3 (48)
'Two groups of the elements, Fire and Water of the same beauty and elegance.'	
Note: There is another model no. 86 in the Price List desribed as *Element Groups* and the above may refer to these.	
'Pastoral Group with antique urn.'	12
'Pair of Sacrifice, finely modeled in biscuit.'	14
'Pair of dancing groups.'	16? 46?
'A fine figure of Garrick in the character of Richard III, in biscuit.'	21
'A pair of figures, Shakespeare and Milton, enamelled and ornamented with gold.,	
'Four muses, Euterpe, Polyhymnia, Thalia and Urania finely modelled in biscuit.'	25–34
'Apollo and 4 muses, Terpsichore, Erato, Clio and Polyhymnia, finely modelled in biscuit.'	
'A large group, Jason and Medea, vowing before the altar of Diana, enamelled and richly finished with gold.'	37
'Two groups Poetry and Grammar, finely modelled in biscuit; two groups Music and Painting and Sculpture, finely modelled in biscuit; two groups of the arts and sciences, viz. painting and sculpture and astronomy in biscuit.'	39–45

APPENDIX VI: SALE CATALOGUES

Description in Sale Catalogue	Possible identification in Halsem Price List
'Pair of elegant groups, Poetry and Music on pedestals in biscuit.'	
'Sitting figures with dog and cat with lace.'	49 (71?)
'A pair of figures enamelled, viz. a sportsman and his companion with his dog and gun.'	50
'Pair of laughing figures dressing a macaroni dog white and gold.'	85? 91?
'Pair of figures, sitting, gentleman singing, lady playing on guitar, with lace.'	
'Bust of Voltaire.'	
'French Horn figures.'	
'Hussar and companion.'	

At this sale in 1773 there were again offered a number of large and lavishly decorated pieces which included, as in the first sale, many 'jars' which commanded higher prices than any other items. Very few are known to-day and the following selection may prove an aid and a spur to their discovery:

'A pair of card toilet bottles (spade) (Plate 115) enamelled with fine pea-green and crimson and richly finished with gold.'

Note: Nightingale gives the following information: 'These card-shaped bottles were not large but bizarre in form. The only decoration consisted of a coloured representation of a court card with mask handles in relief'. At a sale at Christie's in 1869 two pairs sold for £100 each pair.

A number of pieces were mounted on pedestals:

'A curious antique jar and pedestal, a fine crimson ground, white and gold curtains, mostly richly finished in gold.'

'A large griffin jar and pedestal with a fine crimson ground superbly finished in gold.' (18 gns)

'A pair of Sphinx jars and pedestals.'

'A pair of ice pails, finely enamelled in Cupids after Boucher in a chased gold frame and fine blue celeste bullrushes.'

'A pair of curious tripods enamelled with a fine jet ground.'

'An altar dedicated to Bacchus, enamelled in figures, a fine crimson ground and superbly decorated with gold.'

'A pair of caudle-cups, covers and stands finely enamelled in compartments with antique jars and crimson and gold curtains.'

'A pair of row waggon bottles, finely enamelled in birds and flowers.'

'Four vine-leaves enamelled in flowers and fine mazarine, blue and gold.'

'A pair of chandelier jars, fine pea-green ground.'

3. THE 1774 TRADE CATALOGUE

In 1773, Duesbury opened a 'commodious Warehouse in Bedford Street, Covent Garden' and in 1774 instead of an auction sale at Christie's he issued a catalogue which was divided into 'The Ornamental Part' and 'The Useful Part' and Bemrose[1] quotes in full the ornamental wares, many of which were large and elaborately decorated pieces and must have been among the most important to have been made by the factory at that time. The following is a selection:

'A set of three vases of crimson ground richly ornamented in white blue and gold; the center vase is of cup form, hung with an oak leaved gilt festoon, supported by two lions faces; two white and gold dragons form its anses[2] and support two festoons, twisting their tails round the under one and holding the upper one of white flowers with their snouts. The cover, with its turban shaped rim is surmounted with an open winged white eagle, it stands on a rich pedestal with four angular couched white griffins, gilt bills, claws and festoon, height of cup and pedestal 16½ ins. The two side vases scallop'd and double festoon'd in gold and white, with four white masks and candle socket tops and surmounted by two corresponding golden sphynxes standing on a matching pedestal, four white foliated masks in the base corners. Height 13½ ins.'

'A long necked sky-blue and gold vase with two twisted gold and white handles adorned with two heart shaped cartouches representing a bouquet of coloured flowers and the fable of Glaucus. Height 14¾ ins.'

[1] W. Bemrose, *Bow, Chelsea and Derby Porcelain*, pp. 52–67.
[2] Anses = two handles.

'A pair of crimson and gold four sided and four legged rich jars edged with a white and gold foliage topped with a white and gold basket-work surmounted with a small coloured bunch of flowers, the four sides representing alternately in colours, groups of flowers, birds, Silenus and Bacchus. Height 13¾ ins.'

'A pair of blue celeste gold edged onion shaped vases with three gold rings and a pierced cover on a tripod with three goats heads and feet in white, flesh colour and gold, from the base of the tripod round a pine arises the Pythian snake. Height 9½ ins.'

'A set of chalices, of three pieces, the center-piece of a trilateral form represents in its three compartments coloured sacred subjects on a white ground; the corners and pediments are sky blue edged in gold, with golden festoons etc.; the top is adorned with three rams heads in gold, three gold lions couched on the pedestal support the whole. Height 11½ ins. The two side pieces of a truncated conical form adorned in the same manner represent three other sacred subjects. Height 9½ ins.'

'A pair of crimson coloured candle Vases with white and gold edge masks and drapery festoons tied with sea-green knots answering the base slabs crowned with a gold edged pine button and corresponding nossels and adorned with white rims, gold festooned edges and white and gold friezes. Height 8 and 9 ins.'

'A mazarin deep blue urn-vase, onion shaped richly ornamented with a white and gold foliated rim, hung with a gold festoon connected with two goats heads and forming two anses above them; white and gold pedestal corresponding. Height 10 ins.'

'A pair of globular skie-blue claw-footed and goat headed tripods with white and gold borders, foliages and top buttons, the covers perforated, fixed to round gold edged pedestals. Height 10 ins.'

'A set of three white long jars with white, blue and gold foliage handles and an open worked white blue and gold bell-cover, the sides painted in enamel in birds and flowring shrubs. Height 13½ and 12½ ins.'

'A pair of cup-formed agate coloured vases with two gilt goats head handles, from the horns of which hangs a white and gold festoon; the white and gold edged neck and cover pierced with long apertures topped with an agate button; the bottom and pediment white and gold fixed to a square gilt slab. Height 7 ins.'

'A pair of pear shaped wide mouthed beakers (amphoras) white and crimson edged with gold, the body adorned with gold framed antique heads imitating white marble medallions, surrounded with laurel wreaths. Height 6½ ins.'

'A sea-green white spotted ground flask vase with white and gold foliage handles; two round cartouches with a coloured bouquet and a Savoyarde teaching her boy to play the viol. Height 13½ ins.'

'A pair of mazarine blue cup formed urns hung with a white drapery, their elongated white necks adorned with blue gold-edged twisted furrows, the top rim with gold nobs is supported by two lions heads, holding a laurel festoon in gold. Height 19 ins.'

'A large beaker sky-blue ground, spotted in white, two dolphins, lion footed standing on white goats heads from the two anses in crimson and white, edged in gold, the mouth of the beaker and the top of the vase are furrowed with twisted crenures in white and gold; the zone of the top is adorned with golden turned towards white and gold masks. The rim of the cup part is a foliated and crenulated friese; round the body of the vase are 8 gold framed heads in chiaroscuro imitating antique cameos-suspended to a festoon in gold with detached pateras; the pediment striped in gold in alternate triangles; the foot covered with gilt leaves, the pedestal has four white sphynxes. Height of the whole with pedestals 20 ins.'

'A very rich pair of beakers or open-mouthed egg-shaped vases (similar in size and form to the last) in a gold veined mazarine blue or lapis lazuli ground, the embossed goats heads lion and mask entirely gold as well as the festoons and the bases of the pediments fixed on a square slab of corresponding lapis lazuli. The body of the vase too rich to receive any additional ornament from medallions etc. no pedestals. Height 16½ ins.'

'A white gallon cask gold-edged hoops adorned with 4 tropies of musick emblems of love, in chiaroscuro surmounted with a young coloured Bacchus seated on the bung, tasting a grape of which he holds a basket full between his legs and a cup in his left hand, the barrel is made to turn round on a pivot fixed in an ormolu pediment, a satyr's mask holds an ormolu cock in his mouth which opens and shuts by a spring. Height 18 ins.'

4. The next catalogue reproduced by Nightingale was for 18th and 19th February 1778 and according to the title page consisted of 'part of the remaining stock of the Chelsea Porcelaine manufactory'.

The items detailed include a large proportion of table and similar wares, many of which were probably Chelsea. Of figures, there are a number in biscuit which must be of Duesbury manufacture.

5. On 5th, 6th and 7th May in the same year, a further sale of Chelsea stock ('The Remainder') took place including a number of vases and table-wares, as well as figures both in enamel and biscuit. Notable among the figures is one of 'His Majesty in a Vandyke dress on a blue and gold basement, supported by four lions leaning on an altar richly ornamented in blue and gold, with hanging trophies the crown, munde and sceptre reposing on a cushion of crimson, and a glass shade for ditto £31. 10s. 0d.' Nightingale comments that a similar figure bearing the Chelsea-Derby mark, was sold at Christie's in 1875 and that it was included in Duesbury's Trade Catalogue for 1773.[1] The figure was modelled after a group of *The Royal Family* painted by Zoffany in 1770 of which the remaining characters were also modelled by Duesbury.

Description in Sale Catalogue	Possible identification in Haslem Price List
'Pair of griffin candlesticks, blue and gold.'	53
'One group of a galantee-show and one ditto playing at hazard, in biscuit.'	93, 94
'Pair of figures, Madona and prudent mother, in biscuit.'	138
'Pair of boys riding on dolphin and swan.'	142, 143
'Pair of figures, Bacchus and Ariadne.'	193, 194
'Set of Grotesque Seasons.'	47
'Hercules and Minerva.'	121, 122
'Large Music Group in biscuit.'	179
'Two Bacchantes dressing Pan with a garland of flowers, in biscuit.'	196
'Pair of Harlequins and Columbine.'	199
'Pair of sitting religious figures.'	

[1] The Trade Catalogue was more likely published in 1774.

169

Description in Sale Catalogue	Possible identification in Haslem Price List
'Figure of Christ.'	
'Four pairs of Sea-faring figures.'	
'Pair of figures Neptune and Amphitrite drawn by 3 sea-horses in biscuit.'	
'Pair of busts, Horace and Chaucer.'	

6. Yet another sale of the 'Remainder of the valuable Stock of the Chelsea Porcelaine Manufactory' took place at Christie's on 5th, 6th, 7th and 9th May 1779. Much if not all was of Chelsea-Derby manufacture.

Description in Sale Catalogue	Possible identification in Haslem Price List
'Pair of groups, Shoemaker and stocking mender in biscuit.'	77, 78
'Figure of Mrs. Macauley, in biscuit.'	88
'A group of Madona and Child.'	137
'A pair of Aesculapius and Hygaea.'	99
'One set of the quarters (Continents).'	200
'Britannia.'	259
'One small Falstaff.'	

Note: The great majority of figures of this model are nineteenth century examples; Chelsea-Derby figures would appear to be extremely rare.

'A figure of Mr. Garrick in biscuit.'

Note: Presumably the actor in the familiar character of Richard III, first issued in 1773.

'A pair of bust, Addison and Virgil.'

'Lambs and swans.'

APPENDIX VI: SALE CATALOGUES

An interesting item of table-ware is 'twenty-four knife handles, blue and white, 11s'. Although cutlery with porcelain handles is fairly frequently met with from Bow and Worcester, Derby specimens do not seem to have been identified.

7. On 17th, 18th, 19th and 20th April 1780 Christie's sold 'valuable produce of the Derby and Chelsea Manufactories'. From the extracts provided by Nightingale the following are of special interest:

Description in Sale Catalogue	Possible identification in Haslem Price List
'Large figure of Justice, sword and scales.'	54
'Andromache weeping over the ashes of Hector.'	100
'Large figure of Time and Cupid.'	124
'One figure of Time.'	222
'Portrait busts, Milton and Horace on gilt pedestals.'	
'Mars and Minerva.'	
'Pair of Deer.'	

Among the useful and decorative wares at this sale may be mentioned the following:

'Pair of Satyr's head drinking cups, blue and gold.'

'Pair of Neptune's head drinking cups.'

'Pair of large fox heads.'

'Twelve double-shape coffee cups, blue Nankin pattern.'

Note: An example of underglaze blue decoration, never common at the Derby factory (see p. 28–30).

'Etruscan shape vase, fine blue ground striped with gold, enamel'd with compartments with Shenstone the poet.'

'A altar-shape vase supported by 3 lions on a pedestal enamel'd in compartments with figures and richly gilt.'

'A beautiful dejune, enamel'd with Cupids and striped with gold.' (£2. 15s. 0d.)

Note: A 'dejune' is a cabaret set consisting of cup and saucer, cream jug, sugar bowl and teapot all on a tray. Nightingale records that a set of this design was sold at Christie's in 1876 for £66.

'Pair of elegant caudle-cups, covers and stands, peacock pattern, fine mazarin blue and gold.'

'Pair of elegant vases, enamel'd in compartments with figures and fine blue and gold, mounted with metal arms for six lights.'

8. Sales of 'Derby and Chelsea Porcelaine' became an annual event and Nightingale gives extracts from those held in 1781, 1782 and 1783 from which the following items are taken:

Description in Sale Catalogue	Possible identification in Haslem Price List
'3 Graces distressing Cupid.'	235
'Tragedy and Comedy, pair of large figures.'	260
'Large group 3 Graces, 2 Cupids suposed to be crowning her Majesty with garlands of flowers.'	
'Shooting Cupids.'	
'Shakespeare bust.'	
'Two Bacchus.'	
'Pair small foxes in biscuit.'	
'Pair of Haymakers.'	
'A set of elegant chimney ornaments consisting of Andromache, a set of antique seasons and 2 small figures.' (£2. 10s. 0d. Lady Cornwall)	

Note: This seems to be the only instance of a number of different models being sold together under the title 'chimney ornaments'.

APPENDIX VI: SALE CATALOGUES

Although the following models are mentioned for the first time in the catalogues of 1781–3 their correlation with Haslem's serial list would suggest that they had been first issued earlier:

Description in Sale Catalogue	Possible identification in Haslem Price List
'Dragon Candlestick.'	52
'Candlestick, Mars & Venus.'	114
'Andromache, Plenty, a pair.'	163
'Poetry group.'	217

The following is a selection of the useful and decorative wares offered at these sales:

'Pair basket work antique handle vases enamel'd with figures Pomona and Prudence on one side and landscape on the other.' (£14 Lord Monson)

'A large dove house ornamented with natural flowers and richly gilt.' (Colour Plate B)

'Pair of uncommonly large octagon jars (near 2 feet high) decorated with natural flowers, finely enamel'd with figures, landscapes etc. the figures represent votaries of Bacchus and Innocence washing her hands at an altar.' (£18. 18s. 0d. Lady Paget)

'Two pair duck sauce boats enamelled and brown edge.'

'Four salts, white and gold
Four salts, green and gold.'

'Pair foxes heads for drinking cups.'

'Two pairs of neat rummers enamel'd with flowers and fine blue and gold vine borders.' (12s. 6d.)

'Elegant large tray for different cheese and butter enamel'd with vauses and fine mazarin blue and gold.'

'Pair of large octagon salad dishes enamelled with flowers and festoons of red husks.'

'One pair hares heads, enamel'd and gilt.'

'Pair of beautiful lamps enamel'd with vases.'

173

'One pair montephs,[1] blue Chantilly pattern.'

'A large coffee-pot, blue Nankin pattern.'

'Set of 8 views in Windsor Park by Mr. Sandby, very fine impression in elegant green and gold frames.' (£9. 19s. 6d.)

Note: Brother of the better known Paul Sandby, Thomas published eight drawings illustrating his alterations and improvements in Windsor Park.

'Pair of elegant girandoles for 6 lights enamel'd in compartments with figures and blue and gold.'

'Six scallop shells, 6 asparagus servers and 6 artichoak cups, blue and white.' (7s. 0d. Dr. Johnson)

'Seven Chelsea compoteers enamell'd Dresden pattern and brown edge.' (£1. 9s. 0d. Dr. Johnson)

'A beautiful large punch bowl enamell'd with groups of coloured flowers and fine blue and gold borders.' (18s. 0d. Dr. Johnson)

'A superb and elegant cabinet cup and saucer enamell'd in compartments with landscapes, fine ultramarine blue ground finished with chased and burnished gold.' (£1. 18s. 0d. Dr. Johnson)

Note: Although it is known that Dr. Johnson took a great interest in the manufacture of porcelain Boswell quotes his complaint that it was too dear and that he could have vessels of silver of the same size as cheap as those in porcelain. His complaint hardly seems to be borne out in the case of the three lots purchased by him at the sale on 9th May 1783.

'A most capital large therm[2] vase richly painted in compartments with figures of Celadon and Armelia and one pair of ewer shaped vases painted in compartments with a Shepherd's boy and girl with a bird cage.' (£16. 16s. 0d.)

'Two large white shells.' (18s. 0d.)

'Four large vases representing the four seasons, in biscuit.' (10s. 6d. Lygo)

Note: Lygo was Duesbury's London agent; perhaps this means they were bought in.

[1] Probably a mistake for 'monteiths'.

[2] 'Therm' here has no connection with heat but is a corruption of the god Hermes, of whom portrait busts were often displayed on pedestals of inverted pyramid shape, and this corruption of the name of the god was used to denote a similarly shaped vase. An alternative derivation is from the Roman name of the same god, 'Terminus'.

9. In 1783 Duesbury ceased to manufacture porcelain at the old Chelsea Factory in 'Laurence Street, near the Church, Chelsea' and much of the equipment etc. was removed to Derby. That which was not taken up to the Midlands was offered for sale by auction 'on the Premises' on 11th, 12th and 13th December 1783 together with some of the stock of the porcelain, as well as a number of figures in 'artificial stone' and some of the moulds. Lygo was the purchaser of a number of the Lots offered.

10. The last sale of 'Derby and Chelsea Porcelain' took place on 17th May 1784 and five following days; few details are given of what must have been a large sale, but Nightingale remarks that a 'large proportion of the lots seems to have been bought in by Mr. Duesbury'.

11. Work at Chelsea having come to an end, Duesbury's annual sale in 1785 was advertised as 'Duesbury's Annual Catalogue of his DERBY Porcelain', the sale being a six day sale held on 23rd to 28th May. There would appear to have been very few if any new models of figures in this last sale and this position seems to have lasted until the arrival of Spengler in 1790 (see pp. 49, 104). There were, however, a considerable number of important items of useful and decorative wares and many of these still await identification. Amongst the most interesting and even tantalising items were the following:

'A beautiful gallon punch bowl enamelled fine ultramarine borders, highly enriched with pearls and burnished gold.'

'A punch barrell enamelled with oak leaves, acorns etc.'

'A very capital DESERT SERVICE highly enamel'd with landscapes of a pure self-colour and richly finished with borders in burnished gold.' (£26. 5s. 0d. Sir T. Wentworth)

'An elegant set of FIVE VASES, the centre one full 12 inches high, hath on one front a beautiful landscape and on another a figure of Sterne's Maria,[1] the two side pieces correspond, on one is represented a group of Damon and Delia, on the other a group of Paris and Oenone, and 2 ewer shaped vases to complete the set.'

'A Derbyshire milk pail and ladle and 6 egg cups, white and gold.'

[1] Joseph Wright of Derby, A.R.A. (1734–1797) painted a picture of *Maria*, the character in Sterne's novel *Sentimental Journey*. This may be copied from his picture, exhibited at the Royal Academy in 1781.

'Twelve coffee cans and saucers, enamel'd fine blue and white.'

'A beautiful model'd CENTRE VASE (about 9½ ins. high) decorated with fine ultramarine blue, enriched with chased and burnished gold, with one front a landscape and on the other a figure of UNA (vide Spenser's Faery Queen) together with TWO VASES finished to correspond the front one represents the Birth of Shakespeare, the front of the other Shakespear's Tomb admirably finished from those sublime composition of A. Kauffman; TWO EWER FORMED VASES to complete the set. The front of one represents an enamel of the Tamborine Boy, the front of the other the Cymbal Girl delicately finished from C. White's beautiful plates.' (£15. 15s. 0d.)

'A grand CENTRE VASE (16 ins. high) magnificently enriched with an ornamental ground of natural flowers inlaid with burnished gold and blue and gold pearl borders, on one front is displayed a Landscape and on the other is a fine enamel of Damon and Musidora from Thompson's Seasons to which is added 2 SIDE VASES about 10 ins. high and two antique ewer forms to complete the set each of which has one front figures representing the 4 periods of the day, MORNING from Shakespear's Cymbeline, NOON from Gray's Elegy in a country churchyard, EVENING from Shakespear's Twelfth Night and NIGHT from Shakespear's Merchant of Venice.' (£34. 13s. 0d.)

Note: Nightingale records 'a suite of five magnificent vases with blue and gold borders, the bowls enamell'd with flowers on a gold ground and painted with subjects in oval medallions—the centre vase with Celadon and Amelia, the two smaller ones with subjects from Shakespeare, the remaining pair, which were ewers, with figures of Damon and Musidora and all marked with the gold anchor'. These were sold in 1872 and fetched the astonishing price of £600.

The purchasers at all these London sales appear to have been largely dealers such as Morgan, and many members of the aristocracy; among the latter figure Lady Fitzwilliam, Lady Weymouth, Sir T. Wentworth, Lady Cornwall, Duchess of Portland, Duchess of Devonshire, Lord Percy, Lord Grimston, Lady Walpole, Lord Bessborough, the Imperial Ambassador, Lady Churchill and Lord Gore.

The 1785 sale, which was the first to be held after the closure of the Chelsea Works, was also the last of that series of auction sales and a letter[1] addressed to Mr. Duesbury Junior throws some light on the discontinuance of these periodical London sales:

[1] Quoted by Bemrose, *Bow, Chelsea and Derby Porcelain*, p. 50.

'Sir,

The gentlemen of the China Trade have directed me to inform you that your promising to discontinue your Spring Sales to the Nobility has met with their approbation. They have desired your acceptance of the thanks of the Society for the same and have unanimously agreed to assist the Derby Manufactory by forwarding the sale of its Manufacture; hoping at the same time Mr. Duesbury will never lose sight of the Interest of the Members of the China Society.

I am, Sir, your most obedient
humble servant,
WM. HEWSON

Aldgate, 19th Oct. 1785.'

APPENDIX VII

ARTICLES OF AGREEMENT

'ARTICLES OF AGREEMENT between John Heath of Derby in the County of Derby Gentleman Andrew Planche of ye same place China Maker & Wm. Duesberry of Longton in ye County of Stafford Enamellor. Made and enter'd into the 1st Jany 1756.

'FIRST IT IS AGREED by ye said John Heath Andrew Planche & Wm. Duesberry to be Copartners together as well in ye Art of making English China as also in buying and selling of all sorts of Wares belonging to ye Art of making China wch said Copartnership is to continue between them from the Date of these Presents for & during ye Term of Ten years from thence and then fully to be completed & ended And to that end He ye said John Heath hath ye day and ye date of these Presents deliver'd in as a Stock ye sum of One Thousand Pounds to be used & employ'd in Common between them for you caryying on ye sd Art of making China Wares And that one third share of Profits arising therefrom It is mutually agreed between all ye sd parties shall be receiv'd by & paid to ye said John Heath till ye said Prinl Sum of £1000 be paid in ALSO it is agreed between ye said parties to these Presents that ye sd Copartners shall not at any time hereafter use or follow ye Trade aforesaid or any other Trade what-soever during ye sd Term to their private Benefit and advantage. And also that ye sd Copartners shall during ye said Term pay and discharge equally and proportionably between them all expenses they shall be at in managing ye Art and Trade aforesaid And also that all Gain or Profit that shall arise from ye Art and Trade aforesaid during ye said Term shall be divided between them ye sd Copartners Share and Share alike And likewise that all such Losses as shall happen by bad Debts Ill Commodities or otherwise shall be borne equally between them AND it is further agreed by ye sd Parties that there shall be kept during ye sd Term Just and True Books of Accounts to wch sd Books any of ye sd Copartners shall have free access without Interruption of ye other AND it is further agreed that at any time hereafter at ye request of ye said John Heath New Articles shall be made & an additional Term of years not less than Ten shall be added with such alterations and additions as may be found necessary AND that ye said Copartners shall from time to time communicate to each other every Secret of ye said Art AND that ye said John Heath shall have it in his power to appoint any other Person to Act for him if he should chuse so to do wch Person shall be as fully impowered to Act with regard to all Covenants herein contained as ye sd John Heath himself. WITNESS OUR HANDS the Day & Year above written.'

The surviving copy of this agreement is unsigned and may, indeed, never have been executed. It is to be found amongst Jewitt's papers in the library of the Victoria and Albert Museum.

APPENDIX VIII

LIST OF GROUPS AND SINGLE FIGURES[1]

No.	Names of Figures and Groups.	Size.	Height, inches.
1	Group of the Virtues	1st	$11\frac{1}{2}$
	Ditto ditto	2nd	
3	The Elements, Stephan (Plate 125)	1st	
	Ditto	2nd	
	Ditto	3rd	$7\frac{1}{8}$
4	Pastoral Group		
5	Four Antique Seasons, in a Set	1st	8
	Ditto ditto	2nd	$6\frac{1}{2}$
	Ditto ditto	3rd	$4\frac{1}{8}$
6	Four Seasons, in a Set		4
7	Gardening	1st	$6\frac{3}{4}$
	Ditto	2nd	5
8	Fruit and Flowers		$5\frac{3}{8}$
9	Music	1st	$6\frac{1}{4}$
	Ditto	2nd	6
	Ditto	3rd	$4\frac{5}{8}$
10	Flute and Cymbal	1st	$6\frac{1}{4}$
	Ditto ditto	2nd	$5\frac{5}{8}$
	Ditto ditto	3rd	$4\frac{3}{4}$
11	Flute and Guitar		$6\frac{3}{8}$
12	Pastoral Group		$12\frac{1}{4}$
13	Cupid and Bacchus riding		7
14	Sacrifice Figures, Pair		
15	Small Prudence and Discretion, with Urns		$9\frac{1}{4}$
16	Dancing Group		$6\frac{5}{8}$
17	Ditto ditto (Plate 129)		$6\frac{5}{8}$

[1] Quoted from Haslem, op. cit., pp. 170–181, where it is called a Price List. However, as no indication is given as to when these prices, ranging from 7s. to 4gns., were current they seem to be of little value to historian or collector and are therefore omitted here. See also pp. 54–5, 113.

No.	Names of Figures and Groups.	Size.	Height, inches.
18 & 19	Names of Figures not given[1]		
20	Fruit and Flowers, Pair	1st	$6\frac{1}{4}$
	Ditto ditto ditto	2nd	$5\frac{3}{4}$
	Ditto ditto ditto	3rd	$4\frac{5}{8}$
21	Garrick as Richard III., Bacon		$9\frac{3}{4}$
22 & 23	Names not given[1]		
25 to 34	Ten Figures of Apollo and Muses, 5 in. in height, 5/3 each		
35	Four Seasons		6
36	Sitting Fruit		5
37	Jason and Medea	1st	
	Ditto ditto	2nd	$12\frac{3}{4}$
	Ditto ditto	3rd	
38	Prudence and Discretion		$5\frac{1}{2}$
39 to 45	Seven Groups of Arts and Sciences, various, at 16/- each, with Pedestals— 14/- without[1]		
46	Dancing Figures and Group		$5\frac{1}{2}$
47	Grotesque Seasons		$5\frac{1}{4}$
48	Elements in two Groups		$8\frac{3}{4}$
49	Cat and Dog Figures		$5\frac{3}{4}$
50	Sporting and Companion		$5\frac{5}{8}$
51	Cat and Dog Figures		5
52	Dragon Candlesticks		
53	Griffin ditto		
54	Justice		$9\frac{1}{2}$
55	Dresden Shepherd	1st	$9\frac{1}{4}$
	Ditto ditto	2nd	$8\frac{3}{4}$
56	Garland ditto	1st	$9\frac{3}{4}$
	Ditto ditto	2nd	9
	Ditto ditto	3rd	$7\frac{5}{8}$
	Ditto ditto	4th	$6\frac{3}{4}$
57	French Shepherds, Pair	1st	
	Ditto ditto	2nd	
	Ditto ditto	3rd	
	Ditto ditto	4th	
	Ditto ditto	5th	

[1] The following have been identified:
19 Child with basket of fruit.
23 Swiss Boy and Swiss Girl.
40 Music.
42 Painting and Sculpture.
43 Astronomy and Astrology.

No.	Names of Figures and Groups.	Size.	Height, inches.
57	French Shepherds, Pair	6th	
58	Piping Shepherd		
59	Set of Five Senses		$7\frac{1}{2}$
60	Singers	1st	
	Ditto	2nd	7
	Ditto	3rd	$5\frac{3}{8}$
61	Four Sitting Seasons	1st	
62	Welch Taylor and Family, large size		
	Ditto ditto small . .		$5\frac{1}{2}$
63	Small Turks		$3\frac{1}{2}$
64	Four Standing Seasons		$5\frac{1}{2}$
65	Diana	1st	
	Ditto	2nd	$8\frac{1}{2}$
66	Venus and Cupid		$6\frac{1}{2}$
67	Venus, Chelsea Model		
68	Group of Four Seasons . . .		$9\frac{1}{4}$
69	Sitting Flute Figures		
70	Figure of Christie		$12\frac{1}{8}$
71	Pair Sitting Figures, with Cat and Dog .		$5\frac{1}{2}$
72	Pastoral Group, with Goat . . .		$5\frac{3}{8}$
73	Ditto ditto with Dog . . .		$5\frac{3}{8}$
74	Dancing Group of two Figures . . .		$6\frac{1}{2}$
75	Group of Cephălus and Procris . . .		$8\frac{1}{2}$
76	Ditto of Renaldo and Armida . . .		$8\frac{1}{2}$
77	Stocking Mending		
78	Shoemaker, Group of two Figures . .		$5\frac{7}{8}$
79	Complimenting, Group of two ditto . .		$6\frac{3}{4}$
80	Spinning Group of two ditto . .		
81	Shoeblack Group of two ditto . .		
82	Fury Group, Broken Fiddle		
83	Ditto Broken Chair		
84	Ditto Hairdresser, two Figures . .		
85	Macaroni		
86	Set of Elements, in Groups of two Figures each		
87	Pair of Salutation Figures		$4\frac{3}{4}$
88	Mrs. Macaulay		
89	Fury Group, Family		
90	Cook and Companion		
91	Female Macaroni		
92	Three Figures learning Music		

No.	Names of Figures and Groups.	Size.	Height, inches.
93	Group of three Figures playing at Hazard .		6
94	Group of three Figures at a Raree Show (Plate 121)		6
95	Sphinx Candlestick		
96	Ditto of a Vase		
97	Griffin ditto		
98	Group of Prudence and Discretion . .		$11\frac{1}{2}$
99	Pair of Figures, Æsculapius and Hygeia .		$7\frac{1}{2}$
100	Andromache weeping over the ashes of Hector	1st	
101	Pair, Grotesque Boy and Girl . . .		$4\frac{1}{2}$
102 to 113	Twelve Figures of Nuns & Monks		
114	Pair of Figures, Mars and Venus . .		$6\frac{1}{4}$
115	Ditto ditto		
116	Apollo		$6\frac{3}{4}$
117 & 119	Pair of Figures, Jupiter & Juno .		$6\frac{1}{2}$
118	Neptune		$6\frac{3}{4}$
120	Diana		$6\frac{1}{2}$
121	Minerva		$6\frac{1}{2}$
122	Hercules		$6\frac{1}{4}$
123	Set of Seasons, from French . .	1st	
	Ditto ditto . . .	2nd	
	Ditto ditto . . .	3rd	
	Ditto ditto . . .	4th	$7\frac{1}{2}$
124	Time and Cupid (Plate 92) . . .	1st	
	Ditto ditto	2nd	
	Ditto ditto	3rd	$7\frac{3}{4}$
125	Set of four Chelsea standing Seasons . .	1st	$6\frac{3}{8}$
	Ditto ditto ditto . .	2nd	$6\frac{1}{4}$
	Ditto ditto ditto . .	3rd	$5\frac{1}{8}$
126	Wilkes		
127	Small Figures		
128 to 136	Nine Figures, names not given		
137	Madonna, a Group		$8\frac{1}{4}$
138	Prudent Mother, a Group . . .		$8\frac{1}{4}$
139	Music Group of two Figures . . .		$6\frac{1}{2}$
140	Ditto ditto ditto . . .		$6\frac{1}{2}$
141	Pair of Fighting Boys		$3\frac{1}{2}$
142 & 143	Pair of small Boys riding on Dolphin and Swan	1st	5 to $5\frac{1}{4}$
	Ditto ditto ditto	2nd	

No.	Names of Figures and Groups.	Size.	Height, inches.
142 & 143	Pair of small Boys riding on Dolphine and Swan	3rd	
144 to 158	Fifteen Figures, names not given		
159 & 160	Pair, Laughing and Crying Philosophers		$5\frac{3}{4}$
161	Antique Figure of Wisdom . . .	1st	$8\frac{1}{2}$
	Ditto ditto . . .	2nd	
162	Ditto of Justice . . .	1st	$8\frac{1}{2}$
	Ditto ditto . . .	2nd	
163	Antique Figure of Plenty	1st	$8\frac{1}{2}$
	Ditto ditto . . .	2nd	
164	Ditto of Peace	1st	$8\frac{1}{2}$
	Ditto ditto . . .	2nd	
165 to 174	Ten Figures, names not given		
175	Pair of Boy and Girl Figures . . .		4
176 to 178	Three Figures, names not given[1]		
179	Music Group of four Figures . . .		$13\frac{1}{4}$
180	Pair of Boys, Autumn and Spring		
181	Name not given		
182	Pair of Cupids riding on Bucks . . .		
183	Ditto Prudence and Discretion . .		
184	Ditto Boy and Girl Figures . . .		
185	Ditto Cupids riding on Swan and Dolphin .		
186 to 188	Three Figures, names not given		
189	Boy riding on Sea-horse		$4\frac{1}{4}$
190	Triton		$2\frac{3}{4}$
191 & 192	Names not given		
193 & 194	Pair, large Bacchus & Ariadne . .	1st	9
	Ditto ditto ditto .	2nd	$8\frac{1}{4}$
	Ditto ditto ditto .	3rd	$7\frac{1}{2}$
195	Group of two Virgins awaking Cupid . .		$12\frac{1}{2}$
196	Ditto of two Bacchantes adorning Pan . .		$12\frac{1}{2}$
197	Cupid riding on Sea-lion		$2\frac{3}{4}$
198	Pair of Haymakers		$6\frac{1}{2}$
199	Ditto Harlequin and Columbine . .		$5\frac{1}{2}$
200	Set of four Quarters of the Globe . .		6
	Ditto ditto ditto . .	2nd	$5\frac{1}{4}$
201 & 202	Pair of Cupids		4
203	Pair of Cupids, with Dog and Falcon . .		

[1] The following have been identified:
176 The Lovers (2).   177 The Lovers (2).

No.	Names of Figures and Groups.	Size.	Height, inches.
204	Pair of Gardeners		5
205 & 206	Pair of Cupids		$4\frac{1}{2}$
207	Sea Nymph riding on a Dolphin . .		$4\frac{1}{8}$
208	Ditto playing the Tabor . . .		3
209	Syren with a Shell		$2\frac{1}{2}$
210	Triton		3
211 & 212	Names not given		
213 & 214	Pair of Cupids, with Dog & Falcon .		$4\frac{3}{8}$
215	Name not given		
216 & 217	Pair, Groups, Music & Poetry . .	1st	$9\frac{3}{4}$
	Ditto ditto ditto . .	2nd	
	Ditto ditto ditto . .	3rd	
218 & 219	Names not given		
220	Pair Basket Figures	1st	$6\frac{1}{2}$
221	Ditto ditto	2nd	$5\frac{1}{4}$
222	Figure of Time		$6\frac{1}{2}$
223 to 226	Four Figures, names not given		
227	Pair Grotesque Punches (Plate 133) . .		7
228 to 230	Three Figures, names not given		
231	Large Falstaff		
232 & 233	Names not given		
234	Group of four Cupids		10
235	Group of Three Graces distressing Cupid .	1st	$14\frac{3}{4}$
	Ditto ditto ditto .	2nd	
236 & 237	Pair of Cupids		4
238	Name not given		
239	The Virgin Mary		$10\frac{1}{2}$
240	Pastoral Group of two Figures . .		$7\frac{3}{4}$
241 & 242	Names not given		
243	Apollo		$9\frac{1}{2}$
244	Plenty		$9\frac{3}{8}$
245	Peace		$9\frac{1}{4}$
246	Name not given		
247	Pastoral Group of two Figures . .		$12\frac{1}{4}$
248	Group of four Seasons, Antique . .		$11\frac{1}{8}$
249 & 250	Names not given		
251	Group of four Cupids . . .		9
252	Ditto of three ditto . . .		
253	Pair of Cupids, with Dog & Birdcage .		$3\frac{3}{4}$
254	Pastoral Group of two Figures . .		$13\frac{1}{4}$
255	Ditto ditto . .		12

No.	Names of Figures and Groups.	Size.	Height, inches.
256	Pasteral Group of two Figure . . .		$12\frac{1}{4}$
257	Group of four Cupids		$9\frac{3}{4}$
258	Pair Sitting Boy Candlesticks . . .		$6\frac{1}{2}$
259	Brittania	1st	
	Ditto	2nd	
	Ditto	3rd	
260	Crying Boy and Laughing Girl . . .	1st	
	Ditto ditto . . .	2nd	$7\frac{5}{8}$
261	No name		
262 to 278	Seventeen Figures of Cupid in Disguise		
279	No name[1]		
280	Pair Pipe and Guitar Candlesticks, with Ornamental Branches . . .		$8\frac{1}{2}$
	Ditto, with Chandelier Branches . .		$8\frac{1}{2}$
281	Pair Spring Candlesticks		$6\frac{1}{8}$
282	Ditto Small Fame and Mercury . .		$8\frac{1}{2}$
283	Ditto Gardener Candlesticks . .		$6\frac{7}{8}$
284	Ditto Pipe and Guitar ditto . .		$9\frac{1}{2}$
285	Ditto ditto ditto . .		8
286	No name		
287	Pair Garland Shepherd Candlesticks . .		$9\frac{1}{2}$
288	Ditto Mars and Venus ditto . .		8
289 & 290	Names not given		
291	Falstaff	1st	
	Ditto	2nd	
	Ditto	3rd	
	Ditto	4th	
	Ditto	5th	
292	Pair of Dessert Gardeners . . .	1st	
	Ditto ditto . . .	2nd	$4\frac{3}{8}$
293	Tythe Pig Group, three Figures . . .		7
294	Group of the four Seasons, with an Obelisk .		8
295	Ditto of the four Quarters of the Globe .		$10\frac{1}{8}$
296	Pair of Haymakers		$9\frac{1}{4}$
297	Milton		$10\frac{5}{8}$
298	Minerva	1st	
	Ditto	2nd	
	Ditto	3rd	

[1] This has been identified as a Pair of Candlestick Figures Shepherd and Shepherdess, in Sotheby Cat. 19 April 1966.

No.	Names of Figures and Groups.	Size.	Height, inches.
299	Neptune on Rock Pedestal . . .	1st	$9\frac{1}{4}$
	Ditto ditto	2nd	
300	Ditto without ditto		$5\frac{3}{8}$
301	Pair, Sitting Pipe and Guitar . . .	1st	
	Ditto ditto . . .	2nd	$6\frac{1}{4}$
	Ditto ditto . . .	3rd	$5\frac{3}{8}$
302	Ditto of Fame and Mercury . . .		
303	Ditto of Pipe and Tabor . . .	1st	
	Ditto ditto . . .	2nd	$6\frac{3}{8}$
304	No name		
305	Shakespeare		$10\frac{1}{2}$
306	No name		
307	Set of four Seasons, sitting . . .		$4\frac{5}{8}$
308	No name		
309	Music Group of four Figures, with an Obelisk		10
310	No name		
311	Pair, Pipe and Tabor Figures . . .		$8\frac{1}{4}$
312	No name		
313	Pair of Sitting Figures		$5\frac{3}{4}$
314	Ditto ditto		
315	Set of four Seasons, Sitting . . .		7
316	Pair, Sailor and his Lass	1st	
	Ditto ditto	2nd	
	Ditto ditto	3rd	
317	Ditto Dancing Figures		
318	Ditto ditto ditto		
319 to 321	Three Figures, names not given		
322	Pair, Hen and Chicken Candlesticks . .		$6\frac{1}{4}$
323	Ditto Cupid and Flora ditto . .		$8\frac{3}{4}$
324	No name		
325	Set of four Elements		$8\frac{3}{4}$
326	Pair of Singers	1st	
	Ditto ditto	2nd	
	Ditto ditto	3rd	
	Ditto ditto	4th	$5\frac{3}{4}$
327 to 330	Four Figures, names not given		
331	Pair of Candlesticks with Bird and Dog .		$11\frac{3}{4}$
332	Set of the four Quarters of the Globe . .	1st	
	Ditto ditto . .	2nd	
	Ditto ditto . .	3rd	
333	Group of four Boys		

No.	Names of Figures and Groups.	Size.	Height, inches.
354	Group of four Boys		
355 to 359	Twenty-five—Described as "Spangler's and Coffee's Figures and Groups," with no further particulars		
360	Johnny Wapstraw and Companion		
361	Pair, Gardener and ditto . .		
362	Ditto, Sitting Cat and Dog, William and Mary		
363	Ditto, Figures, with dead Bird . .		8
364	Group of Figures Waltzing . . .		6½
365	Pair of Dancing Figures		
366	Spanish Group		
367	No name		
368	Pair Dancing Figures		
369	Shepherd and Shepherdess . . .		
370	Belisarius and Daughter, Spangler . .		
371	No name		
372	Sailor and Lass		7½
373 to 377	Five Figures, names not given		
378	Pair, Scotchman and Lass, Coffee . .		
379 to 389	Eleven Figures, names not given. No. 384 is on a Statuette, probably of Lord Howe or Lord Hood, 12 inches in height; and 385 is on a Figure, probably of Hygeia, 10 inches[1]		
390	Group of Gaultherus and Griselda . .		

THE FOLLOWING ARE ALSO IN THE LIST BUT ARE NOT
NUMBERED

Pointer and Setter, per pair, Coffee	.	.	.		
Large Pug Dogs	ditto	ditto	.	.	.
Large ditto	ditto	ditto	.	.	.
Less ditto	ditto	ditto	.	.	.
Small ditto	ditto	ditto	.	.	.
Begging Pugs	ditto	Chelsea	.	.	
Ditto, French Dogs, do.	ditto	.	.	.	

[1] The following have been identified:
      380 3 female Figures—Poetry, Science, Art.
      388 4 Figures—Seasons.
      397 Cupid embracing Virgin.

APPENDIX VIII: HASLEM PRICE LIST

Names of Figures and Groups.			Size.	Height, inches.
Large Sheep and Lambs, per pair, Holmes	.		.	
Sheep lying down ditto	ditto	.	.	
Standing Sheep ditto	ditto	.	.	
Ditto ditto, two smaller sizes	ditto	.	.	
Lambs with Sprigs, per pair, Chelsea	.		.	
Ditto, without ditto each	ditto	.	.	
Canary Birds, each	ditto	.	.	
Tomtit ditto	ditto	.	.	
Linnet ditto	ditto	.	.	
Birds on Branches, two sizes	ditto	.	.	

THE FOLLOWING ARE FROM BOW AND CHELSEA MODELS

Large Stags, per pair

 Ditto, two smaller sizes

Large Sitting Cat

Cat lying down

 Ditto, with gold collar

Cow and Calf, per pair

 Ditto ditto, lying down

Large Swan

Two smaller sizes of same, 1/- & /10 each

Large Squirrel

Two smaller sizes of same, 1/- &/10 each

Large Boy—Four other sizes of the same were made, prices respectively 1/9, 1/6, 1/3, 1/-, &/10 each. This is a naked boy, standing with basket of flowers, usually white and gold

Satyrs' Heads, each

Small Neptune's Heads

Large Duck Boats, gold dontil edges

Small ditto ditto

Trouts' Heads, with mottoes—"Angler's Delight," &c.

 Ditto, two smaller sizes, 5/- & 3/6 each

Hares' Heads, each

Foxes' ditto ditto

 Ditto, two other sizes 4/- & 3/6 each

Mice, each

Poodle Dogs and Fleecy Sheep, each

Lowing Cow, each

189

Names of Figures and Groups.	Size.	Height, inches.
Sitting Foxes, per pair		
Pointers' Heads, each		
Tulip Egg Cups, each		
Inkstands, on Cats, &c., each		
Large Panthers		
Small ditto per pair		
Large Duck Boats, & several smaller do. . .		
Pigeon Boats		
Set of five Senses		
Foxes, per pair		
Small Turks, each		
Basket Boys, enamelled and gilt, pair . .		
Set of Season Busts		
Cupids grinding, from the Element Group . .		
Dogs from the Dresden Shepherd, each . .		
London Pointer and Greyhound, each . .		
Season Vases, each		
Vases, Common Festoons		
Vases, Best Festoons		
Fountain Vase, on Pedestal		
Cupid Sleeping, on Pedestal, from Spangler's Group		

THE FOLLOWING ARE MODELLED BY EDWARD KEYS

Paris Cries, Set of six Figures		
Archers, per pair		
Large Elephant, with Driver		
Ditto with cloths, no Driver		
Peacock		
Large Napoleon		
Small Napoleon		
Lean Cows, per pair		
Small Elephant		
Key's Fancy Figures, per pair . . .		
New Sitting Pugs, on Cushions . . .		
Small Sitting Foxes		
Tragedy and Comedy		
Bust of Nelson		
Vicars, Curates and Wardens		
Large Monkey Musicians		

Names of Figures and Groups.			Size.	Height, inches.
Small Monkey Musicians				
Dusty Bob and Africa Sall				
Doctor Syntax Walking				
Ditto	in Green Room			
Ditto	at York			
Ditto	at Booksellers			
Ditto	Drawing			
Ditto	Going to Bed			
Ditto	Tied to a Tree			
Ditto	Scolding the Landlady			
Ditto	Playing the Violin			
Ditto	Attacked by a Bull			
Ditto	Crossing the Lake			
Ditto	Mounted on Horseback			
Ditto	Landing at Calais			
Doctor Syntax's Landlady, No. 8				
Grimaldi as Clown, Thomas Griffin				
Liston as Paul Pry, S. Keys				
Ditto as Mawworm, S. Keys				
Vestris in Buy a Broom, S. Keys				
Bucks and Does				
Small Standing Sheep				
Rabbits on Plinths				
Ditto without Plinths				
Large Horses				
Pony				
Set of Tyrolese Minstrels				
Canton Girls				
Liston as Domine Sampson, S. Keys				
Industrious Boy & Girl	ditto	per pair		
Cats on Cushions, large	E. Keys	each		
Ditto ditto small	ditto	ditto		
Lion and Lioness	ditto	ditto		
Worcester Mice	ditto	ditto		
New Poodle Dogs	ditto	ditto		
New Cats with prey	ditto	ditto		
Billy Waters, the Black Fiddler	ditto	ditto		
Small Fruit Basket		ditto		
Sheep in Fold		ditto		
Pair of Topers Douglas Fox		ditto		

A number of other figures were published which are not entered in this list, the keeping of the list probably having ceased at the time they were modelled. Thus Louis Bradley modelled two Dancing Figures, and John Whitaker, between 1830 and 1847, among others modelled the following:

An Eastern Lady	Boy with Greyhound
Guitar Player	Girl with Falcon
Child in Arm Chair	Bust of Queen Victoria
Virgin Mary	Ditto of Duke of Wellington
An Angel	Group of Stags
Boy and Dog	Ditto of Dogs
Girl and Dog	Leaping Stag
Sleeping Nymph	Peacock among Flowers
Mazeppa on Wild Horse (Plate 176)	Parrot

APPENDIX IX

LIST OF FIGURES ATTRIBUTED
TO ANDREW PLANCHÉ[1]

A catalogue of the recorded figures attributed to Planché is likely to become out of date almost as soon as compiled. Nevertheless, it may be useful to attempt such a record here together with a few details concerning the items listed.

I HUMAN FIGURES

A Seated Woman on a bun base, white, with applied flowers on dress. The same applied flowers occur on the dress of the woman in the *Lovers and Clown*,[2] the latter being perhaps post-Planché.

A Fluter. A coloured example illustrated in E.C.C. *Catalogue*, no. 304 (Evill Collection). Another, from Mr. Humphrey Cook's Collection, is illustrated by Gilhespy, *Crown Derby Porcelain*, Fig. 138.

A Dancing Man. In white, at the Victoria and Albert Museum. This figure evidently continued in production for some years; a 'patch-mark' example is in Derby Museum (Plate 51) and a still later coloured version is marked 'N318', which number is in the Derby Price List, described as *A Pair of Dancing Figures*.

A Dancing Lady. On a rococo moulded base with applied flowers having 'hot cross bun' centres. In white. An example was formerly in the possession of the late Mr. W. Pease, of Nottingham, and the model appears again as a 'patch mark' figure on a rococo base (Plate 51).

A Dancing Lady. She holds a mask in her right hand. A 'dry-edge' coloured version is illustrated by Hackenbroch.[3]

A Shepherd with Bagpipes. He has a dog at his feet and is illustrated in E.C.C. *Catalogue*, no. 299[4] (Lord and Lady Fisher Collection).

[1] See Chapter I, pp. 3–5, 7–12.
[2] Hackenbroch, op. cit., Plate 272.
[3] Op. cit., Plate 271.
[4] English Ceramic Circle, *Commemorative Catalogue of an Exhibition held at the Victoria and Albert Museum, 1948.*

APPENDIX IX: PLANCHÉ FIGURES

A Shepherdess. Known as *The Dancing Shepherdess* and the companion to the preceding model. Illustrated in E.C.C. *Catalogue*, no. 300 (Lord and Lady Fisher Collection). Both this and the companion figure are coloured and another coloured example of the *Shepherdess* is at the Victoria and Albert Museum, no. C.115–1938 (Plate 4).

A Pair of Bagpipers. Formerly in the Wallace Elliot Collection and illustrated in *The Connoisseur*, September 1927.

Lady with a Lute. (Perhaps emblematic of 'Hearing'.) An example at the Victoria and Albert Museum, no. C.679–1925, has a dress painted with a star pattern in puce. Another example is at Derby (Plate 9). The same model was used as emblematic of 'Taste' in a set of *Senses*. (See below.)

Kitty Clive in the character of Lethe. A white example in the Schreiber Collection at the Victoria and Albert Museum (Cat. I, 1a) (Plate 3). All examples of this figure were until recently believed to be of Bow manufacture, although some were known to be non-phosphatic. These latter are now recognised as early Derby, having affinities with the marked Derby cream jugs, notably the applied prunus sprigs on the 'star-shaped' bases of the figures, which are very similar to those on the cream jugs.

St. Thomas, also variously called the *Roman Soldier* or *King Lear*. White examples in the Schreiber Collection, (Cat. I, 287), and in Derby Museum (Plate 7); a post-Planché specimen also at the Victoria and Albert Museum, no. C.298–1940.

St. Philip, the companion figure to the above. Both white and coloured versions exist. An example of the latter at the Victoria and Albert Museum, no. C.36–1944.[1] Post-Planché examples also exist, e.g. Victoria and Albert Museum, no. C.299–1940.

A Group of a Hunter and Companion. A white example in the collection of Dr. and Mrs. Statham is illustrated in Lane, Plate 56B.

The Five Senses:
  (i) *Feeling: A Lady holding a Parrot*. A white example is at Derby and a charming coloured one is at the Fitzwilliam Museum, Cambridge (Plate 8).
  (ii) *Taste: A Lady with a Basket of Fruit*. This is basically the same figure as the *Lady with a Lute* (see above). A white version is in the Schreiber Collection (Cat. I, 286), whilst coloured examples are at the Victoria and Albert Museum (Broderip Collection, no. C.1410–1924), and in the Fitzwilliam Museum (Plate 8). The coloured specimen from

[1] Lane, op. cit., Plate 59.

194

the Broderip Collection has slight gilding round the hem of the skirt.

(iii) *Sight: A Man with a Bird.* An example was illustrated in *Apollo*, December 1928, p. 322, no. IX.

(iv) *Smell: A Man with a Snuff Box.*

(v) *Hearing: A Woman with a Birdcage.*

The whereabouts of the two last-mentioned models is unknown to the authors.

The Four Seasons:

(A) Four *Putti* seated. A set of white figures is illustrated by Lane, Plates 56A and 57A. A White figure of *Autumn* is at the Derby Museum (Plate 12), where can also be seen a later candlestick utilising this Planché figure.

(B) Eight standing *Seasons* in pairs.

(i) *Spring: A Gardener and Companion.* A coloured version in Lord and Lady Fisher's Collection (Plates 14 and 15), illustrated in Gilhespy, *Crown Derby Porcelain*, Figs. 182 and 183. The painted flowers on the base of the *Gardener* correspond closely with those on a pair of *Bulls*, and a *Stag and Doe* in the Derby Museum.

(ii) *Summer:* A pair of *Harvesters.* A white example of the male figure is in the Derby Museum (Plate 5) and the companion figure was formerly in the Foden Collection (Plate 6).

(iii) *Autumn:* A pair of *Peasants* with large hats and grapes (Arthur Hayden, *The Lady Ludlow Collection*, no. 242).

(iv) *Winter:* An *Old Man* and *Old Woman* warming their hands over a brazier. Coloured examples are illustrated from the collection of Mrs. W. D. Dickson by Lane, Plate 60B. A white figure of the *Old Woman* was formerly in the Gilhespy Collection (Plate 11).

Street Sellers:

A pair of figures on shell-moulded bases in colour are at the Victoria and Albert Museum, nos. C.408 and 409–1928, and are illustrated by Lane, Plates 61B and C. They are inspired by a Meissen set of *Paris Cries* and are painted in pale colours.

Classical Figures:

(i) *Mars.* A figure in armour. A coloured example is in the collection of Dr. and Mrs. Statham and is illustrated in the E.C.C. Exhibition *Catalogue*, no. 306, Plate 67.

(ii) *Venus and Cupid*. The companion to the preceding. Both this and the figure of *Mars* were also made in the succeeding periods of the factory's history, though somewhat modified in later times. A 'patchmarked' *Venus* of the early model is illustrated in Gilhespy, *Crown Derby Porcelain*, Fig. 141.

(iii) *Pluto and Cerberus*. Perhaps emblematic of 'Earth' from a set of *Elements*. Later versions are not uncommon; a 'pale' period example is in the Derby Museum (Plate 47).

(iv) A figure perhaps representing *Apollo*. A young god with emblems of the Arts; a coloured example, formerly in the F. B. Gilhespy Collection was sold at Sotheby's on 30th May 1967 (Plate 10). There is a white example at the Fitzwilliam Museum, Cambridge.

Other possible Planché classical figures, at present unrecorded, are *Juno and the Peacock*, *Jupiter and the Eagle*, and *Neptune*, all of which are mentioned in William Duesbury's London Account Book although the factory of origin is not named. Such figures normally formed sets of *Elements* of which *Pluto and Cerberus*, mentioned above, is another.

Chinoiserie 'Elements':
Water and Air. Represented by a pair of Chinese boys, coloured and fitted with painted metal branches. A pair sold at Sotheby's on 12th October 1965 has porcelain flowers fitted to the branches (Plate 13). The figure representing *Water* has the word 'Water' incised on the base. The costumes have a star-shaped pattern painted in puce. It is probable that both the metal branches and the French flowers were added by Duesbury himself.

Chinese 'Senses':
(i) *Feeling*. A figure of *A Chinaman striking a Boy*. All the recorded examples are uncoloured, and may be seen in the Schreiber Collection (Cat. I, 284), the Cecil Higgins Museum (no. C361) and the MacHarg Collection (illustrated in the *Catalogue* of the English Ceramic Circle Exhibition, 1948, no. 295).

(ii) *Taste*. *A Chinaman and Boy*, sometimes called the *Quack Doctor and Assistant*. The 'Doctor' is holding a phial of medicine and the 'Assistant' leans over a basket of medicines, holding a bottle in his hand. Two examples are recorded, both coloured, one at the Victoria and Albert Museum (C.103–1938), the other in the Untermyer Collection.[1]

(iii) *Sight. A Woman holding a Bird gesticulating to a Chinaman* (seated beside her). Coloured examples are in the British Museum, and the Untermyer Collection.[2] There is a white specimen at the British Museum (Plate 16).

(iv) *Smell. A Standing Figure* with a flowing robe holding a flower to her nose whilst a boy, seated beside her and leaning backwards, reaches for it. A white specimen is at the British Museum (Plate 17), and a coloured one at the Metropolitan Museum of New York, illustrated by Arthur Lane, Plate 58.[3]

(v) *Hearing. A Chinese Woman* standing and holding a lyre with a seated child. A coloured example is at the British Museum, formerly in the Wallace Elliot Collection.

Other Chinoiserie:

A rococo candlestick with two Chinese boys, one on either side. A pair in the Untermyer Collection is there attributed to the pre-Duesbury period and the models of the boys have all the Planché verve. Other similar candlesticks are more likely to be 'transitional', about 1756 in date. One recorded example has the head and shoulders of the left hand figure missing, and the remaining torso coloured over in contemporary colours to simulate rockwork.[4]

II ANIMAL FIGURES

A Pair of Boars. One is seated, one trotting, the base with acorns in relief. White examples are not uncommon and may be seen, *inter alia*, at the Derby and Victoria and Albert Museums (Plates 18 and 19). There is a coloured pair in the Untermyer Collection[5] and another at the British Museum.[6] This pair of figures has been faked in recent years with sufficient accuracy to deceive.

A Pair of Birds on Branches with a Dog Below. There is a coloured specimen at the Victoria and Albert Museum (Herbert Allen Collection), illustrated by Gilhespy,[7] whilst a white example, also at South Kensington, has ormolu branches and white china flowers.[8]

[1] Hackenbroch, op. cit., Plate 270.
[2] *Ibid*, Plate 269.   [3] Lane, op. cit.
[4] Sotheby Sale Cat., 4th March 1958, Lot 53. Also illustrated in *Apollo*, June 1946 (H. B. Lancaster, 'Early Specimens of the Derby Factory').
[5] Hackenbroch, op. cit., Plate 279.
[6] Gilhespy, *Crown Derby Porcelain*, Plate 136.   [7] *Ibid.*, Plate 189.
[8] *Ibid.*, Plate 190. Another pair similarly ornamented.

APPENDIX IX: PLANCHÉ FIGURES

A Stag at Lodge. The Derby Museum has a coloured example.

A Doe at Lodge. The companion to the preceding, one in the Derby Museum is similarly coloured. Perhaps such figures were inspired by the arms of the town of Derby (Plate 21).

A Pair of Charging Bulls. A coloured pair in the Derby Museum (Plate 20). A very vigorous model and apparently derived from similar Meissen figures after an engraving by Elias Ridinger. The painting of flowers and herbage on the bases is similar to that on the *Stag* and *Doe* in the Derby Museum and likely to be by Duesbury. Another pair is in the Untermyer Collection.[1]

A Pair of Goats Suckling Kids. A coloured example is at the Victoria and Albert Museum.[2]

A Dog and a Cat. There are coloured specimens at the Victoria and Albert Museum.

A Group of Sheep. A white example is in the Derby Museum.

Reference has been made above to some modern fakes of these, and other, early figures. These reproductions possess a rather greasy looking glaze, not unlike that of some genuine Planché models, screw-holes, and in all probability a dirty foot to simulate the 'dry-edge'. Their modelling lacks the vigour of the originals and in the case of human figures the limbs may be too thin. Among the latter may also be mentioned some *Italian Comedy* figures purporting to date from about 1756 to 1760. They constitute a danger to the less experienced and any allegedly early figures offered should be examined with the above in mind, particularly if the price asked be below that which would normally be expected.

[1] Hackenbroch, op. cit., Plate 278.
[2] Also illustrated in Gilhespy, *Crown Derby Porcelain*, Plate 137.

BIBLIOGRAPHY

John Haslem, *The Old Derby China Factory*, London, 1876

Llewellyn Jewitt, *The Ceramic Art of Great Britain* (2 vols.), London, 1878

J. E. Nightingale, *Contributions towards the History of Early English Porcelain from Contemporary Sources*, privately printed, Salisbury, 1881

W. Bemrose, *Bow, Chelsea and Derby Porcelain*, London, 1898

R. L. Hobson, *Catalogue of English Porcelain in the British Museum*, London, 1905

W. Moore Binns, *The First Century of English Porcelain*, London, 1906

Herbert Eccles and Bernard Rackham, *Analysed Specimens of English Porcelain*, Victoria and Albert Museum, London, 1922

Bernard Rackham, *Catalogue of the Herbert Allen Collection*, Victoria and Albert Museum, London, 1923

F. Hurlbutt, *Old Derby Porcelain and its Artist Workmen*, London, 1925

Edward Hyam, *The Early Period of Derby Porcelain*, London, 1926

Bernard Rackham, *Catalogue of the Schreiber Collection*, vol. 1, Victoria and Albert Museum, London, 2nd ed., 1928

F. Williamson, *The Derby Pot Manufactory known as Cockpit Hill Pottery*, reprinted from the *Derbyshire Archaeological Society's Transactions*, 1930

Mrs. Donald MacAlister, *William Duesbury's London Account Book 1751–1753*, English Porcelain Circle Monograph, London, 1931

W. B. Honey, *Old English Porcelain*, London, 1948 ed.

English Ceramic Circle, *Commemorative Catalogue of an Exhibition held at the Victoria and Albert Museum, May 5—June 20, 1948*, London, 1949

Ernst Rosenthal, *Pottery and Ceramics*, Harmondsworth, 1949

F. Brayshaw Gilhespy, *Crown Derby Porcelain*, Leigh-on-Sea, 1951

BIBLIOGRAPHY

J. L. Dixon, *English Porcelain of the 18th Century*, London, 1952

George Savage, *18th Century English Porcelain*, London, 1952

Yvonne Hackenbroch, *Chelsea and Other English Porcelain, Pottery and Enamel in the Irwin Untermyer Collection*, Cambridge, Mass., 1957

Bernard Watney, *Longton Hall Porcelain*, London, 1957

Arthur Lane, *English Porcelain Figures of the 18th Century*, London, 1961

F. Brayshaw Gilhespy, *Derby Porcelain*, London, 1961

C. L. Exley, *The Pinxton China Factory*, Derby, 1963

Bernard Watney, *English Blue and White Porcelain of the 18th Century*, London, 1963

R. J. Charleston (ed.), *English Porcelain*, London, 1965

English Porcelain Circle Transactions (E.P.C. Trans.), 1928 to 1932

English Ceramic Circle Transactions (E.C.C. Trans.), 1933 to 1969

INDEX

INDEX

206

1. CREAM JUG
Incised on base 'D 1750'   Height $3\frac{1}{2}$ in.
Victoria and Albert Museum   See page 4

2. BOWL
Date about 1756   Height $2\frac{5}{8}$ in.
Derby Museum   See page 8

5. KITTY CLIVE
Date about 1752   Height 9¾ in.
Victoria and Albert Museum   See pages 8 and 194

4. SHEPHERDESS

Date 1750–55   Height 6⅞ in.   'Dry-edge'

Victoria and Albert Museum

See page 194

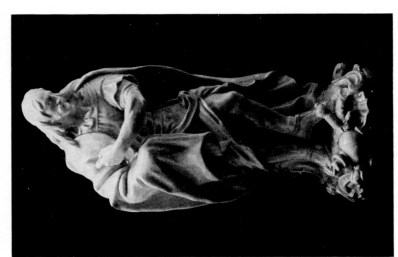

7. KING LEAR
Date 1750–55   Height 9½ in.
Alan F. Green Collection
See page 194

6. HARVESTER'S COMPANION
Date 1750–55   Height 6 in.
Derby Museum
See page 195

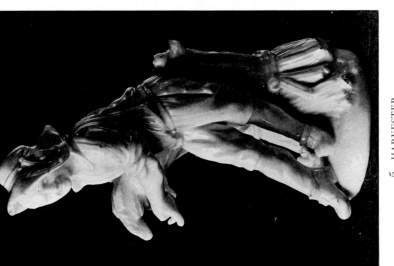

5. HARVESTER
Date 1750–55   Height 6 in.
Derby Museum
See page 195

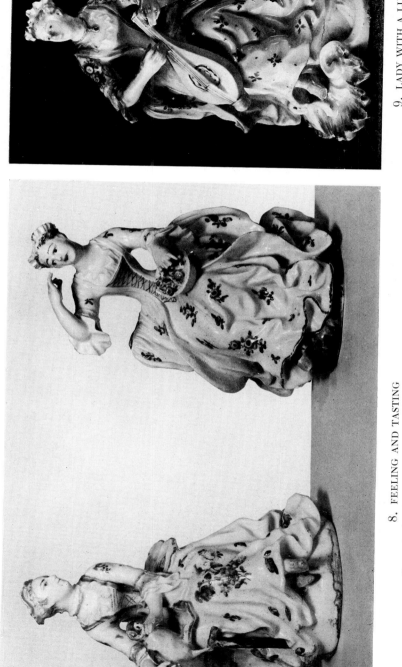

9. LADY WITH A LUTE
Date about 1755   Height 6 in.
'Patch marks'
Derby Museum
See page 194.

8. FEELING AND TASTING
Date 1750–55   Height 6½ in.   'Dry-edge'
Reproduced by permission of the Syndics of the Fitzwilliam Museum, Cambridge
See page 194

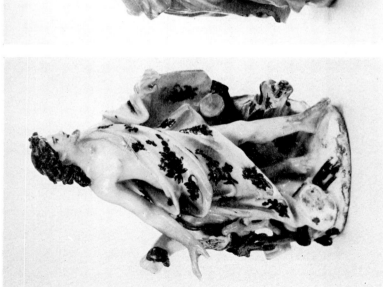

10. APOLLO
Date 1750–55   Height 6½ in.
'Dry-edge'
Royal Crown Derby Porcelain Company
Museum
Photo Sotheby's, London
See page 196

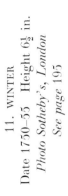

11. WINTER
Date 1750–55   Height 6½ in.
Photo Sotheby's, London
See page 195

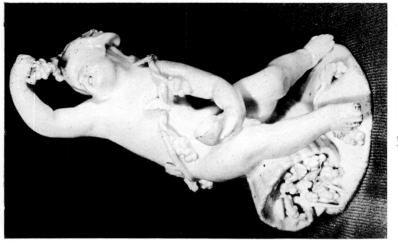

12. AUTUMN
Date 1750–55   Height 5 in.
Derby Museum
See pages 7 and 195

13. CHINOISERIE FIGURES REPRESENTING WATER AND AIR

Date 1750–55   Height 8 in.   'Dry-edge'

H. J. Hyams' private Collection   Photo Sotheby's, London

See pages 11, 12 and 196

14. GARDENER
Date 1750–55   Height 7½ in.   'Dry-edge'
Reproduced by permission of the Syndics of the Fitzwilliam Museum,
Cambridge
See page 195

15. GARDENER'S COMPANION
Date 1750–55   Height 6¾ in.   'Dry-edge'
Reproduced by permission of the Syndics of the Fitzwilliam Museum,
Cambridge
See page 195

16. CHINOISERIE FIGURE REPRESENTING SIGHT
Date 1750–55   Height 7¼ in.   'Dry-edge'
British Museum
See pages 8 and 197

17. CHINOISERIE FIGURE REPRESENTING SMELLING
Date 1750–55   Height 8½ in.   'Dry-edge'
British Museum
See page 197

18, 19. PAIR OF BOARS
Date 1750–55   Height 4 in.   'Dry-edge'
Victoria and Albert Museum
See pages 10 *and* 197

20. PAIR OF CHARGING BULLS
Date 1750–55   Height 5½ in.   'Dry-edge'
Derby Museum   See pages 11 *and* 198

21. STAG AND DOE
Date 1750–55   Height 5 in.   'Dry-edge'
Derby Museum   See pages 11 *and* 198

22. WALL BRACKET
Date about 1752   Height 6¼ in.
Victoria and Albert Museum
See page 9

23. TAPERSTICK IN THE FORM
OF A CRESTED PHEASANT
Date about 1756   Height 8½ in.
Formerly in the
Eckstein and Foden Collections
See page 14

24. CYBELE
Date about 1756   Height 8½ in.
Victoria and Albert Museum
See page 14

25. CHINESE BOY IN A TREE
Date about 1760   Height 8¾ in.
Reproduced by permission of the Syndics of the Fitzwilliam Museum,
Cambridge
See page 15

26. YOUTH WITH DOG
Date 1756–60   Height 6 in.
Reproduced by permission of the Syndics of the Fitzwilliam Museum,
Cambridge
See page 15

27. SHEPHERDESS
Date about 1756–60   Height 7½ in.
Derby Museum
See page 15

28. 'PARFUM' VASE
AND COVER
Date 1760–65
Height 8½ in.
Royal Crown Derby
Porcelain Company
Museum
See page 15

29. ROCOCO VASE WITH
FIGURE PAINTING
Date about 1756
Height 5 in.
'Patch marks'
Formerly in the
Barrett Collection
See pages 15 *and* 21

30. CANDLESTICK GROUP
Date 1756–60   Height 10 in.
Derby Museum
See page 15

31. PLATE
Date 1756–65   Diameter $7\frac{5}{8}$ in.
Derby Museum
See pages 16, 21, *and* 22

32. PLATE
Date 1756–65   Diameter $7\frac{1}{4}$ in.
Derby Museum
See pages 16 *and* 21

33. CUP AND 'TREMBLEUSE' SAUCER
Date 1760–65   Diam. of saucer $5\frac{1}{2}$ in.
Derby Museum
See page 16

34. SAUCEBOAT
Date about 1760   Length $6\frac{1}{2}$ in.
Derby Museum
See page 16

35. TEAPOT
Date 1756–60   Height 5 in.
Norwich Castle Museum   See page 16

36. TEAPOT
Date about 1758   Height 5½ in.
Derby Museum   See page 16

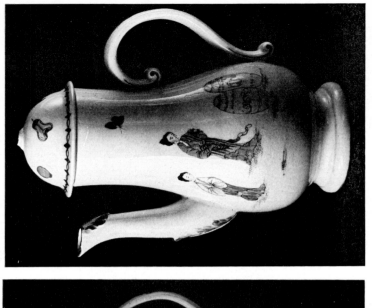

59. COFFEE POT
Date 1760–65   Height 7¾ in.
'Patch marks'
Derby Museum
See page 17

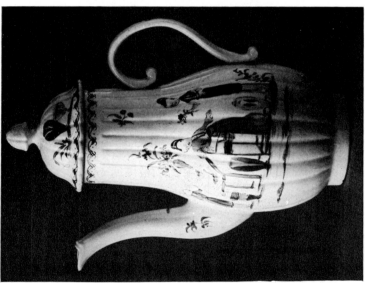

58. COFFEE POT
Date about 1760   Height 9½ in.
Derby Museum
See pages 17 and 27

57. TANKARD
Date 1760–65   Height 4 in.
'Patch marks'
Mr. and Mrs. F. A. Barrett Collection
See page 17

41. SUNFLOWER DISH
Date 1756–58   Diameter 6½ in.
Derby Museum
See pages 17, 21 and 22

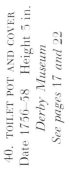

40. TOILET POT AND COVER
Date 1756–58   Height 5 in.
Derby Museum
See pages 17 and 22

42. PLATE
Date 1760–65   Diameter 8¼ in.   Signed (on a moth's wing) 'Thos. F . . .'
Large (added) gold anchor
Victoria and Albert Museum   See page 31

43. DETAIL OF SIGNED PLATE

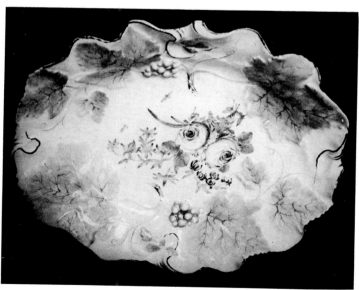

44. PLATE
Date 1760–65   Diameter 8½ in.
Dr. and Mrs. Bold Collection   See page 17

45. VINE-LEAF DISH
Date about 1758   Length 7 in.
Derby Museum   See pages 17 *and* 21

46. JUG
Date about 1760   Height 6¼ in.   'Patch marks'
Dr. and Mrs. Bold Collection
See page 17

47. PLUTO AND CERBERUS
Date about 1760   Height 7 in.   'Patch marks'
Derby Museum   See pages 18, 19 *and* 196

48. PAIR FROM A SET OF SEASONS
Date about 1758   Height 4¼ in.
Derby Museum   See pages 11 *and* 18

49. FIFE PLAYER
Date about 1760
Height 5¼ in.
'Patch marks'
Derby Museum
See page 18

50. AUTUMN
Date 1756–60
Height 8½ in.
Derby Museum
See pages 18 *and* 21

51. DANCERS
Date 1756–60   Height 6¼ in. and 6 in.   'Patch marks'
Derby Museum
See pages 18 and 193

52. PAIR OF SEASONS
Date about 1760   Height 4¾ in.   'Patch marks'   Incised 'New D'
Derby Museum   See page 19

53. SHEPHERDESS
Date 1756–60   Height 10 in.
Derby Museum   See page 18

54. PAIR OF TOMTITS AND A DOVE
Date about 1760   Height of tomtits 4¾ in.
Victoria and Albert Museum (Schreiber Collection)
See page 19

55. PARTRIDGE TUREEN
Date about 1760   Length 8¾ in.
Cecil Higgins Museum, Bedford

56. SPRING
Date about 1765   Height 9½ in.   'Patch marks'
Reproduced by permission of the Syndics of the Fitzwilliam Museum,
Cambridge
See page 23

57. GROUP OF LOVERS AND A CLOWN
Date 1765–70   Height 12 in.
Royal Crown Derby Porcelain Company Museum
See pages 18 *and* 23

58. CANDLESTICK
Date 1756–60   Height 9 in.
Derby Museum
See page 21

59. LEDA AND THE SWAN

Date 1765–70   Height 11½ in.   'Patch marks'

Derby Museum

See page 24

60. VENUS AND CUPID ON A DOLPHIN
Date 1765–70   Height 8¾ in.   'Patch marks'
Derby Museum
See pages 24 and 27

61. YOUTH REPRESENTING WAR
Date 1765–70   Height 8½ in.
'Patch marks'
Cecil Higgins Museum, Bedford
See page 24

62. JAMES QUINN AS FALSTAFF
Date about 1765   Height 5¼ in.
Royal Crown Derby Porcelain
Company Museum
See page 25

63. DAVID GARRICK AS TANCRED AND A STREET SELLER
Date about 1765   Height 8½ in.   'Patch marks'
Derby Museum   See pages 25 and 26

64. HARLEQUIN AND COLUMBINE
Date about 1760   Height 6 in.
Victoria and Albert Museum
See page 25

65, 66. PAIR OF BLACKAMOORS
Date about 1760   Height 8¼ in.
Royal Crown Derby Porcelain Company Museum
See page 25

67. TITHE-PIG GROUP
Date 1765–70   Height 6 in.   'Patch marks'
Derby Museum   See page 25

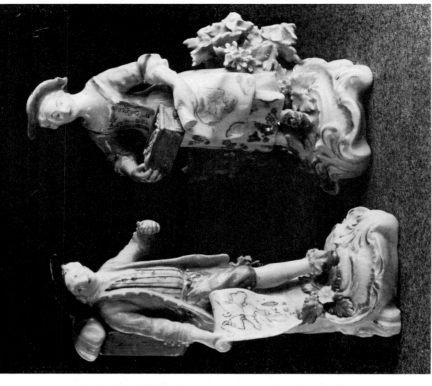

68. THE DUET SINGERS   Height 9 in. and 8¾ in.   'Patch marks'

Derby Museum

Date 1765–70   *See page 25*

69. THE MAPSELLERS   Height 6⅛ and 6¾ in.   'Patch marks'

Derby Museum

Date about 1760   *See page 26*

70. SUMMER
Date 1765–70   Height 9¼ in.   'Patch marks'
Miss Margaret Ward Collection
See page 26

71. AUTUMN
Date about 1760   Height 6¼ in.
Royal Crown Derby Porcelain Company Museum
See page 26

72. MUSICIAN IN AN ARBOUR
Date 1765–70   Height 12 in.
Derby Museum
See page 23

73. SUGAR CASTER (WITH SILVER TOP)
Date about 1760   Height 6⅞ in.
Derby Museum
See page 27

74. CHESTNUT BOWL
Date about 1765   Height 6½ in.
Derby Museum
See page 26

75. PAIR OF ROCOCO VASES
Date about 1765   Height 9 in.   'Patch marks'
Derby Museum
See page 17

76. 'FRILL' VASE
Date about 1765   Height 11¾ in.   'Patch marks'
Derby Museum
See page 28

77. VASE
Date about 1758   Height 9½ in.   'Patch marks'
Derby Museum   See page 28

78. PAIR OF CORNUCOPIA
Date about 1770   Height 9½ in. and 10 in.
William M. Moss Collection   See page 28

79. DISH WITH CHINESE DECORATION
Date about 1760   Length 9½ in.
Derby Museum
See page 30

80. WRITING SET
Date about 1758   Length 7½ in.
Derby Museum
See page 30

81. JUG WITH MASK LIP
Date about 1765   Height 7½ in.   'Patch marks'
Derby Museum
See page 29

82. BASKET
Date 1765–70   Length 7 in.   'Patch marks'
Derby Museum
See pages 17 and 29

83. BUTTER DISH
Date 1765–70   Length 6½ in.   'Patch marks'
Royal Crown Derby Porcelain Company Museum
See page 29

84. SHELL CENTREPIECE IN TWO PARTS
Date 1765–70   Height 10½ in.   'Patch marks'
Derby Museum
See page 27

86. INTERIOR OF BOWL

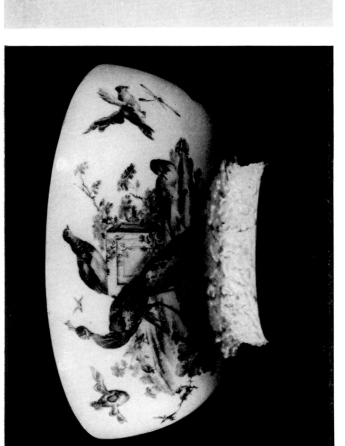

85. BOWL WITH 'RUSTICATED' FOOT

Date about 1770   Diameter 10 in.

William M. Moss Collection

See pages 138 and 139

89. BOY WITH A DOG

Date about 1775   Height 6¼ in.

Derby Museum

See page 43

88. PUTTI

Date about 1785   Height 4½ in. and 5¾ in.

Derby Museum

See page 42

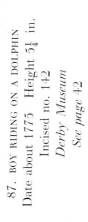

87. BOY RIDING ON A DOLPHIN

Date about 1775   Height 5¼ in.

Incised no. 142

Derby Museum

See page 42

91. JUPITER
Date about 1775
Height 7¼ in.
Incised no. 117
Derby Museum

JUNO
Date about 1775   Height 6½ in.
Incised no. 119 and incised triangle
Derby Museum
See page 42

90. THE SACRIFICE
Date about 1772   Height 6 in.
Incised no. 14 2nd size
Derby Museum
See page 45

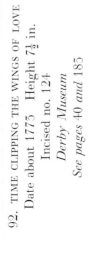

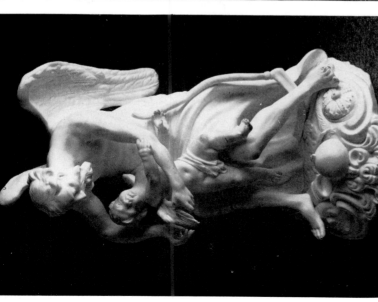

94. GROUP OF FOUR CUPIDS
Date about 1785   Height 9 in.
Incised crown, batons and dots
over D; incised no. 254,
script N and triangle
Derby Museum
See pages 40 and 42

95. CALLIOPE
Date about 1780   Height 6 in.
Derby Museum
See page 42

92.   TIME CLIPPING THE WINGS OF LOVE
Date about 1775   Height 7½ in.
Incised no. 124
Derby Museum
See pages 40 and 185

96. NEPTUNE

Date about 1780   Height 8 in.

Incised no. 229, 2nd size, star and letters T U T

Derby Museum

See page 45

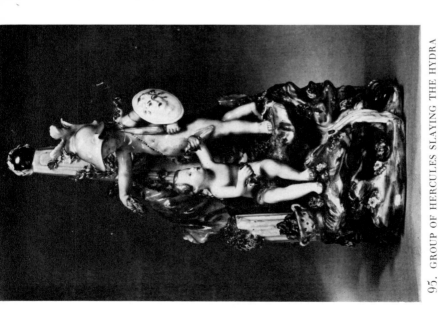

95.   GROUP OF HERCULES SLAYING THE HYDRA

AND MINERVA CROWNING CONSTANCY

Date about 1771   Height 11 in.

Incised no. 1

Birmingham Museum and Art Gallery

See page 40

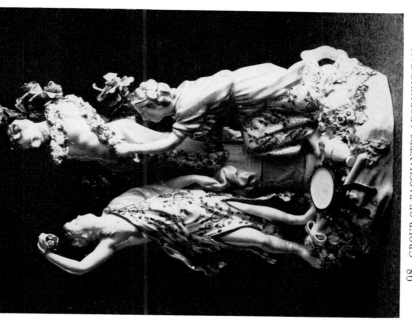

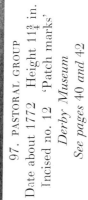

98. GROUP OF BACCHANTES ADORNING PAN
Date about 1775   Height 11 in.
Incised no. 196 and script G
Derby Museum
See page 40

97. PASTORAL GROUP
Date about 1772   Height 11¾ in.
Incised no. 12   'Patch marks'
Derby Museum
See pages 40 and 42

100. GROUP OF GARDENERS
Date about 1780   Height 8 in.
Mr. and Mrs. F. Peel Collection
See page 40

99. GROUP OF THREE GRACES DISTRESSING CUPID
Date about 1775   Height 15 in.
Incised no. 235
Derby Museum See page 40

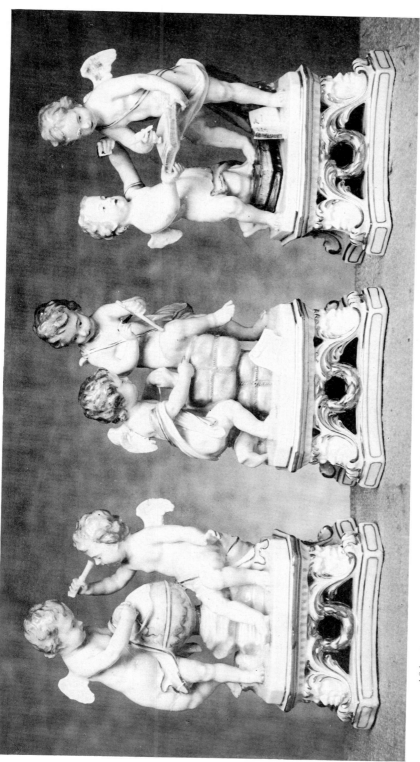

101. GROUPS OF CUPIDS EMBLEMATIC OF (a) ASTRONOMY AND GEOMETRY, (b) COMMERCE, (c) ARITHMETIC,

FROM A SET OF ARTS AND SCIENCES

Height 7 in.

Victoria and Albert Museum (Schreiber Collection no. 345)   *See page 41*

102. ASTRONOMY
Date about 1787   Height of barometer 68 in.
Victoria and Albert Museum
See page 50

103. CUP AND 'TREMBLEUSE' SAUCER
Date about 1780   Height of cup 4 in.; diameter of saucer $6\frac{1}{4}$ in.
Mark 5: gold anchor and script N
Derby Museum   See page 56

104. BOWL, COVER AND STAND
Date about 1775   Diameter of bowl $4\frac{3}{4}$ in.
Derby Museum   See page 47

105. DISH
Date about 1775   Diameter 9 in.   Mark 5: conjoined anchor and D in gold
Derby Museum   See page 45

106. PLATE
Date about 1775   Diameter 7 in.   Mark 5: crown over anchor in gold
Derby Museum   See page 45

107. TEAPOT
Date about 1775   Height 6 in.   Mark 3: conjoined anchor and D in gold
Derby Museum   See page 47

108. TEAPOT
Date about 1775   Height 4½ in.   Mark 3: conjoined anchor and D in gold
Derby Museum   See page 46

110. CUP AND SAUCER

Date about 1785 Height of cup $2\frac{7}{8}$ in.;
diameter of saucer $5\frac{1}{2}$ in.

Mark 9 in puce Pattern no. 54

Impressed 'B' on cup

Derby Museum See page 47

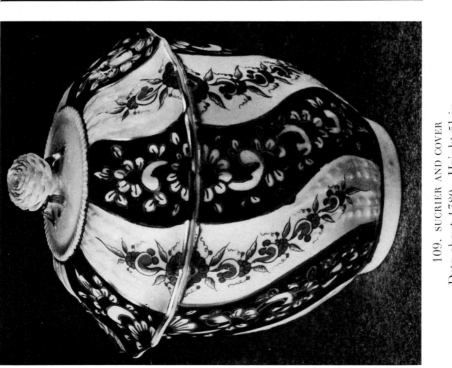

109. SUCRIER AND COVER

Date about 1780 Height $5\frac{1}{2}$ in.

Mark 5: conjoined anchor and D in gold

Derby Museum

See page 46

112. MASK JUG

Date about 1780   Height 9½ in.   'Patch marks'

Mark 4: conjoined anchor and D in gold

Derby Museum

See page 47

111. PLATE

Date about 1782   Diameter 8½ in.

Imitation Chinese seal mark in blue

Derby Museum

See page 47

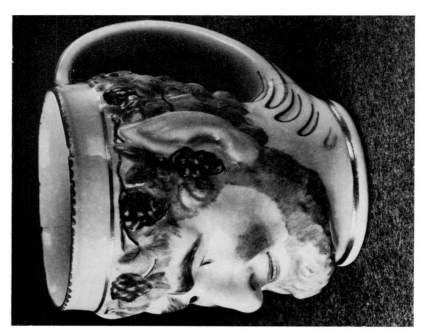

114. BACCHANTE'S HEAD MUG
Date about 1780   Height 4 in.
Mark 6: crown over D in blue
Derby Museum
See page 48

115. MUG
Date about 1780   Height 5 in.
Mark 4: conjoined anchor and D in gold
Derby Museum
See page 47

116. GROUP OF TOYS

Date about 1775   Height about 1 in.

Victoria and Albert Museum

See page 38

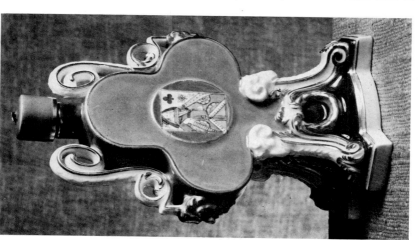
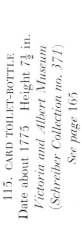

115. CARD TOILET-BOTTLE

Date about 1775   Height 7½ in.

Victoria and Albert Museum

(Schreiber Collection no. 371)

See page 165

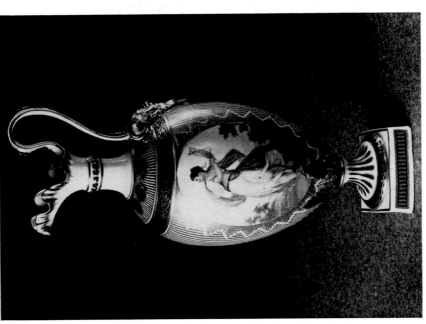

118. EWER

Date about 1775   Height 11 in.   Incised no. 92

Derby Museum

See page 46

117. PAIR OF VASES

Date about 1775   Height 11¼ in.

Derby Museum

See page 46

119(a) TEA-BOWL AND SAUCER
Date about 1775 Height 2 in.;
diameter of saucer 5 in.
Mark 5: conjoined anchor
and D in gold

(b) COFFEE CUP AND SAUCER
Date about 1775 Height 2½ in.;
diameter of saucer 5 in.
Mark 6: crown and D in blue

(c) TEA-BOWL AND SAUCER
Date about 1775 Height 2 in.;
diameter of saucer 5 in.
Mark 5: conjoined anchor and
D in gold

Derby Museum See pages 46, 79 and 80

121. GROUP OF THREE FIGURES AT A RAREE SHOW

Date about 1820   Height 6 in.   Mark 10 in red   Incised no. 94

Derby Museum

See page 185

120. GROUP OF THE SEASONS

Date about 1800   Height 10½ in.

Incised no. 388

Derby Museum   See page 51

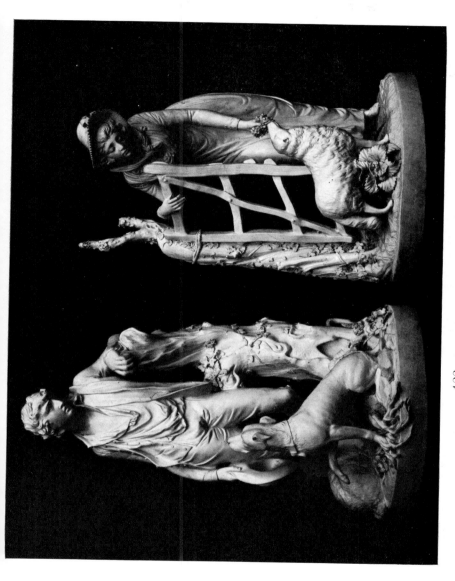

122. SHEPHERD AND SHEPHERDESS

Date about 1795   Height of shepherd 13 in.   Incised no. 369

British Museum

See page 50

124. WELCH TAYLOR'S WIFE

123. WELCH TAYLOR
Date about 1800   Height 10½ in.
'Patch marks'

Derby Museum   See page 55

125. THE ELEMENTS

Date about 1830   Height 6½ to 7 in.   Crossed swords mark in blue   Incised no. 5
Royal Crown Derby Porcelain Company Museum
See page 180

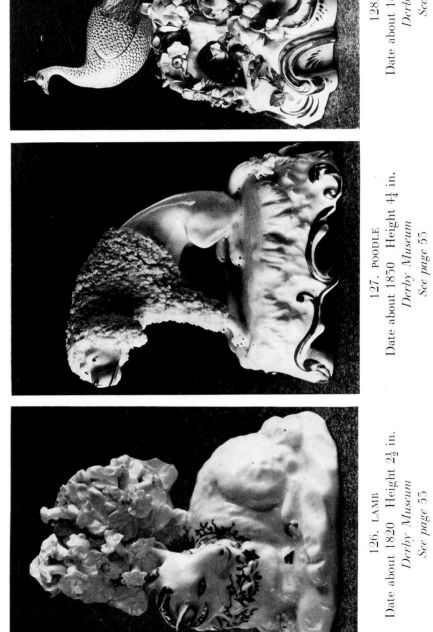

128. PEACOCK
Date about 1850   Height 6½ in.
Derby Museum
See page 55

127. POODLE
Date about 1850   Height 4¼ in.
Derby Museum
See page 55

126. LAMB
Date about 1820   Height 2½ in.
Derby Museum
See page 55

151. SHOEMAKER
Date about 1835   Height 7 in.
Pseudo Sèvres mark in blue (mark 27)
Gilder's mark no. 10
Derby Museum   See page 54

130. GIRL WITH A GUITAR
Date about 1825   Height 6⅝ in.
Incised no. 11
Derby Museum
See page 54

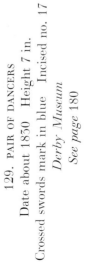

129. PAIR OF DANCERS
Date about 1830   Height 7 in.
Crossed swords mark in blue   Incised no. 17
Derby Museum
See page 180

132. MONKEY MUSICIANS
Date about 1825   Height 4¼ in.
Derby Museum
See page 53

133. GROTESQUE PUNCHES OR
'DERBY DWARFS'
Date about 1820   Height 7 in.
Incised no. 227
Derby Museum
See pages 42 and 185

134. CUP AND 'TREMBLEUSE' SAUCER
Date about 1793
Height of cup and cover 5 in.;
diameter of saucer 6½ in.
Mark 9 in puce   Numeral '1'
in footrim on cup and saucer
Derby Museum
See page 77

135. TEAPOT
Date about 1793   Height 6½ in.
Mark 9 in puce   Pattern no. 320
Derby Museum
See page 57

157. COFFEE CAN

Date about 1790   Height 2½ in.   Pattern no. 260

Derby Museum

See page 57

156. COFFEE CAN

Date about 1792   Height 2½ in.   Mark 9 in puce

Derby Museum

See page 156

140. PLATE
Date about 1792   Diameter 8⅞ in.
Mark 10 in puce
Numeral '7' against footrim
Derby Museum
See page 59

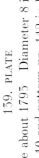

159. PLATE
Date about 1795   Diameter 8 in.
Mark 10 and pattern no. 142 in blue
Derby Museum
See page 60

158. PLATE
Date about 1790   Diameter 8 in.
Mark 9 in puce   Numeral '5' in blue,
'8' in puce on footrim
Mr. and Mrs. F. Peel Collection
See page 59

141. PRENTICE PLATE

Date about 1794   Diameter 8¾ in.   Mark 10 in puce   Pattern no. 158

Derby Museum

See page 59

142. DISH
Date about 1790   Width 9 in.   Mark 9 in puce   Pattern no. 157
Miss Margaret Ward Collection
See page 59

143. CENTRE PIECE
Date about 1790   Width 14½ in.   Mark 10 in puce   Pattern no. 100
Miss Margaret Ward Collection
See page 59

144. COFFEE CAN
AND SAUCER
Date about 1792
Height 2½ in.
Diameter of saucer 5¼ in.
Mark 10 in puce
Pattern no. 211
Miss E. A. L. Rose
Collection
See page 60

145. COFFEE CUP
AND SAUCER
Date about 1800
Height 3⅛ in.;
diameter of saucer 5¾ in
Mark 10 in blue
D. A. Hoyte Collection
See page 62

147. PLATE

Date about 1815   Diameter 8½ in.   Mark 10 in red
Numerals in footrim '75' in puce, '9' in red, '58' in grey
Derby Museum
See page 147

146. PLATE

Date about 1815   Diameter 8½ in.   Mark 9 in gold
Derby Museum
See page 66

149. PLATE

Date about 1815   Diameter 8¾ in.   Mark 10 in red
'Martagon Lily, Wood night shade and Monk's hood'
Derby Museum
See page 65

148. DISH

Date about 1815   9 in. square   Mark 10 in red
'Near Buxton, Derbyshire'
Miss Margaret Ward Collection
See page 64

150. PLATE
Date about 1815   Diameter 10 in.   Mark 10 in red
'65' in footrim in puce
Derby Museum
See pages 66 *and* 96

151. PLAQUE SIGNED 'E.S.'
$5\frac{3}{4}$ in. × 8 in.
Derby Museum
See page 66

152. ICE-PAIL
Date about 1798   Height 14 in.   Mark 10 in blue
'China Aster, Dwarf Double Poppy and Hyacinth Eastern Poppy and
Piquette Carnation'
Derby Museum
See page 65

153. TWO-HANDLED CUP
Date about 1800   Height 5¾ in.   Mark 10 in blue
'The Woodman's Return'
Derby Museum   See page 84

154. PLATE
Date about 1797   Diameter 9 in.   Mark 10 in blue
Pattern 67   Numerals '5' and '1' in footrim   'Hafod'
Derby Museum
See page 63

155. TEAPOT
Date about 1800   Height 4⅞ in.   Mark 10 in blue
Miss E. A. L. Rose Collection   *See page 62*

156. CREAM JUG
Date about 1800   Height 3¾ in.   Mark 10 in blue   'A Calm'
D. A. Hoyte Collection   *See page 61*

158. MUG WITH LID
Date about 1795   Height 4 in.   Mark 10 in puce
Miss E. A. L. Rose Collection
See page 67

157. PLATE
Date about 1795   Diameter 12 in.
'Plum' coloured mark 10   Pattern no. 268
Derby Museum
See page 67

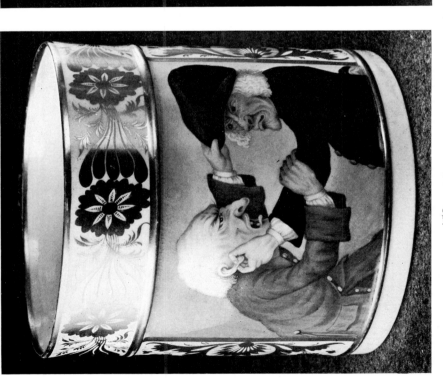

159. MUG

Date about 1815   Height 5 in.   Mark 10 in red
Royal Crown Derby Porcelain Company Museum
See page 88

160. CUP AND SAUCER

Date about 1815   Height 2¼ in.;
diameter of saucer 5½ in.   Mark 10 in red
'In Leicestershire'
Derby Museum   See page 98

162. PLATE
Date about 1815   Diameter 9½ in.   Mark 10 in red
Numerals '22' in red and '29' in grey in footrim
Derby Museum
See page 69

161. PLATE
Date about 1850   Diameter 10½ in.
Mark 24: printed imperial crown and ribbon
Derby Museum
See page 69

164. PLATE

Date about 1815   Diameter $8\frac{1}{2}$ in.   Mark 10 in red

D. A. Hoyte Collection

See page 67

165. PLATE

Date about 1820 or even 1825   Diameter 9 in.

Mark 10 in gold

Mr. and Mrs. F. Peel Collection   See page 66

165. PLATE
Date about 1815   Diameter 8½ in.   Mark 10 in red   Pattern no. 397
Derby Museum
See page 67

166. PLATE
Date about 1800   Diameter 9½ in.   Mark 10 in gold
Derby Museum
See page 69

167. BOUGH-POT
Date about 1815   Height 5½ in.   Mark 10 in red
Commander G. L. Pendred Collection
See page 64

168. BOUGH-POT
Date about 1810   Height 5 in.   Mark 10 in red
Incised no. 376   Repairer's mark an incised star
Derby Museum   See page 66

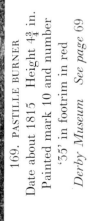

169. PASTILLE BURNER

Date about 1815   Height 4¾ in.
Painted mark 10 and number
'55' in footrim in red
Derby Museum   See page 69

170. MUG

Date about 1830   Height 4½ in.; diameter 4¾ in.
Printed circle mark (25) and 'Matlock High Tor' in red
Miss Margaret Ward Collection
See page 64

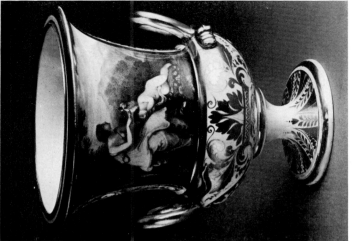

173. VASE   Date about 1815   Height $6\frac{1}{2}$ in.
Mark 10 in red
Miss E. A. L. Rose Collection
See page 69

172. VASE   Date about 1815   Height $15\frac{1}{2}$ in.
Mark 10 in red
D. A. Hoyte Collection
See page 69

171. VASE   Date about 1815   Height $6\frac{7}{8}$ in.
Mark 10 in red
Derby Museum
See page 65

174. VASE
Date about 1850   Height 21 in.
Mark 23: printed imperial crown and circle
Derby Museum
See page 64

175. DR. SYNTAX'S DEBARQUEMENT AT CALAIS
Date about 1830   Height 4¾ in.   Incised no. 11
Victoria and Albert Museum
See page 52

176. BISCUIT FIGURE: MAZEPPA
Date about 1835   Height 5½ in.
Derby Museum   See pages 108 and 192

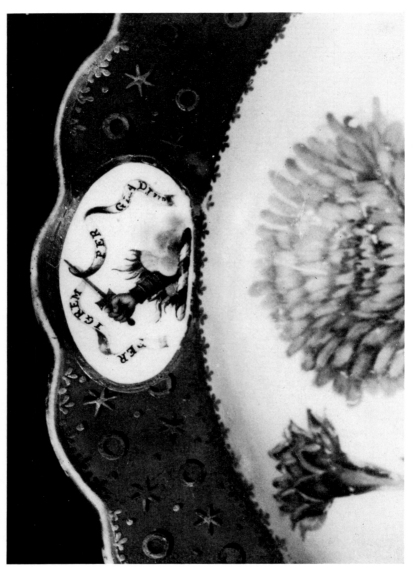

177. PLATE WITH BORDER AND CREST

Date 1794/5

See pages 65 and 150